**W9-AOG-011**

"Here is economic wisdom for humans with habits and desires, immersed in patterns and practices. Here is a model of economic discipleship that doesn't just tell you what to think but how to practically live in an economy of the kingdom. Here is a book that refuses idealism but is fueled by resurrection hope. But you can't pull this off on your own, so buy copies for your family, friends, and congregation."

—**James K. A. Smith**, professor of philosophy at Calvin College; author of *You Are What You Love*

"This book is an incredibly helpful tool for all Christians who desire to live a countercultural life for the common good, especially as it relates to their money and resources."

—**Gabe Lyons**, coauthor of *Good Faith*; founder of Q

"The authors show how biblical mandates work justice and equality in the real world. Their testimonies, grown out of their own experiences, will be life-giving for any reader who cares about economic neighborliness."

—**Walter Brueggemann**, professor emeritus at Columbia Theological Seminary; author of *The Prophetic Imagination*

"In this book, Fikkert, Rhodes, and Holt . . . remind us that if we're really serious about helping the poor, without simultaneously hurting them, we need to discipline ourselves in the basics of working, earning, spending, saving, and giving. This is a powerfully practical book."

—**Joel Belz**, founder of *WORLD Magazine*

"This book is good—really good. I found myself thinking differently about the economy, the marketplace, the kingdom of God, his Word, and even why God put me here. I am a richer man for having read this, and I recommend it to all."

—**Henry Kaestner**, managing principal of Sovereign's Capital; cofounder and former CEO of Bandwidth

"We've bought into a shallow and insufficient view of economics, one that believes our highest goals are merely expanding material prosperity and increasing leisure. *Practicing the King's Economy* is a transformative book with a radical message—that we were created for so much more. Through biblical wisdom, inspiring stories, and actionable practices, this book will lead you to a life of greater joy, impact, and generosity."

—**Peter Greer**, president and CEO of HOPE International; coauthor of *Mission Drift*

"The Bible teaches that 'it is required of stewards that they be found faithful' (1 Cor. 4:2 ESV). *Practicing the King's Economy* is more than just a clarion call to faithful stewardship; it is an eminently practical guide and a spiritual inspiration to that awesome responsibility. The seed that *Practicing the King's Economy* sows promises to blossom into a generation of faithful stewards, whose work and witness are a foretaste of the kingdom to come."

—**Dr. Jordan J. Ballor**, senior research fellow, Acton Institute for the Study of Religion and Liberty

"I am bothered by this book. I bet you will be too. For all the right reasons. *Practicing the King's Economy* provides us a way out of the idolatry and abundant-less materialism of our age. The authors convict without condemning. They hold out the possibility of living life as God intended."

—**Reggie McNeal**, author of *Missional Renaissance* and *Kingdom Come*; city coach with GoodCities

"Simply wonderful, solidly biblical, marvelously practical. This book charts a clear path through one of the greatest challenges (and failures) of the American church. A must-read."

—**Ron Sider**, author of *Rich Christians in an Age of Hunger*

"Michael, Brian, and Robby help believers understand how to leverage their everyday financial, relational, and time resources to help the most vulnerable among us. Not many of us have thought through the most effective, biblical, and lasting ways to come alongside the poor like they have, and they invite us to experience new joy in the kingdom economy of our heavenly Father."

—**Daniel Darling**, vice president of communications at the Ethics and Religious Liberty Commission of the Southern Baptist Convention; author of *The Original Jesus*

"For all its positive aspects, a major negative of globalization is that it has exported consumerism to every part of our planet. Certainly, in the West, consumerism is the major idol of our day, and Western idols ricochet around the globe. So pervasive is consumerism that it often seems as if there is no other option. However, the three multitalented authors of this book join together to show again and again that it doesn't have to be this way—and it shouldn't be this way. Jesus and his kingdom point in a different direction, a far more human one that leads to genuine flourishing."

—**Rev. Dr. Craig Bartholomew**, director of the Kirby Laing Centre for Christian Ethics, Cambridge, UK

"Michael, Robby, and Brian are rare in that they are both theologians and true practitioners. As a result, *Practicing the King's Economy* is full of potent ideas and practical tools for living them out!"

—**Dave Runyon**, coauthor of *The Art of Neighboring*

"While many believers have been inspired and challenged by the idea that Christ has claimed lordship over every square inch of our world, we often don't know how that relates to the day-to-day realities of our pocketbooks, neighborhoods, and supermarkets. Enter pastors and practitioners Michael Rhodes, Robby Holt, and Brian Fikkert, who give us not one key but six, which help us unlock not only a more faithful life of following Jesus but also a more just relationship with God's world."

—**Dr. Sean Michael Lucas**, senior minister, Independent Presbyterian Church, Memphis, TN; chancellor's professor of church history, Reformed Theological Seminary

"*Practicing the King's Economy* is an extraordinarily thoughtful and well-written book urging God's people to adopt economic practices that would transform our nations and communities. Highly recommended."

—**Bruce Ashford**, provost and professor of theology and culture at Southeastern Baptist Theological Seminary

"This richly insightful book shows American Christians how to disentangle ourselves from American consumerism and our often unexamined economic practices. It provides practical examples for change and real-life stories of people who have changed—to show us that it's possible. I hope its message reaches thousands of churches."

—**Dr. Amy L. Sherman**, author of *Kingdom Calling*

"If loving God does not impact the way we manage our finances, then we must ask if we really love him at all. This book challenges us to live out our gospel convictions and our worship with the money that we do—or do not—have. I love the six keys that apply Scripture and can unlock a deeper and more meaningful encounter with God. If your checkbook has been the most significant book in your life, then you need to read *Practicing the King's Economy*."

—**Dr. Krish Kandiah**, founder of Home for Good; author of *God Is Stranger*

"*Practicing the King's Economy* explores the 'why' behind our economic choices and presents practical, genuine steps for positively impacting our families, neighborhoods, and communities. I recommend this book to anyone seeking to live authentically in a world where our deeds must lead the conversation on faith."

—**Stephan Bauman**, executive director of Cornerstone Trust; former president/CEO of World Relief

"In this prophetic and inspiring book, the authors put forth a vision for the healthy, faithful, life-giving use of resources that can, if heeded, make us not only observers of but participants in Jesus's vision to heal the world."

—**Scott Sauls**, senior pastor of Christ Presbyterian Church, Nashville, TN; author of *Befriend* and *From Weakness to Strength*

"*Practicing the King's Economy* provides a radical and wonderful blueprint for a new economic order that's closely aligned with my interpretation of Jesus's teachings and in stark, uncomfortable conflict with many aspects of twenty-first-century America. On these three issues—worship, community, and equity—and more, the authors highlight daunting problems with our current economic paradigm and offer hopeful solutions for getting us back on track."

—**Jonny Price**, senior director of Kiva US

"Michael, Robby, and Brian have unlocked truths with keys from ancient biblical Scripture that are absolutely relevant today. A must-read for business leaders and entrepreneurs who are interested in bringing their faith into the marketplace in a new, fresh, and relevant way!"

—**Wes Gardner**, CEO of PrimeTrailer

"The six keys outlined in *Practicing the King's Economy* provide a paradigm-shifting framework and the action steps we need to experience a world in which everyone flourishes. This is a must-read for every business and community leader who is longing for something more but can't quite put their finger on it. You will certainly find it in this book."

—**David Spickard**, president of Spickard Consulting; former CEO of Jobs for Life

"*Practicing the King's Economy* is one of the most soul-satisfying works I have encountered in my Christian life. I am measuring my words carefully as I make that statement. It is richly exegetical and biblically rooted. It is disarmingly practical and engagingly accessible. It is searching in its application and hope-filled in its perspective. Such a fusion is a significant authorial accomplishment. I did not want it to end."

—**Joseph Vincent Novenson**, Lookout Mountain Presbyterian Church, Lookout Mountain, TN

"I am thrilled to see the release of *Practicing the King's Economy* as it builds on the positive shifts in poverty-alleviation ministry that have developed over the last few decades. This book should prove to equip the church more fully to minister to vulnerable people within our communities. We must first free ourselves from the often-unseen economic captivity so pervasive in our

Western context. Then we will be positioned to minister more effectively from a place of unimagined freedom."

—**J. Ryan West**, PhD, Send Relief

"As a pastor who wants his church to see how the kingdom of God influences every aspect of our lives, I'm thankful for this book. It helps us think holistically about how our lives can be lived in light of God and his kingdom in such a way to bring him glory. I hope you'll read it!"

—**Micah Fries**, senior pastor of Brainerd Baptist Church, Chattanooga, TN

"In this passionate and compelling book, the authors give us a glimpse of what God's economy could truly look like, if only we took the Bible seriously. Grounded in Scripture and full of inspiring stories, this book encouraged, excited, and deeply challenged me. The good news of Jesus Christ brings whole-life transformation, including economically and financially."

—**Nigel Harris**, CEO of Tearfund

"Beautifully exegeted. *Practicing the King's Economy* reintroduces a wide-ranging, timeless, and distinctive approach to economics that only the body of Christ can display."

—**K. A. Ellis**, Cannada Fellow for World Christianity, Reformed Theological Seminary

"Jesus tells us that there is a connection between our hearts and our treasure. Even those of us who believe him need a great deal of help understanding and stewarding what God has provided. Deeply rooted in God's Word and shaped by rich experience in God's world, *Practicing the King's Economy* is a marriage of gracious words and prophetic insight."

—**Jason B. Hood**, PhD, assistant professor of New Testament and director of advanced urban ministerial education, Gordon-Conwell Theological Seminary

PRACTICING THE KING'S ECONOMY

HONORING JESUS IN HOW WE WORK, EARN, SPEND, SAVE, AND GIVE

MICHAEL RHODES AND ROBBY HOLT
with BRIAN FIKKERT

BakerBooks

a division of Baker Publishing Group
Grand Rapids, Michigan

Published by Baker Books
a division of Baker Publishing Group
PO Box 6287, Grand Rapids, MI 49516-6287
www.bakerbooks.com

Printed in the United States of America

Library of Congress Cataloging in Publication Control Number: 2017048999

ISBN 978-0-8010-7574-2

The Proprietor is represented by the literary agency of Wolgemuth & Associates, Inc.

18   19   20   21   22   23   24   7   6   5   4   3   2   1

From Michael

To the staff of Advance Memphis and all my South Memphis neighbors, whose friendship gave me the first glimpses of the King's economy . . . and to my beloved Rebecca, the South Memphian without whom I would never have begun to practice it.

From Robby

To all the saints, along with the deacons and especially the "Map Team" of North Shore Fellowship. May God make us cornucopias of righteousness for his glory . . . and to John and Gaye for the Hiding Place—to write and rest, to B&B—who taught me generosity before I could speak . . .

but most especially to my tenacious love—The OG Nova—and our dear friends who honored her.

CONTENTS

Contents

FOREWORD

I love this book.

I love it because it humbles me. And it humbles me in both of the ways we sometimes use that expression. On the one hand, paradoxically, we sometimes claim, "I'm truly humbled" when we have received some honor or flattering recognition. And sure, the authors kindly acknowledge the influence my writings have had on their thinking and practice. But let's be clear. None of what they have thought, risked, planned, and actually *done* is because "Chris Wright told them to." It's because of what they heard from God in God's Word and then decided to practice as the "obedience of faith." My role was merely to shine a little light on the immense resources God has invested in the Scriptures "for our learning" (though, tragically, in much of church history, "for our neglect").

The book humbles me also, however, in a much more challenging way. For it holds up to me a whole dimension of biblical teaching and a remarkable array of down-to-earth practical implementations of biblical principles, where I confess that I fall far short myself. I sometimes say I live a coward's life in my primary calling as a Bible teacher and writer. I hate the phrase "armchair theologian," and maybe a "desk-and-computer-theologian" is not much better. However, a book like this not only exposes that painful truth but also happily counterbalances it with the massive personal encouragement that there are at least *some* people who have found in my biblical reflection guidance for the kind of integral mission engagement you will marvel at in these pages. I love this book because it fills my heart with joy and thanksgiving to God for such truth and such stories, and because it inspires me to have a go in at least some of what it advocates.

Here are a few other reasons why I love it.

It is biblical. Every section is saturated with biblical passages and teaching. But this is far from merely a dry marshalling of texts. The Bible comes alive as we are helped to understand not only *what* God expected from his people but also *why* and *with what potential outcomes.* And as we understand the radical distinctiveness of the community God sought to create (in Old Testament Israel and the New Testament church), we can readily follow the connections the authors make with contemporary outworkings of the biblical principles and models. It is impossible to dismiss the kind of personal and community life as well as practices advocated here as mere left-leaning liberal idealism. On the contrary, the authors are clear that the economics of the kingdom of God in Jesus Christ provides a trenchant criticism of the whole spectrum of modern political and economic visions. And they do this from demonstrably biblical foundations.

It is gospel-centered. There is good news! The whole Bible tells the story of God's purpose for creation and humanity, promised in the OT Scriptures; accomplished by the life, death, and resurrection of Messiah Jesus; and awaiting its glorious completion in the new creation. And all that this book teaches and advocates is a way of living *within* that biblical story and *for* the good news embedded in that story. The authors love Jesus Christ as Savior, have submitted to him as Lord and King, live their lives as a demonstration and proclamation of that gospel, and long for others to come into the joy of the same saving and transforming relationship with Christ. That, surely, is gospel-centered living.

It is, therefore (that is, because it is gospel-centered), integrally missional. This book refuses to put asunder what God has joined together—word and deed, communication and demonstration of the gospel, believing the gospel and living it, etc. This integrated response to the gospel is, as the apostle Paul called it, the obedience of faith. The book impresses upon me something I have witnessed elsewhere in the world, which is that, when Christians respond to the realities of the world with the love of God, mind of Christ, and dynamic of the gospel, they do so with a kind of *intuitive* holistic mission. Ordinary Christians in Lebanon, for example, don't have to be taught what integral mission means before they reach out in compassionate care and generosity toward traumatized Syrian refugees, invite them into their churches, and see many of them coming to faith in Jesus. The work of their hands and the witness of their words simply go together. I see the same kind of instinctive response in this book, alongside the enriching support of some great theological and practical "keys" that are deeply grounded in Scripture.

It rejoices in "small things." It is easy to become obsessed with or dazzled by the search for (or the advocacy of) grand, global strategies for world evangelization. We are sometimes tempted to think that if we can't find the ultimate solution that will fix things on a grand scale, we are failing in our missional obedience to the Great Commission. We want things *big*—and we want them *now*. But didn't Jesus tell us stories about God's kingdom that point in a very different direction? It's about mustard seeds; grains of yeast; one lost sheep, coin, or son; a narrow gate; a transformed tax collector; a forgiven prostitute; and much more. And so, in this book, I rejoice in the multiplicity of personal stories, projects, initiatives, opportunities, and actions, which in and of themselves may seem small in the grand scheme of things. Yet they are prophetic signs of how God's kingdom works, pointers to a better way, and evidence of the transforming power of God in Christ through the gospel and the presence of the Holy Spirit. What if they were multiplied even more? What if many more churches and Christians followed the examples and suggestions outlined here? What if the yeast can permeate the whole dough and produce the satisfying bread of life for many more? May this book inspire such multiplication, for God's glory and human blessing.

Christopher J. H. Wright
Langham Partnership

ACKNOWLEDGMENTS

The multitude of names on the cover of this book makes clear that the pages you hold in your hands are the result of a communal process, a conversation over many years between Robby, Brian, and Michael. However, the names of the "great cloud of witnesses" without whom this book could never have existed could fill many books of their own. Without any hope of being exhaustive, we would like to acknowledge some of those witnesses.

I, Michael, must begin by acknowledging those academics and writers who have personally invested in me, beginning with Chris Wright, who, in addition to writing the foreword for this book, has graciously spent time listening, talking, and responding to these ideas. Moreover, Chris's lifetime work on mission, ethics, and the study of Scripture has given me a model that I can only aspire to in my own scholarship.

Thanks also to Rollin Grams, who first got me thinking about practices and became a beloved mentor and friend throughout my time at Gordon-Conwell. Of course, I am deeply indebted to Craig Bartholomew for not only taking me on as a PhD student but also putting up with a student who set out to try to write a book like this "on the side." Craig, you are a mentor and a friend beyond what any student deserves.

Ryan O'Dowd read and responded to early work on kingdom economics and provided me with the sort of incisive feedback one always covets. Dru Johnson's friendship, responses to wordy emails, and Skype calls have been a much-needed shot in the arm. D. Stephen Long's *Divine Economy* was absolutely paradigm shifting for me, and I'm so grateful that he later agreed to be a second supervisor on my PhD. Jason Hood and Kelly Kapic started investing in this project long before it began through their work with Generous Giving and have continued that investment through their friendship and advice. Joel Green kindly agreed to oversee an independent study on ethics and Scripture while I was in seminary, an experience that continues to shape my thinking deeply. Without any hope of being exhaustive, Lance Wescher, Steve Corbett, Russell Mask, Mark Glanville, and Bob Goudzwaard have all contributed to my thinking on these issues in ways that leave me deeply in their debt and grateful for our conversations.

Thanks also to all those who have shepherded me through this journey over the last ten years or so of exploring the King's economy. Sandy Willson's preaching and pastoring began shaping my imagination almost as far back as I can remember. Joe and Elfi Muutuki, George and Martha Mixon, Hash and Deepa Gudka, Alvin and Nancy Mbola, the entire Khisa family, and Sabia and the late Shafkat Khan (of whom the world was not worthy) all pastored Rebecca and me during our very formative time in Kenya. Since our return, I cannot say enough about how much we have depended on the pastoring and shepherding of Richard and Rachel Rieves, Chris Davis, Michael Davis, and Crystal and Derrick Oliver, among others. Downtown Church has been an incredible gift, given through the ministry of these saints. I also remain convinced that God used Steve Klipowicz's spiritual formation course and Chris Pekary's counseling couch to renew and restore me in ways that will last a lifetime.

Thanks to those who gave me the opportunity to present portions of this content in various formats: Dave Clark's friendship and invitation to speak at the CCDA National Conference in Memphis and the Market Solutions for Community Transformation team in LA; Neighborhood Church; Hope for the Inner City; EdenThistle Farms; Grace Evangelical Church; Second Presbyterian Church; and Ed Rambo, Dan Johnson, and the generous team of folks at Taylors First Baptist Church in Greenville.

Thanks also to Andrew Wolgemuth for his help in every step of preparing and submitting this manuscript, as well as to Bob Hosack, Amy Ballor, and the rest of the Baker team for their willingness to accept this project and work hard to make it the best it possibly can be. I owe a debt of gratitude to those whose stories fill these pages, and especially Christian Man, whose life and friendship are unceasingly encouraging to me; Wes Gardner, whose creative embodiment of God's economy in his business confirmed to me that neither of us was completely crazy; Randy White, whose faithfulness and ingenuity are awe-inspiring; Noah and Allyson Campbell and Scott and Erica Cobb, founders of the Memphis Center for Food and Faith, whose work embodies an economic imagination shaped by the kingdom; Marshall and Katherine Teague, who have created a refuge for the Rhodes family through their life and love, as well as been an example of kingdom living to which we can only aspire; Hal Bowling, whose friendship and encouragement have been absolutely essential; Marlon Foster, a friend and a hero in our community; and of course to the Chalmers Center, and in particular Mark Bowers, Jerilyn Sanders, Michael Briggs, Justin Lonas, and Tim Mahla. Your friendships mean more to me than you can possibly know.

I cannot neglect to mention some of the many friends who've loved and supported us so well. To the entire New Years Crew, including the Wilsons, Harrisons, Banners, Feigls, Noveys, Pettits, Peppers, Ottolinis, Normans, Charleses, and so many more: I hope you know we wouldn't survive without you. Thanks to Krue and Hollee Brock, who challenged us to go at the pace of love and use work as a way to be with friends. Andrew and Haley Vincent, Brandon and Lily Russell, Ethan and Grace Knight, and Tyler and Lydia Lund have been friends beyond all our deserving. Allen Halliday, Kevin Rea, Mike Harris, Tee Shipmon, John Wepfer, and Frank and Jeanne Jemison have been generous conversation partners, co-collaborators, and friends. The South Memphis Community Group has been a source of constant blessing, not least thanks to the Biggers, Anna Hollidge, RP and Loni Proctor, Erin Brinkman, and so many others. Furthermore, some of our best glimpses of the potluck economy of God have come alongside all those, past and present, who have participated in this intentional community experiment of ours, including Daniel Warner, Nate Kirsch, Pie Boaz, Pete and Catherine Nelson, Chris and Kandis Oliver, Laura Neal, Kellee Newell, Bryce (who read and commented helpfully on much of this book) and Bethany Stout, Michael and Gretchen Shaw, and "the Interns": Callie Riddle, Grace Cowart, Morgan Opgenorth, and Josh Fikkert.

I owe a tremendous debt to the staff of the Memphis Center for Urban and Theological Studies past and present, and especially to Joe Caldwell, Sharon Smith, Troy Miller, Murlene Beauregard, DiAnne (and Isaac!) Malone, Cicely Wilson, Audwin Sprouse, Marsha Young, Cathy Miller, and of course, Rob Thompson, whose friendship, encouragement, and general scheming I find invaluable and irresistible. I might also mention Martell Hixson, DeAnna Cullum, Al Blanks, Kim Wheeler, Edward Richardson, Andre Manning, Sherman Helton, Antwoine Clark, Trey Gamble, and so many other students who have welcomed me to MCUTS and made me fall in love with the place.

I am forever grateful to my family. To Katie and Brantley, whose energy and encouragement are so appreciated; Grandad, Grandma Pat, Mompsee, and Grandy (now with Jesus), whose generosity at every level has made many of our experiments in the King's economy possible; Mark, Marian, and the whole Sasscer clan, who've welcomed me into their family and loved us well; and most of all, to my parents, Mike and Gay Rhodes. Words cannot express how much I love you and am grateful for your love, support, kindness, care, conversation, and friendship.

I dedicate this book to my South Memphis neighbors. That umbrella category must include all those historic residents who have welcomed our family with open arms, especially Betty Isom, Betty Massey, Bettie Miller, Rhoda Baines, Larry "Honie" Chatman, Tim and Kim Gardner, and Donald and Jean Jenkins. It also includes the staff of Advance Memphis, past and present, and especially, in addition to those already mentioned above, Kate Lareau, Cindy Chapple, Juanita Johnson, Laron Trip, Ann Brainerd, Molly Aiken, Thelma Polk, and Brittany Taylor. And what shall I say about Steve Nash, without whom the snapshot of God's economy that is Advance Memphis would never have even been imagined, much less brought into reality? You, the staff of Advance, and the people of South Memphis, changed the course of my life forever, not least by giving me my first and best glimpses of the King's economy. I'm forever grateful.

But finally, I must thank my nearest South Memphis neighbors, the ones with whom I share a home: Isaiah Jemison, Patrick Amos, Nova Hope, and Jubilee Ruth: my love for you is beyond words. You inspire me to desire

God's kingdom more fervently. Last mentioned but first in importance save God himself alone, I must thank Rebecca, bride of my youth, my chief co-conspirator, the one without whom I would never have imagined, much less begun, the journey of practicing the King's economy. Rebecca, you have all my love. May Jesus graciously lead us "further up and further in" to his kingdom.

I, Robby, must begin by acknowledging the people who raised and rescued me through persistent prayer and nearly endless patience—my mother and father. My parents were converted to saving faith in Jesus Christ when I was very young. I don't remember many details of those earliest years, but I do remember and give God thanks for the ethos of our home. We were God's people. Commitment to God's Word and his church were never up for grabs. Their lifelong devotion to keep me both rooted and grounded bears fruit beyond my present limitations and persistent failures.

Craig Bartholomew has been a significant influence in my life for well over a decade now. I cannot overestimate the joy of discovering a mentor who loves the true King's lordship over *all* of life and therefore loves the Scriptures, loves the church, loves philosophy, loves the creation, and hungers for spiritual growth and—as a serious introvert—works so diligently to build community for believers in the church and the academy. Along with Craig, my most cherished teachers and mentors have included Knox Chamblin (now with the Lord), Ray Clark, Steve Kaufman, Michael Pettit (who, since the 80s, has helped me take inventory of my deepest hopes and commitments), Hal Bowling, Lurone Jennings, Joe Novenson, Frank Hitchings, Sandy Willson, Alfred Johnson, and Andy Mendonsa. Two others who deserve special mention are Carl Ellis Jr. and Roger Lambert.

Carl Ellis preached at my pastoral ordination service years ago. He did not disappoint—Acts 6 still rings in my ears! May God make us a people devoted to prayer, to his Word, and to practicing mercy *justly*. Moreover, may God's people appoint more and more leaders from among those who have walked faithfully with the true King while in cultural, social, and ecclesial positions of subdominance. Carl's example of faithful long-suffering in the far-from-perfect church has challenged and encouraged me.

When I was installed as the senior pastor at North Shore Fellowship, Roger Lambert charged me with Proverbs 29:25: "The fear of man lays a snare, but whoever trusts in the LORD is safe" (ESV). Along with these apt words he chose for my heart and that occasion, he has taught me as much as any other person. Moreover, his willingness to translate Greek and Hebrew texts with Crispy, TJ, me, and others most weeks for many years makes him, next to my parents, my longest-standing teacher (even though I did have that *lamentable* start).

One's companions shape one's life, and great friends have shaped mine. Should I fail to acknowledge Fred, Chris, Will, Bill, and Krue (K-Diddly Broccolinni), it would be a theft of sorts. Every error in this book is *definitely* and collectively your fault. What's next?

Other friends who have wrecked my thinking include Jamie Grant, Matt Novenson, Aubrey Spears, Jason Hood, and Brian Fikkert.

The "Map Team" mentioned in the dedication includes Dick "Snack Daddy" Allen, Dave "The Masonite" Masoner, Liz "E-Liza" Edrington, Chris "Crispy" Powell, and John "JC/JT" Tomberlin II. If you're praying that I will become a wise and soft-hearted listener, always pray and never give up! Your faithful and diligent partnership makes occasional writing and daily hope possible. HD and Berda1—welcome to the team! The whole loyal, diligent, flexible, "all hands on deck," and fun-loving staff at NSF deserve my gratitude. Yes, Miguel, we're friends. EEnafit, people like me get by with (a lotta) help from our (firstborn) friends.

While I have preached about generosity, John and Gaye Slaten and Jim and Catherine Eldridge have practiced it toward me and my family in very concrete ways. Much of my messy contributions were first written at the Slatens' cabin *Hiding Place*, where I spent "study leave" time more than once.

Ultimately, without the Super-Nova, My Novacious Bride, I would probably only write (and speak and think and ponder) abstractions. You keep my feet on the ground, girl! You are a great wife, a great mother, and a great pastor's wife. Your passion for Scripture is as irresistible as your smile. If Shug, Clickity, LD, or Ellie Bellie were writing these acknowledgments, they would each write a long book about you! Speaking of and now to those four humanoids—I'm very glad to be your BFD. Perhaps you could mention the second adjective less frequently? Clark, your passion for God's good creation comes through in chapter 9. Thanks for teaching us to compost.

Michael and Rebecca—you sure did eat a lot of our cookies. As you and your kids get older, these words will make more sense: "Run on now. It's your turn to set the pace and show us the way. Chrissy (OG Nova) and I have our eyes on you!"

PREFACE

This book truly represents a three-way collaboration that's the fruit of countless conversations between the three of us over the last twelve years. Each person has influenced every page before you. In terms of the actual writing, Michael served as primary author for the introduction and the chapters on the Worship Key, Community Key, Work Key, and Equity Key, while Robby served as the primary author for the chapters on the Creation Care Key and the Rest Key. Brian helped shape the overall concept of the book and provided editing and feedback on each chapter and the book as a whole. In case you're interested, we wanted to tell you a little bit about ourselves and why this book is so important to us.

I, Michael Rhodes, first really got to thinking about the kingdom of God as good news for the marginalized while studying economic development at Covenant College under Brian Fikkert and being pastored by Robby Holt. So this book is the result of more than a decade of my learning from these two heroes of mine. After graduating from Covenant, my wife, Rebecca, and I got to work trying to love low-income people in South Memphis (where we currently live). I worked for Advance Memphis, an incredible neighborhood community development ministry, and was involved with job training, financial literacy, entrepreneurship, GED classes . . . you name it. I spent a lot of time working with the business community to find jobs for Advance's Work Life program. My last eighteen months at Advance were primarily dedicated to helping South Memphians start small businesses, mobilizing local entrepreneurs to serve as mentors, coaching our neighbors in the basics of launching a successful business, and helping these startups connect with resources and potential customers.

Because I grew up in Memphis in an affluent community, I found myself regularly talking to and teaching middle-class groups about how God's Word demands that we dive in to sacrificial love of neighbor. I prophetically pointed to God's radical call and was regularly disappointed with the results in my own life as much as in anyone else's.

Then one day I read James K. A. Smith's *Desiring the Kingdom* and realized I didn't get up in the morning to try to love my neighbor (primarily) because God commanded it. I got out of bed in the morning because I'd fallen in love with God's vision of a world in which everyone sits under their own vine and fig tree, and "none shall make them afraid" (Mic. 4:4 KJV). My imagination had become captivated by something in Scripture called the Jubilee (which we can't wait to talk about in this book). My desire had been reshaped by the stories of the early church and the practice of trying to create community and become a neighbor among the materially poor. Smith's book, along with Chris Wright's work on biblical ethics,[1] changed the way I shared about God's kingdom with others and the direction of my studies as a graduate student at Gordon-Conwell Theological Seminary–Charlotte.

That journey led my family to look for and do our best to embrace a series of what I now call formative economic practices. We hired low-income neighbors to help with home renovations and invested in businesses aimed at the common good, watching our hearts get shaped toward these people and causes as a result. We wrestled with Ron Sider's graduated tithe (giving a higher percentage of your income whenever your income goes up) and found our hearts freed up and filled with joy. We tried to deepen our practice of neighboring as white outsiders living in a majority black neighborhood and learned to love the abundance of our block.[2] And we threw ever-larger Christmas and Easter feasts in an attempt to tie together worship, community building, and celebration. Many of the practices recommended in this book reflect our experiences trying to practice the King's economy.

Brian, Robby, and I have experienced all this as a total gift from Jesus. Such practices have begun to free our hearts for love of God and neighbor.

We cannot say this clearly enough: *entering into these practices has been a gift of God's grace to us.* As we began to dream about sharing these practices through a book, we came up with new ideas. Indeed, this book is another step in our own journeys of asking how we, as a community and as a family, can embrace God's kingdom. This has been one of the most rewarding and challenging aspects of our lives with Christ. We are so grateful to those who have inspired us to start this journey and walked in these practices with us.

Today I have the incredible privilege of working as an instructor and the director of community transformation for the Memphis Center for Urban and Theological Studies (MCUTS), an accredited Bible college in the heart of Memphis whose typical student is a bivocational African American pastor serving in our city. MCUTS is an incredible institution that works to equip pastors and leaders with tools to love their neighbors and neighborhoods well. That work includes helping neighborhood churches in Memphis welcome and walk with the materially poor, not least by proclaiming and pursuing the good news of the King's economy.

The Rhodes family is far from perfect, nowhere near "arrived," and writing this book has challenged us to consider ways we continue to fall short of the life Jesus invites us to live. We pray God will give us the grace to recognize our sin and live toward his redemption. We pray also that this book will play some small part in encouraging all of us to grow into a church that carries in its own life the gift of God's good kingdom economy.

I, Robby Holt, spent many formative years in Lookout Mountain, Tennessee, my father's hometown. It's possible that you have heard of Lookout Mountain because the Chalmers Center is located there and you have read *When Helping Hurts.* Or perhaps you have heard of it due to its legacy as a place of collected, generational wealth. Or maybe the place sounds familiar because it happens to be one of those places Martin Luther King Jr. called on to "let freedom ring." It's all those places. And it's my hometown.

When I was in high school (especially during 1985–87), my dad began to take me to "Adopt-a-Block" gatherings hosted and organized by Inner City Ministries (a nonprofit community development organization now called Hope for the Inner City) and New City Fellowship, the local church founded by Randy Nabors, which birthed the nonprofit. The block was Fort Negly on the Southside of downtown Chattanooga. The street where I always worked was Mitchell Avenue. I had no real skills, so I repeatedly landed the job of sweeping up broken bottles, used syringes, and also some unmentionables. I often began on the corner of 16th Street and Mitchell and swept down toward 17th Street. I regularly swept in front of New City's "Fellowship House," where all kinds of good meetings happened.

It may have been my first or second time helping at Adopt-a-Block when my dad left me to sweep while he helped other men with plumbing or carpentry or similar work. As I swept along, a young adult man with blue jeans, long blond hair, and a burly beard invited me to join him and others on the porch of the Fellowship House. Remember, I was from affluent Lookout Mountain in the 1980s. People like this guy—Andy Mendonsa— only existed in pictures . . . of the hippies. I'll never forget his message to me and whoever else was up on that porch with me that day:

> Religion that God our Father accepts as pure and faultless is this: to look after orphans and widows in their distress and to keep oneself from being polluted by the world. (James 1:27)

Can you picture me? The men in my world were white, wealthy, and frequently wore bow ties. My dad had the wisdom and kind of heart that got me on that street with a broom in my hand. But I had never seen anyone like Andy Mendonsa. And I had never heard that Scripture before. It worked through me like lightning through a flagpole. Its truth reached my toes and caused my hair to stand up straight. The Word resonated with the new heart of hearts God had given me by his limitless grace. Over the next couple years, I watched Andy like a hawk, drove to meet him at homes of various widows, and soaked up all the wisdom I could.

Around this time, Andy launched Chattanooga Widows Harvest, a ministry to largely poor and neglected widows in urban Chattanooga and its region. One summer during college, I volunteered with the youth training program at Inner City Ministries. My "work crew" served Andy and his widows, and two of the guys on the crew came from Mitchell Avenue.

After attending college, starting a family, and going to seminary, I landed one of those jobs that would make me irresistible to Michael Rhodes. My good friend Krue Brock knew Lurone Jennings was searching for partners at the Bethlehem Center for Community and Economic Development, aka "the Beth," in Chattanooga's Alton Park neighborhood. Lurone wanted to plant a church to hum at the center of the Beth's life. Krue connected us, and Lurone became my boss for eighteen wonderful months as we co-labored to plant the Bethlehem Community Church on 37th Street in Alton Park.

Worshiping and feasting with this body at the Beth proved invaluable to my whole family. One of the biggest lessons I learned from my brothers and sisters there came from worship. We regularly sang a song during the offering, a part of the service deeply celebrated by some of the poorest people in Chattanooga. One line had us all singing, "Give! And it will come back to you, a good measure pressed down, shaken together, running over . . ."

This song bothered me. See, I had been to seminary and was afraid it was theologically suspect. So imagine my surprise when I read Luke 6:38 shortly after arriving at the Beth from seminary and wondering how I'd fix this "problem." Jesus said:

> Give, and it will be given to you. A good measure, pressed down, shaken together and running over, will be poured into your lap. For with the measure you use, it will be measured to you.

I did then and still do reject the health and wealth gospel. But that moment was a good reminder of just how much I had to learn from those who were unlike me. I came to teach. To lead. To help. Now I knew I had come to learn, to be shaped by others, to receive help.

Well, eventually I began a PhD program, studying in the United Kingdom with Craig Bartholomew. Luke's Gospel challenged my wife, Nova Christine (Chrissy), and me throughout our first year there when, at the end of that year, we received two phone calls that altered our course once again. First, Andy Mendonsa called to tell us his board wanted to sell the Fellowship House, which had become the offices and center for Widows Harvest. The next week Joe Novenson called to tell us my home church, Lookout Mountain Presbyterian, planned to plant a church in Chattanooga.

He thought somehow I was part of that plan. Both men knew we were one year into a three-year commitment to study with Craig in the United Kingdom. Then the next week Craig called me and four other students into his office to tell us his time at that university was coming to an end. The math wasn't hard from there!

Our story really has come full circle. I have been doing gospel ministry at that church, North Shore Fellowship, since 2003. (Michael worshiped with us, helped with our youth group, and ate our cookies—often!—from 2004 through 2008.) We live in that house on Mitchell Avenue, the same one where I swept up trash as a teen and heard Andy talk about the widows. And Michael is doing doctoral work with Craig.

And 1603 Mitchell Avenue is still a fellowship house. We have a revolving door, and later in the book we will tell a couple stories of the people who've shaped us by spending time feasting at our table. Some of those people are Michael and Rebecca Rhodes and their three children, Isaiah, Amos, Nova Hope (named after my wife, Nova Christine Holt), and their fourth, Jubilee, who arrived shortly after we submitted the manuscript for this book.

I, Brian Fikkert, am the coauthor with Steve Corbett of *When Helping Hurts*.[3] That book is an extension of my work as the founder and president of the Chalmers Center for Economic Development at Covenant College, where I also serve as a professor of economics and community development.

The Chalmers Center's vision is for local churches to declare and demonstrate to people who are poor that Jesus Christ is making all things new. Toward that end, the center equips churches to walk alongside people who are poor, helping them break free from the spiritual, social, and material bonds of poverty. I am absolutely delighted that this book is the latest resource to be published under the auspices of the Chalmers Center, for it contains messages the church desperately needs to hear, messages I desperately need to hear. Let me explain.

The opening chapter of *When Helping Hurts* is titled "Why Did Jesus Come to Earth?" The chapter explains that few Christians answer this question the way that Jesus did, saying, "I must proclaim the good news of the *kingdom of God* to the other towns also, because that is why I was sent" (Luke 4:43, emphasis added). The book goes on to explain that the church's lack of familiarity with the full implications of the kingdom of God often makes our efforts to help the poor both anemic and ineffectual. In other words, we first need to be transformed by the kingdom before we can declare and demonstrate that kingdom where Jesus did: among the poor and marginalized (see Luke 7:22–23).

And that's where this book comes in. In the past several years, Michael and Robby have been confronting me with the truth that the kingdom of God is radical in nature and that most of us—myself included—are living highly nonradicalized lives, particularly in the space of economics. You see, globalization is subtly shaping all of us in a particular way of thinking and behaving in our economic lives that is, in many respects, antithetical to the economics of the kingdom of God. I already believed this, but Michael and Robby have shown me more implications of the King's economy than I had ever considered before. And to be completely honest, I find these implications to be somewhat irritating. In fact, if Michael and Robby weren't such great guys who love on me so much, I'd probably just tune them out.

You see, I am a specialist in international economics, meaning I have been trained to love global finance, international trade, the spread of market capitalism, and economic growth. Indeed, I love many aspects of globalization, not the least of which is that it has caused an unprecedented reduction in global poverty in the past twenty-five years. In addition, I don't want to be challenged this much! I want to be left alone. I like shopping wherever it's most convenient to me, and I tend to think recycling is just kind of, well, cute. But Michael and Robby keep taking me back to Scripture, showing me in new ways how radically different the vision of the King's economy is from the vision of the global economic order. And slowly, very slowly, I am trying to put these ideas into practice, believing by faith that the gospel of the kingdom—in all its radical fullness—is truly good news for me too.

I don't know what all this means, nor do Michael and Robby. However, I am convinced we need to be reshaped by the goals, narratives, and practices of the kingdom of God, whose economy is far more radical and conducive to human flourishing than that of the kingdoms of this world. So take this book as our imperfect attempt to improvise what the economics of the kingdom of God looks like in the twenty-first century. We don't have it all figured out, and you may very likely take issue with many of the practices we suggest in this book. That's fine. Then develop your own practices. Just work to ensure your practices are shaping you to function well in the King's economy, which is already replacing the current global economic order, for "the kingdom of God is at hand" (Mark 1:15 KJV).

INTRODUCTION

PRACTICING THE KING'S ECONOMY IN OCCUPIED TERRITORY

Caught between Two Kingdoms: A Prostitute's Story

Remember Rahab? She was the prostitute living in the walls of Jericho when the Israelite spies showed up. Even though they were her people's enemies, she hid the spies from her fellow countrymen. "I know that your God has given you the land," she told the spies, "for we've heard how he dried up the Red Sea before you, how he destroyed the kings who stood against you. We're terrified, because we know your God is 'God in the heavens above and on the earth beneath.' So please, swear you will spare my family and me when you conquer our country!" (Josh. 2:9–13, paraphrase).

This may not seem like the most promising place to start exploring how to live in the King's economy, but just go with us for a moment. Rahab lived in a kingdom. Jericho had its own rulers and rules, its own economic policies and social arrangements, and of course, its own gods. Rahab's entire life had been shaped by this kingdom, although if her job as a prostitute is any indication, the Jericho regime hadn't always been friendly. Then one day she looked out the window and saw another kingdom invading, a kingdom with another king, a different economic policy, other sorts of social arrangements, and even, if she could believe the stories, a God strong enough to overcome the most powerful empire on earth. This God, known in Israel by his name *Yahweh*, was on his way.[1] Rahab had to answer the question, *Whose side am I on?*

Rahab chose the kingdom of Yahweh at least in part because she believed that, at the end of the day, the kingdom that would still be standing when the dust settled would be different from the one in which she currently lived.

She was right. Her family was spared, but more than that, this pagan prostitute became a heroine of righteousness and faith (see Heb. 11:31; James 2:25). She even became an ancestor of the ultimate King, Jesus himself (see Matt. 1:5). And perhaps, strange as it might seem, she also provides us with a parable for understanding Jesus's economy—and how we might practice it in occupied territory.

Here Comes the King

When King Jesus came on the scene, he confronted people in a similar situation to Rahab's. Jesus came proclaiming the good news of the kingdom of God (see Mark 1:14–15) to a people suffering under the bad news of the kingdom of Caesar and the Roman Empire (see Luke 3:1). Indeed, Jesus announced, planted at the cross, and inaugurated at the resurrection the reign of God over the entire universe.

The kingdom of God isn't just a minor footnote in the Gospels. On the contrary, the arrival of King Jesus and his kingdom is the centerpiece of the biblical story that runs from Genesis to Revelation.

This story begins with an amazingly generous King—the Triune God—who is the Creator of heaven and earth. Out of his incredible generosity, this King created human beings in his image and invited them to rule over his creation with him. Think about it: human beings were created to rule with the Creator King over his kingdom, cultivating it, unpacking its potential, and developing it into a flourishing empire. The same generous God who called lions, fruit-bearing trees, and coral reefs into existence generously gave all these to his people to enjoy, protect, and develop. Humanity's high calling is nothing less than coruling and co-loving everything our God and Father has made.

In other words, because people are made in the image of a creating and creative God, we are called to (1) *preserve and protect* the natural world and

(2) *create culture* and *economic flourishing* by stewarding the natural world (this is what some scholars call the "cultural mandate"). This is, in many ways, the theological foundation for our economic lives: God *wants* and *requires* us to work to bring out the unexploited potential of his world as part of our vocation. Unpacking the economic potential of God's creation in ways that reflect his character is part of our divinely sanctioned "job description."

But our first human parents, Adam and Eve, rejected their God-given vocation and rebelled against God's good and generous kingdom in the Garden of Eden, bringing sin and suffering into every corner of the world. The snake in the grass tricked our ancestors into disobedience by causing them to doubt the goodness of the King's gifts: "God's holding out on you,"[2] the serpent suggested. "He doesn't want you to be like him." Adam and Eve's rebellion was a rejection of God as their generous King and a rejection of their roles as coworkers in his kingdom.

This rebellion resulted in humans being thrown out of God's kingdom and joining the kingdom of darkness where Satan reigns (see Eph. 2:1–2; Col. 1:13). As we all know, the results have been devastating. Designed for an intimate and trusting relationship with our generous God, we find ourselves running from him and feeling far from his love. Designed to serve alongside our fellow image bearers, we find our relationships are marked by competition, fear, and distrust. Designed to see ourselves as unique, gifted reflections of the Great King, we vacillate between soul-crushing shame and outlandish pride. And designed to rule this King's world on his behalf, we instead spend our lives abusing, neglecting, or worshiping God's stuff rather than caring for it.[3]

In the face of human rebellion, our generous Creator amazingly promised that his best gifts were yet to come. Right there in the garden—on the very scene of humanity's rebellion against his kingship—God promised to send a Savior, a conquering King who would crush the serpent and free humanity from the serpent's reign.

To fulfill this promise, God called a childless pagan named Abraham and promised to give him a kingdom of descendants living in a flourishing land. Even more miraculously, this generous God promised that through this nomadic nobody's kingdom, he would bring blessing to the whole world (see Gen. 12:3).

Much of the Old Testament tells the story of God's relationship with Israel, the kingdom God created from Abraham's offspring. Again and again, God gave the Israelites good gifts and a high calling. Where Adam and Eve rebelled, Israel was to be a kingdom of "justice and righteousness" through whom God would bring restoration to his world (see Gen. 18:19).

By the way, this is why we'll spend a fair amount of time exploring the Old Testament. In the Old Testament, we encounter Israel as God's chosen community, called to embody his rule and reign. The story of God's relationship with Israel gives us pictures of his heart for all humanity and even creation itself. Indeed, the New Testament actually teaches that the story of the Old Testament is essential for the spiritual life of the church (see Rom. 15:4; 1 Cor. 10:6). We cannot understand God's kingdom unless we learn from his establishment of "a kingdom of priests and a holy nation" (Exod. 19:6) through Israel in the Old Testament.

But though God gave the Israelites everything necessary to fulfill their calling, like Adam and Eve, they ultimately fell short of living fully as faithful members of God's kingdom. When God came looking for the kingdom of justice and righteousness he had expected and longed for, he instead found violence and oppression (see Isa. 5:1–7). Once again, the generous King's plan to rule his world through his chosen, royal representatives appeared to have stalled out.

Nevertheless, God kept his promises by sending his Son, Jesus, a descendant of Abraham, as the conquering King who freed God's children from Satan's dominion. In his life, death, and resurrection, Jesus announced and inaugurated God's rule over everything (see Luke 4:43). And he invites all humanity to become, in him, what they were always meant to be: members of God's royal, priestly family, coworkers and rulers in God's glorious kingdom, joining with him in preserving, protecting, developing, and cultivating the created world. In Jesus, God shows up and claims what's rightfully his: every square inch of the cosmos. In Jesus, God makes clear that he has not and will never turn his back on his good world or on his plan to fill it with sons and daughters who reign over it with him.

Many of us miss much of this wonderful, earth-shattering announcement because we are so accustomed to thinking about the gospel exclusively in narrow, legal terms. Don't get us wrong. No one should skip over or diminish the following aspect of salvation: "For all have sinned and fall short of the glory of God" (Rom. 3:23). Moreover, due to God's righteous wrath (see Rom. 1:18–32), "the wages of sin is death" (Rom. 6:23). But thanks be to God, on the cross, Jesus Christ "died for the ungodly" (Rom. 5:6)! "God shows his love for us in that while we were still sinners, Christ died for us" (Rom. 5:8 ESV). We had a terrible and, left to ourselves, unsolvable relational problem: alienation from God. This alienation included a major legal dynamic. But God has acted to reconcile us to himself. This is truly good news. "God was reconciling the world to himself in Christ, not counting people's sins against them" (2 Cor. 5:19). The one true God "has rescued us from the dominion of darkness and brought us into the kingdom of the Son he loves, in whom we have *redemption, the forgiveness of sins*" (Col. 1:13–14, emphasis added). Our forgiveness is "in him" because God saved us "by canceling the record of debt that stood against us with its legal demands. This he set aside, nailing it to the cross" (Col. 2:14 ESV). God, in his grace, sent his Son to become one of us and rescue us from, among other things, our sin and guilt and his righteous wrath toward sin, evil, and injustice (see Rom. 3:21–26).

However, the good news is even more than this!

Look at what Paul writes right before "in whom we have redemption, the forgiveness of sins": God the Father has "rescued" us from one kingdom of darkness to live in the kingdom of his beloved Son. God has brought us out of one kingdom and into another.

Now look at Colossians 1:15–20 to see what Paul writes right after that wonderful line about "redemption, the forgiveness of sins." God is reconciling all things to himself through Christ on the cross.[4] To "reconcile" is to put things into right relationship again, and Christ is doing this with respect to "all things" in heaven and earth. This is the good news of the kingdom of God for all those who repent and believe.

This book seeks to celebrate the gospel. We believe that, at its heart, the gospel is the good news that God is both bringing his kingdom and welcoming his people into that kingdom through forgiveness and reconciliation. We believe that the (great) news of God's kingdom and the (great) news that God offers forgiveness from sin so that people might enter that kingdom should both be kept in view, as they are different aspects of the same overarching story. The true King is our only Savior, and forgiveness from sins welcomes us into his kingdom.

The good news of the gospel, then, is more than our souls being snatched away from this world to another world where our disembodied souls—that are now legally safe—play harps for all eternity in some never-ending choir rehearsal. Think about what happened to Jesus on Easter morning. His soul didn't fly off to heaven; his body rose to new life! It was really him, all of him, body and soul. And just as Jesus reclaimed his physical body, clothing it in power and glory, *Jesus will reclaim our physical bodies and the entire created world* (see Phil. 3:20–21). What happened to Jesus will happen to us and to the whole world.[5]

Jesus's resurrection life is the firstfruits of his kingdom reign. Our King isn't rescuing us *from* creation. He's bringing a kingdom that will reclaim every square inch of the cosmos. He's launching a new world in which every person who is in Jesus might live, reign, work, and worship in the resurrected and renewed heaven and earth. And he's creating a people marked by his justice and righteousness, united to him by his Spirit. Now *that's* the Good News—the gospel—of the *kingdom of God*! And this good news of God's kingdom was the central message of Jesus and his apostles (see Luke 4:43; 9:1–6; Acts 28:23–31).[6]

Ever since Jesus's ascension, then, we have lived in the next-to-last act of this incredible drama. As the church united to our faithful King, God calls us to become the people he always intended for us to be, bearing witness to the justice, righteousness, mercy, and love of our generous King in our still-broken world. We do this work by the power of our King and in the shadow of his coming kingdom. For one day, the King will return and claim what's his in full, driving out sin "far as the curse is found" and welcoming all his children into a renewed and resurrected creation.

A Kingdom within a Kingdom

Today, then, each one of us is a bit like Rahab. We live in one kingdom, a kingdom of this world. When we look out the window and see King Jesus and his kingdom headed our way, we're confronted with the same question

Rahab faced: Whose side am I on? Nobody can swear ultimate allegiance to more than one king. "No one can serve two masters" (Matt. 6:24).

Actually, our situation is a bit more complicated than Rahab's. Jesus has already invaded the city. Furthermore, Jesus hasn't come simply to obliterate the human kingdoms we've grown up in; he's come to conquer *and* reclaim them. After all, every throne, dominion, ruler, or authority—on earth and in heaven—was created *by* and *for* him (see Col. 1:16–18). And at the end of the biblical story, we find the "kings of the earth" bringing their "splendor" into the new heavens and new earth (Rev. 21:24). And most importantly for our purposes in this book, our role isn't simply to accept the invading King and then abandon the communities in which we live. Our role is to swear allegiance to Jesus and become, as the church, an outpost, a colony of the Jesus kingdom, amidst the kingdoms of the world.[7] We are to declare in our words, our actions, and our lives together that "there is another king" (Acts 17:7), and he's on his way to reclaim what's his. Through lives lived under the rule of Jesus, we invite every other kingdom to join us in pledging allegiance to our world's rightful Lord.

This means that those of us who are followers of Jesus live in earthly kingdoms that cannot and should not claim our primary allegiance. We live in the United States or Sudan or China or South Korea or Switzerland. But while different aspects of these earthly kingdoms may be closer to or further from God's design, *all of them fall short of his kingdom.*

Every earthly kingdom has its own way of doing things, its own customs and policies regarding food, sex, family, and religion. And *every* kingdom has an economic policy. But when Jesus welcomes us into his alternate kingdom, something strange happens. We discover a whole new world. As we encounter this strange new world, we discover that the Jesus kingdom looks very different from the kingdoms to which we've grown accustomed.

Perhaps you have grown used to thinking about this dynamic in terms of God's sexual ethics or emphasis on honesty and integrity. Many of us sense that our United States kingdom, for instance, has an entirely different "marriage and family" policy than the one Jesus calls us to embrace. Many of us also sense that when our culture's approach to family or sex conflicts with God's approach, we must choose to "obey God rather than men" (Acts 5:29 ESV).

> In the West, our prevailing economic worldview sees people as self-interested individuals with limitless desires in a limited world, who seek to increase consumption and leisure by earning as much money as possible.

But King Jesus also has his own unique economic policies, his own economic program. In the West, our prevailing economic worldview sees people as self-interested individuals with limitless desires in a limited world, who seek to increase consumption and leisure by earning as much money as possible.

Then there's Jesus, with:

- His parables of well-dressed lilies that neither labor nor spin and wealthy farmers punished for saving too much.
- His commands to lend without expecting return and to invest in heavenly dwellings.
- His establishment of communities in which "no one claimed that any of their possessions was their own" (Acts 4:32).

Suddenly we sense that Jesus might teach Economics 101 quite a bit differently than our high school teachers did. We have a hunch that if economics is, at its most basic, a discussion around consumption, production, and the exchange of goods and services, Jesus might call us to very different patterns of consumption, production, and exchange than those to which our Western world invites us.

For example, consider the definition of economics in the opening pages of a popular introductory textbook: "Economics is concerned with the efficient use or management of limited productive resources to achieve maximum satisfaction of human material wants."[8] This field sounds like a materialist, humanist manifesto! We suspect that if the same Jesus who said, "Seek first the kingdom of God" were writing this textbook, he might define this field a bit differently. He might propose something like the following: Economics is the study of humanity's consumption, production, and exchange of goods and services in order to steward King Jesus's creation.

When faced with such discrepancies between Jesus's approach to our economic life and our culture's approach, many of us sense we are falling short of the life God intends for us.

There are good reasons for our misgivings. Nearly 43,000 Americans commit suicide *every year*, making it the tenth highest cause of death in the country.[9] Indeed, between 1950 and 1999, a period of serious economic growth in America, suicides among people under the age of twenty-four increased by 137 percent.[10] Nearly 43 *million* Americans experience some form of mental illness each year.[11]

> Economics is the study of humanity's consumption, production, and exchange of goods and services in order to steward King Jesus's creation.

Or consider these stats on substance abuse:

- "In 2013, 30.2 percent of men and 16.0 percent of women 12 and older reported binge drinking in the past month."[12]
- 17.3 million Americans reported alcohol addiction or serious problems related to alcohol use in 2013.[13]
- 4.2 million Americans met clinical criteria for dependence based on marijuana use in 2013.[14]
- Life expectancy is currently *decreasing* for white, middle-aged Americans, driven by high rates of suicide and substance abuse.[15]

All this is happening in the wealthiest nation that has ever existed on earth. Indeed, substance abuse, mental illness, and depression seem to have risen right alongside our rising incomes. In fact, some research even suggests that our pursuit of these rising incomes is actually causing the explosion in mental illness.[16] When we consider our unprecedented wealth *and* our increasing inner despair, we wonder whether our approach to economics, like that of the rich young ruler before us, has tempted us to walk away sad from our Lord's invitation to come and follow him.

The problem with our Rahabesque situation may be that the kingdoms we live in just seem more real than the one we encounter in the Bible. If we're honest, the Bible's approach to our economic lives doesn't just look foolish; it looks entirely implausible. When we read the Bible, we sometimes feel as though we're reading about a parallel universe. Like the older children in C. S. Lewis's *The Lion, the Witch, and the Wardrobe*, we find it incredibly difficult to believe in Narnia, a land with talking animals and walking trees, when our own world seems so different. And yet Jesus's triumph over death on the cross and at his resurrection invites us to believe, against any evidence to the contrary, that another "Narnia" is real. Indeed, God is bringing a kingdom far more real than any earthly power or authority we experience today.

If Jesus is welcoming us into this kingdom and calling us to live as colonies of that kingdom within the nations and places we reside, how do we possibly begin to embrace our King's economic program?

Walking through the Wardrobe: Six Keys to the King's Economy

We believe the first step is simply to take a look around this strange world of the Bible and grow better acquainted with the neighborhood. Like the kids in the Chronicles of Narnia, we must "walk through the wardrobe" and wander around in this foreign land, learning its customs, acknowledging its alternate reality, and embracing its authority. And then we need to live like we are in Narnia back on this side of the wardrobe, because Narnia is invading our world.

Lucky for us, the God-breathed Bibles on our shelves invite us to do just that. When we read Scripture with an eye to its economic vision, we enter into the world of God's economy. The time we spend exploring that Narniaesque world prepares us to welcome the kingdom of God in our daily lives as well.

To help you take this journey through the wardrobe (or to help you in your journey "further up and further in" to this grand country), we'll discuss six keys to the King's economy. Each of these keys represents a biblical theme we believe captures an important element of God's heart for our economic lives. Think of these keys as tools to help you "unlock the wardrobe" and enter into the alternate universe of God's economy in Scripture. We'll discuss the following six keys:

1. "God, Not Mammon" ‖ The Worship Key
2. "One Table, One Baptism, No Distinction" ‖ The Community Key
3. "Work and Wages, Gleaning and Giving" ‖ The Work Key

4. "No Poor among You" || The Equity Key

5. "The Heavens Declare the Glory" || The Creation Key

6. "The Lord Has Given the Sabbath" || The Rest Key

Of course, we would never suggest that these themes exhaust all there is to say about the biblical economic vision.[17] We hope that by exploring Scripture through these keys, we will open up new avenues to explore God's economy in God's Word—and God's world—today.

Practicing the King's Economy in Occupied Territory

Short visits to this parallel economic universe contained in Scripture, though, aren't enough; we're called to bear witness to this world in our own lives and communities. We've got to come back through the wardrobe, bringing glimpses of God's kingdom reign, including his alternative economic program, into our own world.

This is hard work for at least two reasons. First, *proclaiming King Jesus in territory occupied by other would-be kings can get us in trouble.* In every culture in which the church has taken root, the surrounding culture simply has refused to accept certain aspects of Jesus's kingdom. Sometimes this leads to marginalization. Sometimes it leads to martyrdom. So while we celebrate when the kingdoms of this world recognize aspects of our King's economic program, and indeed work to help them do so, we also recognize that the King's economy will always be countercultural.

Second, *we ourselves have been deeply deformed in our economic lives by living in kingdoms that fall short of God's kingdom.* To illustrate this, imagine for a moment that you are a star offensive lineman for the Dallas Cowboys. You have studied the rules of football for a lifetime. You have watched countless hours of the sport, and all your heroes are those stars who have come before you and whose stories encouraged you to persevere in the hard times. You have spent even more countless hours practicing to be an offensive lineman in scrimmages and practice drills and have adhered to a complex diet and exercise regimen. All this practicing is designed to form you into a particular sort of player: a 300-pound man capable of running the forty-yard dash in under six seconds and bench-pressing 225 pounds twenty-five times in a row. That's what you're training for because that's how you succeed in the game you're playing.

But what if you woke up one day and realized you were supposed to be an Ironman triathlete? Even though you might be one of the top athletes in the world, all your training hasn't prepared you to get on that bike. In fact, much of your training has actually *deformed* you: all that bulk and mass just won't do on a 26.2-mile run (let alone the 2.4-mile swim and 112-mile bike ride).

If you wanted to stand a chance of even qualifying for an Ironman, you'd have to launch an entirely different training program altogether. You'd have to find a new diet and exercise regimen, one that would help you slim down and increase your endurance. You'd have to learn new rules, rules that make an Ironman an Ironman but have no parallel in football. You'd have to attend triathlons, get new heroes, find new coaches, and essentially fall in love with an entirely different sport.

We believe this strange sports parable can speak to us about how to begin to live toward Jesus's coming kingdom. You see, we've spent the better part of a lifetime practicing to be offensive linemen through:

- Intense training in the world's stories, practices, and rules.
- Admiring and imitating the world's heroes.
- Listening to the world's coaches.

If we want to announce another king and another kingdom, all that must change. We've got to start practicing for this new kingdom.

That's why, in this book, we don't just give you a chapter on each key to the King's economy that will enable you to explore God's economy in Scripture. We also include a second chapter on each key that contains stories of fellow sinners who've brought bits and pieces of that economy to life in our world. These stories will help you encounter each key. And most important, these chapters will also include a set of formative practices, a training regimen, if you will, that we believe will help you embody the King's economy back on this side of the wardrobe.

By formative practices, we mean actions you can take as an individual, together with your family, as a church, or in the marketplace, that explicitly illustrate this economy. Think of them as spiritual disciplines for your economic health. We believe these formative practices will do three things:

1. Act to bring about the healing brought by our King in the midst of our hurting world.
2. Express something to the world about the kingdom and our King.
3. Form our own hearts, habits, visions, and imaginations to see, bear witness to, and welcome this kingdom.

As an example of this, one scholar points out that when members of the early church shared bread and wine with one another at the Lord's Supper, they were simultaneously doing justice (people were fed who otherwise wouldn't be), declaring something about God and his world (God desires for all people to have enough of his good creation), and forming the hearts of those who ate together across lines of race and class to recognize one another as brothers and sisters who ought to take care of one another.[18] These formative practices enabled members of the church to act in line with the King's economy, declare the good news of the King's economy, and exercise their hearts, minds, and even bodies to pursue the King's economy.

Jesus actually assumed something like this in his command in Matthew 6:20–21: "Store up for yourselves treasures in heaven," Jesus said, "for where your treasure is, there your heart will be also." We often read this verse as saying, "Where your *heart* is, there your *treasures* will go." But while that's true too, Jesus makes the opposite point here. "Where you put your stuff," we might paraphrase, "will determine what happens to your heart." Contrary to our expectations, Jesus declared that if we obey him by investing in his kingdom, then our hearts will be moved toward his kingdom. Our practice of giving shapes our hearts for God. And this practice, this exercise in heart formation, is essential precisely because two kingdoms are waging war for our allegiance. Or as Jesus put it just a few verses later, "You cannot serve both God and money" (Matt. 6:24).

We believe, then, that formative practices like the ones we will recommend alongside each of the six keys to the King's economy will help us to do what God calls us to do, say what God calls us to say, and become what God calls us to become.

Almost none of these practices are prescriptive commands. They didn't come down Mount Sinai with Moses. They are more like strategies to help us creatively become more and more like Jesus in our economic lives. You may find some more or less helpful or you may even come up with your own, and that's okay. But what we *can't* do is expect to become faithful economic disciples of Jesus without some sort of economic exercise regimen. You might think of these formative practices as spiritual economic disciplines for economic discipleship.

Two Caveats

Now, for some caveats.

Caveat #1: at this point, you might be thinking, *This talk of formative practices is legalism. God changes our hearts, we don't. This is just works righteousness.* We want to say two things about this.

First, the Bible teaches us that every good thing we do is all unearned grace and a gift from God to us. We *are* saved to do good works, but we are *not* saved by them (see Titus 2:11–14; 3:3–8). We believe that any good done by us is a result of God's grace at work within us. In other words, not only is our justification by grace but our sanctification and our good works are also by grace. That's why in Ephesians 2:10, Paul writes that we are "created in Christ Jesus to do good works" that God has already "prepared in advance for us to do."

We don't believe for a minute that the practices we recommend in this book have the power to do anything at all if they are done simply out of our own strength. Furthermore, let us say it here loud and clear: doing these practices cannot earn merit before God or save us from our sins. Only God can save us. Far be it from us to ever suggest our actions could somehow earn us favor with God.

But that doesn't mean we shouldn't engage in formative practices or that these disciplines don't actually shape our hearts, minds, affections, moral vision, and habits.[19] Think of it this way: right now invisible radio waves are flying through the air all around you. They are present regardless of any action on your part. However, if you want to hear those radio waves, *you have to raise an antenna.*

We believe formative practices help us to raise the antenna, tuning us in to the transforming power of the Spirit that is always all around us and all ours in Christ. As we walk in the Spirit in love, we become more deeply attuned to Christ Jesus (Philem. 6). Indeed, one scholar speaks of practices as "habitations of the Spirit."[20] Perhaps this is something like what Paul meant when he said to the Galatians, "Since we live by the Spirit, let us keep in step with the

> We believe formative practices help us to raise the antenna, tuning us in to the transforming power of the Spirit that is always all around us and all ours in Christ.

Spirit" (Gal. 5:25). The Spirit is at work among us, leading us to discern together, in practice, new ways of serving the Lord, King Jesus (see Rom. 12:1–2; Phil. 1:9–11; Col. 1:9–14; Philem. 6).

Even here, though, the analogy breaks down. Because unlike with radio waves, the presence of God sometimes breaks through and we hear the music even though our antennae are broken off completely. That's the miracle of salvation! Furthermore, without God saving us and renewing our hearts, we can't "raise the antenna" on our own. Without the Holy Spirit's work in salvation, the practices are powerless to deepen our life with Christ. None of this, though, means we aren't called to engage in disciplines of discipleship in response to God's love. We believe God's grace thoroughly changes whole people. Grace renews us as thinking, loving, willing, acting humans.

Second, despite our difficulty explaining theologically how it is that God does all the work and yet also calls us to work out our salvation (Phil. 2:12–13) through practicing his ways, Scripture clearly exhorts us to engage in what we're calling formative practices. God told the Israelites to feast before him "so that [they] may learn to revere the LORD [their] God always" (Deut. 14:23). David told God he had practiced meditating and memorizing Scripture so that he might not sin against him (see Ps. 119:11). Jesus told his followers where to store up treasures not least because it would affect their hearts (see Matt. 6:20). Paul told the Corinthians to be like athletes who exercise self-control so as to be capable of winning the prize (see 1 Cor. 9:24–27; 2 Tim. 2:4–6). Many more examples could be given, but hopefully we've made the point. It's dangerous to ignore the commands of Scripture because we can't completely understand how they work.

Ultimately, the way God graciously enables us to engage in good works that shape our hearts toward him in sanctification is a mystery we can't fully fathom. "Work out your own salvation with fear and trembling," writes Paul, "for it is God who works in you, both to will and to work for his good pleasure" (Phil. 2:12–13 ESV).

Caveat #2: this is a book about how to live economic lives that are more in line with the righteousness, justice, mercy, and generosity of our King Jesus. Many times when we have discussions about how to do a better job living kingdom-centered lives in relationship to economics, we quickly move to partisan political debates about the best type of economic system: free-market capitalism, socialism, or some hybrid of the two. The question of which system we vote for becomes the litmus test of whether we're really faithful to the economics of the Bible.

In this book, we won't engage in any of these arguments about the best economic system, even though they are extremely important discussions. Instead, we'll focus on formative practices God's people can perform together within their communities. We'll do this for at least three reasons.

First, there is plenty of important economic work to be done that we believe members of the body of Christ from across the political spectrum can embrace. Far too often, discussions of how to care for the poor or to bring justice to our communities divide neatly along political lines and separate Christians from one another. We hope this book provides ways for people of differing partisan persuasions to work together for King Jesus.

Second, we believe God's Word primarily speaks to the church as the body of Christ and that God has given the church a special mission to embody God's kingdom through our lives together. Don't get us wrong; we fully believe Christians are called to proclaim the kingdom of God in word, deed, and sign to every person and every sphere of society. We believe this will require us to do the hard work of figuring out questions such as: What role do markets play in a just economy? What should government do to promote justice and liberty? What sorts of systems best allow for human flourishing for everybody?

However, we also believe the church has a unique role as the "pilot run," "God's beachhead in the world as it is; the down payment, the prototype, the herald, the midwife of the new world on the way."[21] In other words, the way we order our way of life as those who explicitly claim Jesus as our King allows us to serve as a colony of the kingdom amidst the world's broken kingdoms. Our work to improve this or that political system depends on our first being faithful to the call to embody the kingdom as the church, demonstrating that this radical kingdom—this Narnia, if you will—actually works in this world, on this side of the wardrobe.

This is part of what Paul meant when he declared that "through the church, the manifold wisdom of God should be made known to the rulers and authorities in the heavenly realms" (Eph. 3:10). Through the church, God makes his wise rule known to earthly kingdoms and even the spiritual powers of our world. We will be more effective in helping citizens of presently rebellious kingdoms begin to welcome this wise rule if, as the body of Christ, we have done the prior work of embodying what God's wise rule looks like.

Third, then, we actually believe we won't be able to serve the world around us in love unless we become, in our lives together, just such an outpost of the kingdom. Somewhat paradoxically, when we live lives invested in God's countercultural community, we become better equipped to serve our broken world. By being formed as faithful economic disciples through "exercising" for the economy of our King, we become people more capable of improving the systems and nations of our world.

People unchanged by the grace of the King stand little chance of effecting change among others locked in the kingdoms of darkness. We can't really work to change the world until we've become changed people. And we don't have much to contribute to the common good unless we're becoming—by God's grace—the uncommonly good people of Jesus.

Let's highlight one economic example of what we're talking about. On the more "conservative" end of the political spectrum, many good people love Jesus and care about the economically poor but believe a government-mandated minimum wage of fifteen dollars per hour would kill more paying jobs than it creates. They tend to suggest allowing the market to operate freely and believe the benefits of the rising tide of markets will benefit everyone.

On the more "liberal" end of the political spectrum, many good people love Jesus and care about the economically poor but believe the rising tide can't help people without boats. In other words, economic growth doesn't always trickle down to help poor people, so government intervention is necessary to enable the poor to benefit from the growth that the rest of us enjoy. They often point to historical market failures and contemporary economic problems to argue that the government should do more to ensure economies work well for everybody.

> We don't have much to contribute to the common good unless we're becoming—by God's grace—the uncommonly good people of Jesus.

The truth is, even the best economists and policymakers don't know for sure how to fix our systemic problems or avoid unintended consequences. Our somewhat audacious claim in this book is that if we begin to follow Jesus in ways consistent with the economy of his kingdom, we will not only honor our King and serve his church but also develop the vision, character, wisdom, and habits that will allow us to see and share new ways of working for better systems. Accepting Jesus's yoke, we will become wiser people better equipped to engage in this important question of public policy and economic justice. By practicing Jesus's generous economy as the church, we will begin to become people capable of contributing to the common good. We will also become more faithful people, people capable of serving our neighbors over the long haul without turning bitter, antagonistic, or violent toward those who disagree with us. In short, once we discover together how to re-enfranchise and empower low-wage workers as Christ followers, one by-product of our efforts is that we'll have more to offer debates about which policies might help the world achieve similar goals.

Walk through the Wardrobe

We invite you, then, to join us in taking up these six keys and using these biblical themes to explore the King's economy in the Bible (in the language of our earlier Narnia analogy, to "unlock the door" and "walk through the wardrobe"). We invite you to hear stories of those who have found ways to make that new economy known in this old one in which we find ourselves, becoming colonies of God's kingdom in the midst of the kingdoms of our world. And we invite you to begin practicing this economy in your church, family, and neighborhood today.

The Shape of the Book

The six keys to the King's economy provide the structure for this book. Each key will be divided into two chapters. In the first, we'll primarily look at Scripture, identifying how God's Word presents each particular economic theme. In the second chapter, we'll share stories of those who are seeking to apply that key in our world and give you ideas for how to begin practicing each key in your own life.

These practices that conclude our discussion of each key are *the heart of this book*. We've tried to provide practical ideas on how to practice each spiritual economic discipline at home, at church, and in the marketplace. Don't try to adopt all these practices at once. Instead, treat these sections like a "choose your own adventure" story. Pick the practice that makes the most sense for where you are right now and get to work. Whatever you do, don't read this book and ignore the practices!

The first two keys, the worship and community keys, identify the way our economic lives are structured around love of God and love of neighbor. We'll discover that the community God is creating is not a soup kitchen where everyone gets fed but a potluck feast where everyone brings a plate. In the work and equity keys, we'll explore biblical themes and practices for bending our marketplace lives toward this potluck God is creating. Finally, in the creation care and rest keys, we'll explore how God calls us to recognize and embrace his design for his world in the ways we pursue our economic lives. Practicing creation care and Sabbath will enable us to pursue the potluck in ways that reflect God's design for his world.

For further resources for using this book and practicing the King's economy in your context, visit the *Practicing the King's Economy* resources webpage at www.PracticingTheKingsEcon omy.org. Also see the resources for further study on page 283.

"GOD, NOT MAMMON"

THE WORSHIP KEY IN SCRIPTURE

All things come from God, are sustained through him, and will eventually flow back to him as the ultimate Owner of everything. . . . Only by affirming that Yahweh is the God of creation, with everything flowing from him, through him, and to him, can we rightly relate to God.

Kelly Kapic

I do not believe one can settle how much we ought to give. I am afraid the only safe rule is to give more than we can spare. In other words, if our expenditure on comforts, luxuries, amusements, etc., is up to the standard common among those with the same income as our own, we are probably giving away too little. If our charities do not at all pinch or hamper us, I should say they are too small. There ought to be things we should like to do and cannot do because our charitable expenditure excludes them.

C. S. Lewis

I see us free, therefore, to return to some of the most sure and certain principles of religion and traditional virtue—that avarice is a vice . . . and the love of money is detestable. . . . But beware! The time for all this is not yet. For at least another hundred years we must pretend to ourselves and to everyone that fair is foul and foul is fair; for foul is useful and fair is not. Avarice and usury and precaution must be our gods for a little longer still. For only they can lead us out of the tunnel of economic necessity into daylight.

John Maynard Keynes, prominent twentieth-century economist

For where your treasure is, there your heart will be also.

Matthew 6:21

The tomatoes caught me off guard. Sitting in a small Anglican church in Kenya, I was prepared for the invitation to give an offering to God as an act of worship. I was not prepared for tomatoes.

But that's what the members of that farming village brought. Tomatoes, mangoes, perhaps some chickens, all brought up and placed on the altar. They brought the literal firstfruits of their small fields, the work of their hands given back to God in gratitude for his blessing on farm and farmer alike.

Few aspects of Christian worship are more controversial than the passing of the dreaded collection plate. Yet in that pile of tomatoes stacked up on the table that held the Lord's Supper, I caught a glimpse of the Father whose gift of his Son reshapes our work and our world. His gift invites us into the King's economy, where all our economic lives are nothing more than one long grateful response to the God who so loved he gave.[1]

Choose This Day: Worship, Idolatry, and Economics

Worship is an economic issue. As discussed in the introduction, from Genesis to Revelation, we see that one of our Creator King's primary qualities is his lavish generosity. We are made in the image of this generous King, wired to reflect his generosity to the rest of creation. Indeed, giving back to God and to his people is part of our DNA, a sign of our family resemblance to our generous Creator. "Giving is what we do best"; "the air into which we were born."[2] Giving signals and solidifies our allegiance to and dependence on God and his kingdom.

Worship is an economic issue.

Idolatry is an economic issue. When we read about the Israelites worshiping the god Baal in 1 Kings 18, we tend to think of them developing a preference for wooden idol images. But the primary attraction to Baal wasn't a pretty statue; it was an economic promise. For the nations around Israel, Baal was the "rider of the clouds," who brought the rains and blessed the earth.[3] When Baal showed up, the heavens rained oil, the rivers ran with honey, mothers gave birth to healthy children, and even the dead could be raised.[4] Little wonder, then, that when King Ahab chose

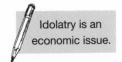

Idolatry is an economic issue.

to marry a woman from Baal territory, the farmers in Israel built a house for this new god and welcomed him to the neighborhood (see 1 Kings 16:31).

Of course, most Israelites probably didn't totally reject Yahweh, the God of Israel. They likely continued going to church, paying their tithes, and saying a prayer or two now and again—especially on holidays. They just added Baal worship to their insurance policy. After all, if you're a farmer, it's only practical to invest in getting the rider of the clouds to like you.

Yahweh would have none of it. He sent his prophet Elijah to tell Israel to stop "limping between two different opinions" (1 Kings 18:21 ESV). Through Elijah, God declared that Baal couldn't deliver the goods and his people couldn't have it both ways.

To win his people back, God demonstrated his power and mocked Baal along the way. Baal promised the rains, so God sent a drought at the word of his prophet (see 1 Kings 17:1). While Baal worshipers went hungry during the drought, God fed Elijah meat and bread delivered to him daily by carrier ravens (see v. 6).

Even on Baal's home turf, people starved while waiting for Baal to bring his promised abundance. Meanwhile, in the midst of Baal country, God made oil and flour overflow for Elijah and his newfound friends (vv. 14–16). When Baal's people died, it was Elijah who raised them to life (v. 22). Yahweh took care of his own while the king who had turned to Baal because of his claim to bring home the economic bacon wandered the countryside hoping to find a bit of grass for the few horses and mules who hadn't died yet (see 1 Kings 18:4–5). Baal's 450 prophets worked themselves into a frenzy, cutting themselves, dancing, and chanting to their god. "But there was no voice. No one answered; no one paid attention" (v. 29 ESV).

But God listened to his prophet. He sent fire from heaven. He sent the rain in torrents. He turned the hearts of his people back to himself. He solicited their allegiance, work, and worship—for himself and his kingdom. The battle for their hearts took place in part on the battlefield of their bank accounts. Worship, after all, is an economic issue.

From Pretty Statues to Silver and Gold: Jesus or Mammon?

Jesus knew all about gods such as Baal. He also recognized, though, that people in his day faced a new, subtler, and perhaps even stronger temptation: to treat money as an idol like Baal, an idol to worship as a god to get what they wanted. But humans cannot serve two kings. Jesus reminds us that when we try, we risk devoting ourselves to money and hating him (see Luke 16:13).

In fact, the New Testament teaches that money and greed are often the loudest and most appealing idols seeking to steal our attention. Paul declares that greed *is* idolatry, that to be greedy is to worship other gods (see Col. 3:5; Eph. 5:3). Once we remember that the Jews saw idolatry as the ultimate sin that put one outside the community of faith, we can hear the full force of Paul's words. Idols had always threatened to steal the love, trust, and service God deserves and demands.[5] By equating greed with idolatry, Paul provocatively told the church they didn't have to go into a rival temple to worship another god. Their greedy hearts created other gods out of every coin in their coffers.

That's why Jesus warned his followers to watch out for all kinds of greed (see Luke 12:15). His parables tell of farmers destroyed in the midst of their prosperity because they hoarded wealth and failed to be rich toward God (see vv. 16–21), of rich men sent to hell for their failure to let go of their wealth for the sake of their neighbor (see Luke 16:19–31), and of eternal judgment declared on the basis of one's willingness to share with those in need (Matt. 25:31–46). All these parables point in the same direction: money wants our worship. But every bit of ourselves we give to our stuff we snatch away from our true King.

Mauled by Money: The Cost of Economic Idolatry

The Bible also teaches us that the wages of our economic idolatry is death. "[People] who want to get rich," Paul declares, "fall into

temptation

and a trap

and into many foolish and harmful desires

that plunge people into ruin

and destruction." (1 Tim. 6:9)

Stop for a moment. Do you believe that? That *wanting to get rich* inevitably causes such destruction? Paul goes even further. He writes that "the love of money is a root of all kinds of evil" that has led some to wander from the faith and pierce themselves with "many griefs" (v. 10). In Paul's opinion, love of money wounds the worshiper, woos them away from the faith, and wells up in all sorts of other evils. "You desire and do not have, so you murder," James writes, spelling out a few of these other evils. "You covet and cannot obtain, so you fight and quarrel. You do not have, because you do not ask. You ask and do not receive, because you ask wrongly, *to spend it on your passions*" (James 4:2–3 ESV, emphasis added).

> Love of money wounds the worshiper, woos them away from the faith, and wells up in all sorts of other evils.

Because our material possessions so often seduce us into worshiping them like gods, they pose possibly the preeminent threat to worshiping Jesus. When we worship money, it mauls us. Money becomes a spiritual power that too often uses us rather than the other way around.[6]

In a truly horrific passage, Jeremiah writes that our worship of idols consumes not only our "flocks and herds" but also our "sons and daughters" (Jer. 3:24). Our idols never stop consuming and destroying that which we hold most dear. In the end, "Those who make [idols] will end up like them, as will everyone who trusts in them" (Ps. 115:8 NET). We said earlier that when we give, we reflect the image of our giving God. But when we worship the idol of money, when our lives are oriented primarily toward earning, getting, and keeping, we become *de*formed, reflecting not the image of Yahweh, Lord of heaven and earth, but money, the god of me and mine. We become increasingly committed to a lifestyle of an abundance of possessions. Such living falls far short of the life Jesus invites us to experience.

The Idol of Our Age

In 1860, a ship traveling from Panama to the United States sank. Four hundred people lost their lives. One of those passengers was a very successful businessman who had two hundred pounds of gold on the ship. Reluctant to lose all this wealth, he strapped as much as he could to himself before jumping into the sea. The gold, of course, dragged him to the bottom. "Now as he was sinking," one author asks rhetorically, "had he got the gold? Or had the gold got him?"[7]

So many of us find ourselves drowning in our worship of stuff. The signs are all around us. Slogans like "It's the economy, stupid!" reflect the belief that gross domestic product is the primary measure of our national success. The General Motors marketing team could have spoken for much of the advertising industry when they declared themselves to be in the business of the "organized creation of dissatisfaction."[8] Everywhere we look we encounter "icons of the ideal" that "subtly impress upon us what's wrong and where we fail."[9] "But don't worry," we're told. "Shopping can solve your problem." This deodorant will summon an army of bikini-clad supermodels to your side. That smartphone will keep you connected to what really matters. This financial adviser will make sure you can retire to a yacht at age fifty-five.

Contemporary economists describe people as *homo economicus*.[10] This view defines people as being, at their core, solitary individuals whose lives are devoted to increasing pleasure through consuming more material goods and increasing leisure. The formula for achieving *homo economicus* happiness is pretty simple: get more services, consume more stuff, and work less.[11] Of course, in many ways, this is a laughably lopsided view of humans, who are so much messier than the model. Even more obviously, nobody who reads Genesis 2 could ever embrace the idea that people were designed simply to walk around finding ways to work less and consume more! The *homo economicus* story falls far short of the big story of God's purposes for his people that we explored in the introduction.

But what if our idolatry is reshaping us in the image of this *homo economicus* idol? What if, by investing our love, trust, and identity in materialism, we have lost the ability to see, value, or pursue much else? What if living life in a world dominated by *homo economicus* has given us training routines that have gotten us into good shape for the *homo economicus* game but left us horribly unprepared for life in the King's economy? John Maynard Keynes, one of the twentieth century's most prominent economists, declared that the gods of avarice and usury could lead us out of the tunnel of economic necessity and into the daylight (see the quote at the start of this chapter). What if our worship of these gods is shattering our souls and leaving us empty and in despair?

> Contemporary economists describe people as *homo economicus*. This view defines people as being, at their core, solitary individuals whose lives are devoted to increasing pleasure through consuming more material goods and increasing leisure.

Evidence shows that this is precisely what's happening. From 1968 to 2001, US per capita incomes *doubled*. During that same time, the average church member's giving fell from 3.10 percent to 2.66 percent of their total income. In other words, "For most of the past thirty-plus years, the percentage [Christians gave] kept falling even though our income kept climbing."[12]

Nor has our wealth made us any happier. As we discussed in the introduction, mental illness and suicide have increased alongside rising incomes over the last fifty years in the United States. Brian Fikkert writes about one effort to explain this phenomenon:

> Seeking to uncover the root causes of the rising rates of mental illness, an expert team gathered at Dartmouth Medical School to examine the leading empirical evidence, mostly from the field of neuroscience, and concluded that ". . . the human child is 'hardwired to connect.'" We are hardwired for other people and for moral meaning and openness to the transcendent. Meeting these basic needs for connection is essential to health and human flourishing. Because in recent decades we as a society have not been doing a good job of meeting these essential needs, large and growing numbers of our children are failing to flourish.[13]

And what has caused this breakdown of relationships with other people and with the "transcendent"? Jean Twenge, professor of psychology at San Diego State University, has explored the causes and concludes, "We have become a culture that focuses more on material things and less on relationships."[14]

How have we become so much wealthier and at the same time more suicidal and less generous? A fairly simple explanation exists: greed *is* idolatry. Designed to find ourselves satisfied through a worshiping relationship with the infinite God, we have instead cultivated an infinite desire for finite stuff. We have cast our lots with gods who can never satisfy, never secure us sufficiently, never make us okay. "Whoever loves money never has enough" (Eccles. 5:10).

We worship material possessions, we cling to them for security, and we are being remade in the image of our gods. Having made material possessions the measure of our lives, we have become better and better at producing and consuming more and more. Meanwhile, we've become worse and worse at connecting, caring, and serving. Drawing on our parable in the introduction, we've become linemen when we were designed to be triathletes.

In the United States, our idolatry leaves us feeling, at best, like we're barely getting by. One politician argued in 1995 that his salary put him in the lower middle class. He made more than $250,000 a year.[15] In 2004, an NBA star turned down a $21 million, three-year contract extension because it wasn't enough. "I got to feed my family," he said.[16] Our ever-rising incomes never bring contentment. Instead, they delude us into thinking we just need a little more. Our idolatry blinds us to the ugly reality of our addiction. My pastor says that after nearly thirty years in ministry, he has never had anyone come to him to confess the sin of greed.

Now, pause for a moment. My guess is that the past five paragraphs have resonated with most readers. We know we're surrounded by materialism and greed. But I have a sneaking suspicion you read these last paragraphs on someone else's behalf. I'm worried you wasted your time thinking about "those rich people out there somewhere." I want to challenge you to confront the idol within. Don't believe you've been had by the Almighty Dollar Idol? Let's take a simple, one-question test:

- Imagine you're offered your dream job, but it pays half your current salary. Would you take it?

My guess is that living on fully 50 percent less than what you currently earn strikes you, *as it strikes me*, as totally and utterly impossible. But according to the stats above (which control for inflation), the average American fifty years ago lived on half what the average American lives on today. The love of money has led us to believe that standards of living that were normal just a generation ago are totally unfeasible today. Never mind the fact that nearly three billion people on our planet live on less than two dollars a day. Our grandparents' "normal" has become our "almost impoverished."

This hit home for my wife, Rebecca, and me when, from one year to the next, our income basically doubled. If you'd asked me just before we made that jump what a difference that extra money would make to our lives, I would have waxed eloquent about how great everything would be in our new financial dispensation. The reality? *We hardly noticed!* We saved essentially no more money, nor did the sense of our "quality of life" dramatically improve. We found ourselves wishing for "just a bit more" just about as much as we had beforehand.

Re-created in the image of *homo economicus* through our idolatry to money, we find ourselves trapped in a "work-spend-work cycle"[17] in which we overwork ourselves to be able to afford ever-increasing affluence, education, and economic security. What we get, we spend up to the point where we feel pressure to get more. Small wonder, then, that the average US household has $7,000 in credit card debt.[18]

Keep in mind this doesn't have to look like "keeping up with the Joneses." It can look like measuring our self-worth against what we get paid, allowing our raises to stoke our egos, and interpreting income that rises more slowly as a sign of our worthlessness or of others' disrespect. It often masquerades as a bastard form of "stewardship" that tricks us into thinking God honestly prefers that we ensure we are shored up against every possible financial disaster *before* opening wide our hands to the marginalized.

This too has proved a perennial temptation for Rebecca and me. For most of the last several years, we have received a significant financial gift. The first year we got one of these checks (worth about half our annual income at the time), my eyes just kind of glazed over. We felt so grateful for this lavish gift. We were able to use a couple of these checks in subsequent years to purchase and renovate our home in South Memphis, an economically depressed community where banks don't like to lend and where we feel called to be neighbors. It was wonderful.

The next time we got one of those checks, we gave what felt to us like a significant percentage of it away. That also felt great. But then, the next year, we didn't get a check at all.

Now, let me remind you: we did nothing for this money. We did not ask for it and in prior years had never imagined receiving it. And yet in its absence, we felt like we'd somehow been wronged! The following year, when we received yet another check, I personally found it much harder to be as generous as we had been previously. Subtly, my version of steward-ship started to sound more like "secure your long-term future at all costs first, then be generous."

The Old Testament mandated a 10 percent tithe, plus significant other gifts and offerings for agrarian peasants living on small, rain-dependent farms. Jesus commanded his followers, poorer by far than any of us today, to "give to everyone who begs from you" (Luke 6:30 ESV). The earliest Christians, living under occupied rulers and oppressed by exorbitant taxes, nevertheless liquidated assets and shared their homes with one another. Paul celebrated the Macedonians for giving out of their Greco-Roman poverty. But today US Christians, the richest people ever to walk the face of planet Earth, give away less than 3 percent of the highest average incomes earned in all of human history.[19] Even when we get financial windfalls—like the big gifts or significant income increases my family has experienced—our first inclination is often to invest in our own security and comfort rather than to spend on behalf of those in need. If the biblical authors thought a peasant's love of money could drag them to hell, what would they have to say to us?

What's the Solution?

The good news is Jesus doesn't just warn us of our idolatry; he gives us a way out of it. By the power of his Spirit, Jesus renews our hearts, rescuing us from dehumanizing idolatry and restoring us as worshipers of Jesus. When we worship the idol of materialism, we become increasingly less human, but thanks be to God, when we behold the glory of our King Jesus, we find ourselves "being transformed into his image with ever-increasing glory" (2 Cor. 3:18). Worshiping God with every part of our being and with all the saints is the ultimate solution to our idolatry.

This transformation doesn't just happen in a single moment though. Even with hearts renewed by salvation, we often find ourselves slipping back into our old ways. Thank goodness, then, that Jesus gives us a practical step, an act of obedience, that when we enter into it by his grace, liberates us from the idolatry of money. You see, just before Jesus warned us we can't serve God and money, he invited us into this powerful practice: "store up for yourselves treasures in heaven, where neither moth nor rust consumes and where thieves do not break in and steal. For where your treasure is, there your heart will be also" (Matt. 6:20–21 NRSV).

It turns out that our economic practices, so often corrupted by our own idolatry, can play a key role in restoring our hearts to true worship. Jesus clearly said that our decision to give our resources to him, to his work, and to those in need is connected to our hearts. But, as we discussed in the introduction, when most of us hear this very familiar passage, we actually hear Jesus saying, "Where your *heart* is, there your treasure will be also." We hear Jesus making the (true!) point that what we do with our money and resources indicates where our hearts are. We hear Jesus like a weatherman offering us a barometer that will measure our affections.

That's not actually what Jesus was saying. In this passage, Jesus doesn't give us a thermometer to measure the temperature of our hearts but a thermostat to *change* the temperature of our hearts. He stands before us like a doctor offering us a prescription that can help heal our idolatry. According to Jesus, when we invest in the kingdom, our hearts follow our investments. If we invest in earthly treasure, our hearts will be in earthly treasure. We'll worry about moth and the stock market destroying our savings, about thieves and the government who might break in and steal. We'll look to the Joneses to see if we measure up rather than to the birds of the air and the lilies of the field (see Matt. 6:26–29). We will end up worshiping money, and it will take the power over our lives that we offer it.

But, said Jesus, if we invest in the kingdom, our hearts will follow. Giving jams a spoke in the relentless wheel of our idolatry. Giving casts down money from the throne of our hearts. When we release our grip on our money, we free up our hearts for worship and our hands for work in God's kingdom. When we give, the Spirit inhabits our generosity and works to reshape us in the image of our generous God.

> Jesus doesn't give us a thermometer to measure the temperature of our hearts but a thermostat to *change* the temperature of our hearts.
> . . . According to Jesus, when we invest in the kingdom, our hearts follow our investments.

Through giving, God changes our hearts. And worshiping hearts lead to open eyes. That's why right after Jesus talked about heart-forming investments, he talked about eyes full of light.[20] Such eyes can see in the birds of the air and the lilies of the field a testimony to God's faithfulness to his creation and an invitation to live in the following ways:

- Free *from* materialism's toxic anxiety.
- Free *for* lives that honor King Jesus and seek first his kingdom.

Our lack of generosity in the midst of overwhelming affluence is both a *cause of* and a *result of* our idolatry. Little wonder, then, that we've given less as we've earned more. The good news is that giving in the King's economy flows out of hearts renewed by God's grace, moving our hearts away from greedy idolatry and toward worshiping the King.

Becoming generous worshipers of King Jesus is good because generosity is good for us. The verdict among those who engage in concrete practices of generosity is clear: it really is more blessed to give than to receive (see Acts 20:35). Our giving is nothing more than the grace of God abounding in us. His generosity flowing through us enriches us and draws our hearts deep into the joy of our Father, who loves us lavishly (see 2 Cor. 9:8–15). As we'll see in the stories in the next chapter, those who follow Jesus regarding generosity testify that participation in God's kingdom through giving is one of the great joys and blessings of their lives.

Good Giving

On one occasion, Jesus told his disciples he had already taken care of the difficult parts of his mission—and without their help, thank you very much. Pointing to the fields around them, he declared: "Others have done the hard work, and you have reaped the benefits of their labor" (John 4:38). Why? Why does Jesus invite his people into the work of witnessing when he's already done the hard work and never needed anyone to bear witness about him in the first place (see John 2:25)? The answer, Jesus said, is simple: "So that the one who sows and the one who reaps *can rejoice together*" (John 4:36 NET, emphasis added).

I remember one time taking my then four-year-old son, Isaiah, to help a friend move. Isaiah could not have been less helpful. Not only could he not carry anything by himself, but he insisted on "helping me" carry such big-ticket items as pillows and tablecloths. And I loved every single minute of it. You see, I didn't invite Isaiah to help me because I needed his little four-year-old frame to help me with the sofa. I invited him so I could see his face light up when I asked him if he wanted to come to work with his daddy. I asked him so I could see the look in his eyes when I put my arm around him at the end of the day and said, "Feels good to help others, doesn't it, buddy?" I asked him because I love my children so much it hurts, and I know almost no moment is more precious to my children than getting to work alongside me.

That's why Jesus invites us into his mission. And that's why giving is so often accompanied by joy. Because when we enter the work of investing in the fields of the Lord, we find Jesus already there, ready to rejoice together with us.

In our day, though, generosity has fallen on hard times. Giving has not only diminished in practice but also developed something of a reputation. And we must admit that some forms of generosity don't reflect King Jesus. Philanthropy often becomes little more than another way to gain power and prestige. Even the Pharisees knew that (see Matt. 6:1–4).

Furthermore, giving often does nothing to reduce the gap between the giver and the receiver; it perhaps even deepens the divide between them. Indeed, Corbett and Fikkert argue in *When Helping Hurts* that the wrong type of giving makes the poor feel like nobodies and the rich feel like gods. Such giving *de*forms our hearts.

Finally, sometimes giving becomes so disconnected from the day-to-day of our economic lives that it becomes an act of hypocrisy. Money earned through injustice and oppression can't be sanctified through giving, and we're rightly revolted by stories of oppressive businesses that make a sudden show of generosity. A few years back, the *Chattanooga Times Free Press* shared one such story in which a payday lending company that skirted the law and got rich off a product that enslaved the poor with 400 percent interest rates used some of those profits to invest in schools and fund missionaries.[21] This sort of giving fails to shape our hearts toward Jesus *and* ends up being false worship. Such giving is like that of the scribes and Pharisees, who tithed their herbs and neglected "justice, mercy and faithfulness" (Matt. 23:23). Jesus pronounced woe on all such giving! Make no mistake: giving a bit off the top of gain unjustly gotten does not please God. Nor can meager economic generosity let us off the hook to live lives essentially oriented toward ourselves.

What kind of giving glorifies God and shapes our hearts for worship? Looking at the Scriptures, we can discern at least four conditions for sharing that shape us for true worship of our King.

1. *Giving shapes our hearts when our gifts are given to God.* We should aim our generosity toward honoring God rather than currying people's favor (see Luke 6:35; Matt. 6:1–4). A gift to the poor is ultimately a loan to God (see Prov. 19:17), and our generosity to the least of these is given to Jesus himself (see Matt. 25:40). Giving in this sense *is* worship: it gives back to God what he has given to us. It is an act of love, trust, and service to the owner of all.

2. *Giving shapes our hearts when our gifts reflect the heart of our King.* Giving must conform to the heart of our King if it's going to form our hearts toward his kingdom.

How are we doing on that? Statistics show that nearly half of church budgets go to staff alone. Certainly many churches do and should pay salaries to their pastors (see 1 Tim. 5:17–18), and some money spent on church programs and buildings is appropriate. Indeed, some churches need to take better care of their leaders and staff. But these same church budget statistics show that in recent years, evangelical churches gave just 2.6 percent of their annual spending to world missions, 5 percent to domestic mission support, and 7 percent to all other ministry and support expenses.[22]

Does this kind of giving reflect the heart of our King? The Bible's answer is a resounding no. Consider just a few passages on God's heart for the poor:

> Religion that is pure and undefiled before God the Father is this: to visit orphans and widows in their affliction, and to keep oneself unstained from the world. (James 1:27 ESV)

> Is not this the fast that I choose:
>> to loose the bonds of wickedness,
>> to undo the straps of the yoke,
> to let the oppressed go free,
>> and to break every yoke?
> Is it not to share your bread with the hungry
>> and bring the homeless poor into your house;
> when you see the naked, to cover him,
>> and not to hide yourself from your own flesh? (Isa. 58:6–8 ESV)

> Be generous to the poor, and everything will be clean for you. (Luke 11:41)

> When Jesus heard this, he said to him, "One thing you still lack. Sell all that you have and distribute to the poor, and you will have treasure in heaven; and come, follow me." (Luke 18:22 ESV)

These are not isolated passages. The call to share with the poor is one of the Bible's primary messages. Indeed, Jesus described his gospel as good news for the poor (see Luke 4:18).

While the church often pits social action for the poor against evangelism, Paul's teaching and example show that such a divide does not do justice to the gospel. Theologian Jason Hood explains that the book of Romans makes clear that Paul delayed his launch of evangelistic ministry to unreached regions in order to deliver the collection for the poor in Jerusalem (see Rom. 15:22–29). "We do not know if Paul achieved this mission [to Spain], but we do know that he delivered the collection. The collection was so vital that its delivery was at that moment a more urgent matter for Paul than his desire to evangelize and plant churches on the missionary frontier among those who were 'without hope and without God in the world.'"[23] At the same time, scholars also believe Romans was, in many ways, a fundraising tract for the apostle, a call to the church in Rome to invest in Paul's efforts on that Spanish missionary frontier. Mission and social action cannot be separated.

In short, giving that reflects God's heart will make care for the marginalized and investment in mission top priorities. Giving that creates more menu items for members in our church programs at the expense of spiritually and economically needy neighbors will not.

The good news is that when we give in line with God's priorities, we experience the reality that it is better to give than to receive (see Acts 20:35). Our hearts become captivated by Christ's kingdom. Through our giving, we can be part of Christ's work of liberating sex slaves in India, bringing clean water to villages in Ethiopia, translating the Scriptures into the mother tongue of an unreached people group, inviting Muslims and Hindus and agnostics to embrace the love of Jesus, and tutoring youth in failing US schools. And as we share in the work of Christ, our hearts grow more and more like the heart of Christ.

3. *Giving shapes our hearts when it builds community*. One of the most damning criticisms against charity is that it increases the distance between the haves and have-nots. But it does not have to be this way! The early church's radical generosity formed a community in which "all who believed were *together*" (Acts 2:44 ESV, emphasis added). As we shall see in later chapters, the generosity demanded by Old Testament law was designed to ensure every family unit could fully participate in the community.

Jesus himself saw almsgiving and sharing food with the marginalized as ways to create community between the haves and have-nots. Scholars tell us the economy of Jesus's day was embedded in social relationships. A gift given to the needy or a meal shared with the marginalized established an economic *and* social relationship between the giver and the receiver.[24] Who one gave to and who one ate with created what scholars sometimes call "fictive kinship" connections. In other words, generosity created family.

In an economic world in which what group you belonged to mattered far more than how much money you made, Jesus's teachings about sharing food and money with the marginalized called his disciples to become family with the most vulnerable and needy in society.

And so it should be in our own day. God's gift of his Son creates fellowship between sinful, impoverished humanity and our King Jesus. If our giving is to reflect the heart of God and form his heart in us, it must create community rather than undermine it.

4. *Giving shapes our hearts when it follows the way of the cross.* In perhaps the most powerful passage on generosity in all of Scripture, Paul called the Corinthian church to give like their King, who "though he was rich, yet for your sake he became poor, so that you through his poverty might become rich" (2 Cor. 8:9). Christ's willing impoverishment at the incarnation and on the cross calls us to share in the world's sufferings through radical, sacrificial generosity. Paul told the Corinthians about the Macedonians, whose extreme poverty overflowed in a wealth of generosity. And he invited them to join in the "circulation of grace,"[25] the overflowing abundant giving of God, through which they had been blessed in every way so that they might be generous on every occasion.

> If our giving is to reflect the heart of God and form his heart in us, it must create community rather than undermine it.

King David once wisely declared he would not offer a gift that cost him nothing (see 2 Sam. 24:24). Too often our own giving costs us so little, a few scraps shoved off tables lavishly filled with an abundant feast to our own desires. But God calls us to follow King Jesus in the way of the cross.

We are often told we ought to be willing and ready to suffer for Jesus's sake. What we've forgotten in the West is that this doesn't just mean being ready to declare Jesus with our lips if anti-Christian terrorists come charging into our church, AK-47s in hand. It means declaring Jesus with our lives, not least by willingly entering into the suffering of the world's poor, taking some of their economic burdens onto our own backs. If we want to know Christ and the power of his resurrection, then costly generosity will be one way we share in the fellowship of his and his church's sufferings. Indeed, in a day when most of us in the United States will never face actual suffering for our faith, embracing voluntary suffering through sharing may be one of the most Christlike acts we ever commit.

What this means is that, as C. S. Lewis said, our giving ought to affect our lifestyles. If there aren't things we'd like to do and can't because we're so invested in God's work, if we're not giving "more than we can spare," then we cannot claim to have entered fully into the movement of divine generosity. Our generosity will not shape our hearts unless it represents a real investment of our *treasure* in the kingdom of heaven.

Generosity can easily get corrupted. Giving can be used for self-promotion, self-justification, self-preservation. But when our giving is truly given to God, given in line with the heart of God, given to build the community of God, and given in the sacrificial way of God, then it has the power to shape our hearts toward the God who impoverished himself for us.

The Worship Key in Scripture: Summary

The Worship Key opens our eyes to the ways that idolatry is, in part, an economic issue, and names money as one of the primary false gods competing for our trust, allegiance, and worship. When we give in to the temptation to worship money and economic power, idolatry wrecks us, consumes our energy and efforts, and, in the end, remakes us in the image of our idol; those who trust in idols become like them (see Ps. 115:8). "Those who desire to be rich fall into temptation, into a snare, into many senseless and harmful desires that plunge people into ruin and destruction. For the love of money is a root of all kinds of evils. It is through this craving that some have wandered away from the faith and pierced themselves with many pangs" (1 Tim. 6:9–10 ESV).

But our generous King has given us an antidote: generosity. When we give back to God from the good gifts he has first given us, we wrench our economic practices away from idols and aim them at worshiping our King. When we give in worship, we experience the joy of loving God and becoming more like him, as the Spirit uses our giving to move our hearts toward Jesus's kingdom. If we want our hearts to reside in God's kingdom rather than in another idolatrous temple, then we must learn to worship our King through giving. "For where your treasure is, there your heart will be also."

THE WORSHIP KEY TODAY
STORIES AND PRACTICES OF CROSS-SHAPED GIVING

In the last chapter, we suggested that worship and idolatry are economic issues and that sacrificial giving is one of Jesus's primary tools for recalibrating our hearts. So how do we begin to live into the Worship Key today?

Yes, You!

More than a hundred years ago, a small group of some of the only Christians in Mizoram, one of the poorest regions in India, made a decision.[1] Every time they cooked anything, they'd throw a handful of rice into a separate container to give to their local church. The church would then sell all the rice to provide for ministers among their neighbors, almost none of whom knew the Lord. This service "done in the corner of the kitchen where nobody sees" raised a whopping $1.50 the first year. Today Buhfai Tham, the practice of giving a "handful of rice," raises $1.5 million annually, allowing Mizo churches to support thousands of missionaries at home and abroad and to bring the majority of their people to saving faith in Jesus. "We are giving what is basic, essential, what is fundamental to your life," one Mizo church leader said. "When I cook for my family," said another, "I cook a meal for the Lord as well." These believers have so entered God's movement of lavish generosity that they practice the reality that "as long as we have something to eat every day, we have something to give to God every day."[2]

On the other side of the planet, Brian Bakke tells the story of a visit to an Argentinian prison named Number 25.[3] Number 25 has the dual distinction of housing both:

- Inmates who have all killed at least two people.
- A thriving church and seminary training program that has eliminated violence within the prison, brought many to faith in Jesus, and prepared some of Argentina's worst criminals to serve Jesus inside and outside the jail cells that have become their homes.

The stories of spiritual renewal in Number 25 are nearly unimaginable, including accounts of these inmates' generosity while incarcerated. Bakke says that when the inmates get food and clothing from their families, they "tithe" a third of whatever they receive, storing it up to share with others. "You see," one incarcerated senior pastor told Bakke, "there are others in this prison that have nothing. Their families cannot come to visit them here. And since the government does not provide food and clothing, these other inmates would be starving and naked. So all of us take the 'firstfruits' from what we are given by our families and we put them in our tithe room."

"The chief of the prison later shared with me that the men would soon be making twenty-four hundred small cakes for the children of the [slum] down the road from the prison as a gift to the slum families," Brian recalls.

We so often equate generosity with a philanthropy reserved for the wealthiest among us. Yet these Mizo women and Argentinian men truly "spearheaded a revolution" by offering what little they had from the basic necessities of life. "Giving was not limited to some individuals," one Mizo leader said. "Everyone contributed: rich or poor, old or young." Today Buhfai Tham is passed on from generation to generation, a radical practice of generosity embodied every day within the home, a sign of God's kingdom economy in the kitchen. Meanwhile, Jesus is using the generosity of

Number 25 to bring the good news of the kingdom to slums and prisons across the country, not least through discipling and training current inmates for ministry once they're released.

The truth is, we can all give, and most of us can give more than we currently do. In fact, it appears that as American Christians, the poorer we are, the higher a percentage of our income we give away. Americans who make $10,000 a year or less give on average 11.2 percent of their income, while those who make more than $150,000 give on average only 2.7 percent.[4] Black Protestants give a higher percentage of their income than their white counterparts (whether liberal or conservative), despite having lower average incomes and net wealth. This was brought home to me personally when an older African American neighbor of ours called me on a Sunday to see if she could borrow some money till she got paid the next day. She had put her last few dollars in the offering plate at church, so she didn't have any money for dinner that night.

Generosity is God's gift to all of us, rich or poor, and participating in God's work is a gift that shouldn't be denied to anybody. In fact, when we truly believe it's better to give than receive, we'll work to make sure everyone gets the privilege of participating in generosity. New Testament scholar Ben Witherington tells how his father recounted the story of a lawyer in their church going around to collect pledges for the church. When he arrived at the home of a retired woman living on a fixed income in a trailer on the edge of town, this is what happened:

> When the lawyer found the lady, he noted the condition of her tiny yard and the trailer, and was growing reluctant to ask her for a pledge of money. . . . As the chat wound down, the lawyer rose to leave without asking for the pledge and the widow said, "Wait just a minute, son, I've got my pledge on the fridge." He muttered in return, "That's all right, ma'am, we understand you are just barely getting by . . ." Before he could finish his sentence she had gotten right up in his face, grabbed him by the lapels, and said, "Don't you take away from me my opportunity to contribute to the ministry of Jesus. Don't you do it, son." Then she handed him her pledge card.[5]

I tear up every time I read that story. This woman had experienced the joy of giving and wasn't about to let anybody take it from her. This isn't super spirituality; it's just reality for those who, despite hard times, share in the joys of God's kingdom through giving.

"We Don't Really Own Anything"

Two families who've embraced sacrificial generosity in the midst of tremendous wealth testify to the joy and power of generosity in their own lives. When Alan Barnhart felt led to work for his family's small business, Barnhart Crane and Rigging, rather than go into the mission field, he spent two years studying what the Bible said about money, business, and wealth. At the end of that time, he'd reached two conclusions: first, God owns everything, and second, he needed to be afraid of the way his wealth could lead him away from Jesus. When he acquired the business from his parents, he took steps to guard against that fear by building intentional financial accountability into his life. "In my church," Alan says, "if I were to come in bragging about cheating on my wife, somebody would rebuke me. But in this area of money, if I were to consume more of it on myself than I should, nobody in my church would confront me about that. I'm afraid they would actually congratulate me!"

Alan told those around him, including those within his business, that the benefits of their company's growth would go to generous giving to others rather than increasing the Barnhart family's lifestyle.

God blessed that commitment. For twenty-three straight years, Barnhart Crane and Rigging experienced 25 percent growth every year. Whatever profits they earned beyond the "enough" the Barnharts set for themselves was invested in other kingdom work. For the last ten years, their company has given away one million dollars *every month*. In 2007, the Barnharts actually *gave* their business away to their charitable foundation. The enormously profitable business they built no longer belongs to them at all. "We never felt that we owned it, anyway," Alan says.

How did the Barnharts decide how much was enough?

Our principle is that the Army cook shouldn't eat a whole lot better than the troops. Those of us who're in a position to generate wealth aren't entitled to a different lifestyle than the rest of the body, the rest of the troops. We may need different tools, just like that cook, but our lives shouldn't be so different.[6]

The Barnharts will tell you that investing in God's kingdom has been one of the great joys of their lives and a tremendous blessing to their children. "Being a kingdom investor is so much more fulfilling than anything we've passed up," Alan says. "We passed some things up. But the trade-off has been so worth it."

Wes Gardner, another entrepreneur, tells how when he became serious about his faith, he started out giving 10 percent of his income. "But gradually I realized that I was treating 90 percent of it like it was mine," he says. Over time, Wes began praying over how God would have him use more and more of his money. "Today I see it as all God's. I try to ask him how he wants us to manage every bit of it."

According to Jesus, what we do with our money shapes our hearts. Alan and Wes followed Jesus in his radical challenge to invest first and foremost in his kingdom. Their generosity has brought them joy and changed the way they view the world. Furthermore, they bear witness to one of the primary arguments of this book: when we practice the King's economy, we exercise our hearts and lives for greater faithfulness in his kingdom. We'll share how each of these men eventually found creative, sacrificial ways to bend their businesses toward those on the margins, creating work opportunities for single moms, former offenders, and addicts. They have created radical new expressions of God's kingdom within their companies, but their journey began with radical faithfulness to God in giving.

They Gave to Anyone in Need: Generous Churches

As the stories we've told already demonstrate, generosity is a team sport. In God's design, the local church is the primary place where we gather to become participants in the generosity of Jesus. Churches around the country are finding powerful, creative ways to practice the King's economy through giving.

Pastor Van Moody, of Birmingham's Worship Center Christian Church, realized that many in his congregation were drowning in payday loan debt.

After a sermon on debt in which Moody dressed in a prison uniform to emphasize the bondage that debt brings, he found out that forty-eight attendees had payday loans totaling more than $41,000. Since payday loans can carry interest rates as high as 400 percent annually, Moody and his team knew they had to do something. So the church had a special offering and committed not only to pay off the loans of these forty-eight folks, some of whom were just visitors, but also to offer workshops and budgeting help to assist those liberated from payday loan bondage to make a fresh start. "We are a church of generosity," Moody says.[7]

In 2006, five pastors began asking themselves how they could help their congregants celebrate Christmas by worshiping fully, spending less, giving more, and loving all.[8] Today Advent Conspiracy is a global movement of churches that choose to spend less on themselves at Christmas to give more to the poor as part of the joyful celebration of the King of Kings and Lord of Lords. Their practice of consumer resistance in the United States, where we spend roughly $600 billion on stuff over the holidays, embodies the King's economy and invites churches to join in on the joy of our generous Jesus. Through sacrificing stuff and investing in the kingdom, participants in the Advent Conspiracy have raised millions of dollars for clean water solutions around the world. (They also inspired my community to get creative in feasting together before the Lord, a story we share in the next chapter.)

In later chapters, we will tell stories of creative generosity by people who throw outlandish parties, create work opportunities, invest in their communities, care for creation, and more. But all these kingdom investments begin with creating a culture of generosity through concrete practices of giving. For where we put our treasure, there our hearts will go!

Practicing Cross-Shaped Giving

If giving is part of God's strategic plan for rescuing our hearts from idolatry and winning them back to worshiping him, how do we get started? And how do we do this in a world where the "default" choices we face in our daily lives are so often oriented toward the love and worship of money? We suggest practicing "cross-shaped giving."

By cross-shaped giving, we mean sacrificial giving that is both costly and community oriented. Such giving reflects the earth-shattering reality that Jesus suffered the horrors of the cross so he might create a new family in which he stands as the firstborn of many brothers and sisters (see Rom. 8:29). Giving that shapes our hearts for his kingdom should foster solidarity among God's people and involve us in sharing in one another's sufferings.

Perhaps the greatest testimony of such giving comes from the early church. About a hundred years after the death of Jesus, Aristides wrote that when a Christian became poor and the church had nothing to spare, they would "fast two or three days for him. In this way, they [could] supply any poor man with the food he [needed]."[9] Such giving embodies the kind of generosity that bears the sufferings of our neighbors and deepens the relationships between us. Practically speaking, we suggest (1) giving up something so you can give more, and (2) seeking to give in such a way that your heart and life become further connected to others.

> By cross-shaped giving, we mean sacrificial giving that is both costly and community-oriented.

In the remaining portion of this chapter, we provide a sort of "choose your own adventure" selection of cross-shaped giving practices for families and churches.

Cross-Shaped Giving at Home

Consider: What are some expenses you and your family could cut back on to free up money for generous giving? What steps could you take to simplify your life so there would be more to share? Keep in mind that in the immediate term, this might require also releasing yourself from debt so you might be freed for greater generosity in the future, "prepared for every good work" (Titus 3:1 LEB). Also consider how you could give the excess you free up in such a way that it draws you into relationships, particularly with those in need.

Some ideas for cross-shaped giving at home include:

- *Fast from something for the purpose of giving more.* Consider a regular meal fast to free up money for generosity. For instance, our dear friends Brandon and Lily Russell recently shared with us that once a week their family eats a very simple meal of rice and beans, and they talk with their three young girls about issues of global hunger. They then give away the money they would have spent on a "normal" meal to Christian organizations addressing hunger locally and worldwide.

Or consider downsizing (rightsizing?) your life. Could a smaller house, a less expensive car, different vacation choices, or even different approaches to saving free up money to serve the poor and support God's church? Consider beginning to make lifestyle decisions that translate into greater generosity. Do a family staycation and use the savings to give a bivocational pastor a vacation. Partner with the deacons at your church to give a car you could do without to a person struggling to come out of generational poverty. Find some way to cut back on yourself so you can splurge on God's kingdom. In doing so, you will find yourself entering into Jesus's way of the cross for the sake of the community.

• *Give in ways that create community.* After hearing about our friends' rice and beans night, our family discovered the Dorothy Day House of Memphis. The Dorothy Day House provides hospitality for homeless families who live in a house together until they're ready to get back out on their own. The house has a communal meal one night a week shared by volunteers, the families facing homelessness, and Sister Maureen and the Dorothy Day staff. We've begun using the money we save from the rice and beans night to prepare that communal meal occasionally. Our rice and beans practice has not only freed up money for giving but also welcomed us into a new community, where people from all walks of life share a meal together.

There are plenty of ways to give that create community. One of the simplest is to volunteer at ministries you support (and support ministries at which you volunteer). Your giving could also help bring the feast practices of the Community Key or the impact investing practices of the Equity Key to life.

• *The graduated tithe.* In his monumental book *Rich Christians in an Age of Hunger*, Ron Sider suggests that Christians should give a higher percentage of their income whenever they experience an increase in income.[10] In other words, families would give 10 percent of their "base living expenses" (for Sider this meant 150 percent of the poverty line, plus the cost of education for his kids). Then, with every $1,000 extra that a family earns above those base living expenses, they would give an additional 5 percent more of this extra income. The end result? You give away a greater percentage of your income as your income rises *and* you implicitly set a "thus far and no further" for your family's finances (because at some point your family would give 100 percent of any increase).

Whether or not you follow Sider's exact method, committing to give a higher percentage of your income as it increases is a powerful way to combat the love of money and the relentless pursuit of more. By planning to practice a form of the graduated tithe, you can protect yourself from the tendency to spend every cent of any new surplus. Indeed, one of the few saving graces of my family's experience of doubling our income was that we simultaneously raised the percentage we gave away. We did not do this because it was easy or immediately appealing. We did this because we had planned to do it because we had been inspired by Sider's graduated tithe. Having done it, we can testify to the exhilarating joy of giving.

Cross-Shaped Giving at Church

Consider: Does your church's current spending line up with the heart of God? Do your teaching and preaching challenge people to worship God and cast down their idols through radical generosity? Does your church's giving practice connect generosity with heart change and community formation?

Some ideas for practicing cross-shaped giving at church include the following:

- *"Right-size" your church's budget.* Reevaluate how your church spends money in light of God's priorities. Are you pushing yourselves to invest in the kingdom through mission and caring for the poor at home and abroad? Or are you busy creating entertainment to keep your sheep from shopping for another church? If you decide you want to give away more or give in ways that align better with God's heart, *tell your congregation.* Make entering the lavish generosity of Jesus a church-wide goal.

- *Create communal giving through "opening the books."* When nobody knows how much we make, what our giving habits are like, or how we spend our money, we give idolatrous money a foothold. All the stories we've shared in this chapter happened in part because people let others into their financial lives and gave their accountability partners the power to challenge the way they managed their money. This doesn't necessarily mean letting every single person read your bank statements, but it does mean being completely vulnerable about your finances with people other than your immediate family members. Jesus's words about not letting our left hand know what our right is doing while giving remind us of the dangers of giving to gain others' good opinions (see Matt. 6:3). But we miss the point if we use that text to live financial lives in the dark, away from the eyes of other believers (people certainly saw Old Testament Israelites bringing their tithes to the sanctuary or early church Christians putting their gifts at the feet of the apostles).

So bring your finances into the light! Form "generosity accountability" partnerships, and encourage small groups to open up about their incomes and generosity patterns. Share testimonies of disordered greed turned to generosity, and invite heroic givers from lower-income backgrounds to share their stories. Offer "greed counseling." One way money exerts power over us is by tricking us into believing we shouldn't talk about it with others. But Paul used his own example, the example of Jesus, and the example of other churches to inspire people to generosity. Church is a team sport. Giving is a team sport. We can't do this alone.

It's also vital that the church preach the good news of God's kingdom economy rather than worldly wisdom dressed up as "stewardship." If we're not careful, we can end up "baptizing" the message of popular financial education materials that encourage good financial practices (such as keeping a tight budget and getting out of debt) but focus on the end of building personal wealth.[11] Staying out of debt so you can be lavishly generous is one thing; staying out of debt so you can be comfortable is another. We're concerned this sort of training falls far short of God's call to take risks *right now* to care for one another and invest generously and sacrificially in God's kingdom. Don't delay generous giving! Indeed, as everyone from our stories would tell you, from the women in India with their rice to Alan trying to figure out how to give his business away to charity, the economic wisdom of our God will often seem like foolishness to the world. We need to stop dissuading people from downsizing, taking economic risks, accepting a job with lower wages, and giving like crazy on those all-too-rare occasions when Christians actually come up with such ideas.

- *Give together.* Encourage small groups to give together, both financially and through acts of service. Encourage them to practice some of the household practices mentioned previously. Many intentional communities practice contributing regularly to a common fund for mercy and justice ministries. They have found that when we invest our treasures in the kingdom *together*, our giving can draw us closer to Christ and to one another. Small groups could mimic this practice by storing up money from the group and then allowing members to suggest ways to bless their neighborhood or community with those funds.

Start Practicing

Before moving on, take a moment to consider where to begin practicing or how to deepen your practice of cross-shaped giving. Spend a few moments in silence and ask Jesus: Where do you want me to begin? Pay attention to what's happening in your heart and what you hear from the Lord. Ask Jesus to replace the hidden greed of your life with the abundant joy of his generosity. Think about who else in your community you might want to talk to about growing in cross-shaped generosity. Before finishing this chapter, identify how you, individually or with a group, can start practicing cross-shaped giving within the next two weeks.

Within the next two weeks, I can practice cross-shaped giving by doing the following:

_____

_____

_____

_____

The Worship Key: Conclusion

The Bible calls us to worship a God so all-encompassing that he requires nothing less than all we have. Our attempts to get security, pleasure, or meaning from material possessions is a perennial threat to true worship. Since before the days of Jesus, possessions have confronted us camels with the impossible task of getting through the needle's eye. G. K. Chesterton memorably quipped that too often we respond to Jesus's words about camels getting through that needle's eye by considering how to manufacture ever-larger needles and breed ever-smaller camels.

What if, instead, we really believed Jesus's words, "With God all things are possible" (Matt. 19:26)? We know to give is far more blessed than to get. We sense the gold in our pockets drags us down. What if the impossible thing made possible by Jesus is liberation from our idolatry and hearts captured for generous, abundant worship and work in his world? What if another way is possible? What if joy, sharing, and richer community could replace anxiety and fear? What if practicing cross-shaped giving is one powerful way to welcome the work of Jesus into our hearts, habits, and wallets?

Talking about generosity is hard. Most of us experience some guilt about our lifestyles, while at the same time feeling stuck about how to make changes. Sometimes we get so caught up in our shame that we shut down. Other times we get defensive and seek to justify ourselves.

If you're feeling that way now, remember the big story—Jesus loves you and gave himself up for you! Remember that becoming more generous means becoming more of who you were meant to be, participating in the very joy of God. We don't give out of obligation; we give because God gave and because in giving we grow in him.

At the same time, by talking about cross-shaped giving, we remind ourselves *that none of us has arrived when it comes to generosity*. Not you, not me, not any of us. We are all pilgrims on the way. Because if our model of generosity is the cross of Jesus, then we can never say, "I've done enough. I've fulfilled my obligation." We're called to imitate a God who gave immeasurably more than we could ever ask or even think to give. How could we ever get comfortable with our giving if we give in imitation of the One who gave himself up on the cross for us? Imitating him will inevitably be a lifelong adventure of gradually growing in the deep joy of becoming ever more like our Lord. Perhaps when we understand this, we can be more open with our friends and loved ones, actively sharing and learning from one another about how better to steward our resources for cross-shaped giving. Perhaps we can become communities that practice the King's economy.

For me, one of the deep joys of writing this book has been getting challenged again to deepen my family's practice of the King's economy. In doing the research for this chapter, Rebecca and I began to take sacrificial generosity more seriously and added a practice or two in our own community. I was convicted by my own shortcomings in cross-shaped giving and inspired to follow after Jesus through some of these economic practices. And we haven't pulled off some practices in this chapter yet. In other words, we're all on this journey together.

Wonderfully, as we, God's people, lay up ever more of our treasures in the kingdom and with our King, he will increasingly open our eyes to his abundant world of well-fed ravens and sharply dressed daylilies (see Luke 12:24) and welcome our hearts to find deeper rest in him.

3

"ONE TABLE, ONE BAPTISM, NO DISTINCTION"
THE COMMUNITY KEY IN SCRIPTURE

It was not simply the promise of salvation that motivated [the first converts to Christianity], but the fact that they were greatly rewarded here and now for belonging. Thus while membership was expensive, it was, in fact, a bargain. That is, because the church asked much of its members, it was thereby possessed of the resources to give much. For example, because Christians were expected to aid the less fortunate, many of them received such aid, and all could feel greater security against bad times. . . . Because they were asked to love others, they in turn were loved. . . . In similar fashion, Christianity greatly mitigated relations among social classes—at the very time when the gap between rich and poor was growing.

Rodney Stark

At the heart of the celebration, there are the poor. If [they] are excluded, it is no longer a celebration. . . . A celebration must always be a festival of the poor.

Jean Vanier

The horizon [in Israel's economy] is not maximum output, it is the feast. If we have a party today, after one day of feasting we're collapsing. In Israel, you had to take the widow and the Levite with you to Jerusalem and spend a full week feasting. That was the horizon of Israel's economy.

Bob Goudzwaard

Let us remember that this sacred feast [of the Lord's Supper] is medicine to the sick, comfort to the sinner, and bounty to the poor.

John Calvin

At the present time, your abundance will meet their need, so that one day their abundance may also meet your need.

2 Corinthians 8:14 NET

New Prospect Missionary Baptist Church, a large congregation serving a predominately African American population in Cincinnati, operated a soup kitchen for homeless people for many years.[1] After a while, though, ministry leaders realized they weren't building relationships with those they served. So they began asking people who came to the soup kitchen about their skills and abilities, their dreams and desires.

The results were shocking: the congregants found "carpenters, plumbers, artists, musicians, teachers, and caregivers, all coming to the soup kitchen at New Prospect."[2] But most astonishing of all was the fact that over 50 percent of these men and women being served food prepared by church leaders listed cooking as one of their talents.

New Prospect got the message. "As Pastor Damon Lynch put it, 'Folks were telling us, "We don't want to stay over here on the receiving side of the table. We're not just recipients. . . . We want to cook and serve, too. We want to belong by contributing."'"[3] And so the homeless people began to cook the food and church members began to receive it. Instead of a soup kitchen, New Prospect created the kind of community that can only emerge once everyone is empowered both to *give* and to *receive* gifts.

The Potluck Party of God

As we discussed in chapter 1, the King's economy calls us to care for those who are struggling economically. But so often, the metaphor for our compassion becomes the soup kitchen. We line up on one side of the serving line and scoop heaping hot resources into the bowls of hungry people standing on the other side. We might ladle out soup or clothes or shelter or education or counseling or spiritual nourishment. We can ladle anything we want so long as we have it, they don't, and they are willing to take it from us.

But what if in God's economy our goal isn't a soup kitchen? What if it's a potluck? A soup kitchen divides us up into haves and have-nots. At a potluck every single person both *gives* and *receives*. Food comes *from* everyone and goes *to* everyone. Everyone gets fed and everyone brings a plate.

Now, I'm not talking about some WASPy millennial potluck either, the kind where you grab potato salad from the grocery on the way. I'm talking about a potluck like the ones we have in my South Memphis neighborhood. I'm talking about sweet potato pie, fried pork chops, and greens . . . with bacon in them. South Memphis potlucks are so good because folks spend all day in the kitchen getting ready. When my neighbor Betty brings a plate to a potluck, it's the best plate of the week. The potluck God invites us to isn't a last-minute compilation of leftovers. It's the party to which everybody brings their very best dish.

In community development circles, we often quote the proverb about giving a man a fish and feeding him for a day versus teaching a man to fish and feeding him for a lifetime. Sometimes we even talk about who has access to the fishing pond. But in Jesus's economy, the primary goal isn't captured by any of these. Eating, fishing, and access are all necessary, but not sufficient. The ultimate goal is to be so vested economically and socially in the neighborhood that you and your neighbor can participate in the potluck fish fry.

This changes the way we think about helping others. If God's economy is a potluck rather than a soup kitchen, our primary problem isn't that poor people "out there" are hungry and hurting. Our primary problem is that *because* of economic poverty and sin, the poor aren't "in here," participating fully in the joyful life of the community, giving and receiving gifts around the Lord's table.

Think about it for a moment: What's the goal of your economic life, of your habits of working, producing, consuming, and investing? Remember the *homo economicus* way of thinking we described in chapter 1? For many, including many who most shape our economic policies and agendas, the present shape of our economy produces people oriented toward selfish ends, so that we aim our economic lives toward self-gratifying consumption.

Isn't that true for most of us? I mean, we probably include a spouse or aging parents or our children in our economic goals, and we certainly would like to tithe when we can, but at the end of the day, our economic agenda primarily serves our individual benefit. Like archers, we aim our arrows at the target of "me and mine" (see figure 3.1).

Figure 3.1

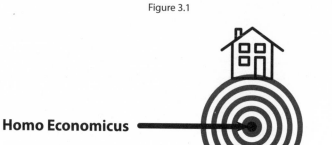

Homo Economicus

Individual success and security

Figure 3.2

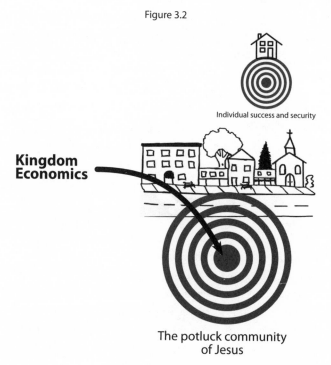

Individual success and security

Kingdom Economics

The potluck community of Jesus

This view works nicely with the soup kitchen. Each family makes sure they've got enough for themselves, however they define it, and then they hopefully have some left over. Those leftovers are just what we need for the soup kitchen! But if what we're after is a potluck, then the potlucking *community* becomes our target right out of the gate (see figure 3.2).[4]

We typically begin conversations about our economic lives by asking what individuals are like and then working our way toward what this means for our community. We in the United States actually represent the extreme end of the spectrum on this issue when compared to other countries and cultures, as depicted below.[5]

Figure 3.3

Concept of Self

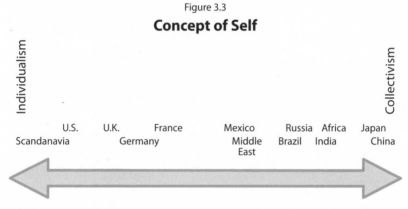

Adapted from Craig Storti, *Figuring Foreigners Out: A Practical Guide* (Yarmouth, ME: Intercultural Press, 1999), 52. © 1998 by Craig Storti. Reproduced by permission of Nicholas Brealey Publishing.

So in our US cultural climate, we tend to think of society as just a collection of individuals; the community itself is more of "a bonus in the background" of our minds. But for God's people in the Old and New Testaments, the pattern "tends to start the other way around."[6] In other words, the Bible sees the community as absolutely essential for the sake of both individual and communal flourishing. Kingdom economics, then, calls individuals to aim at the community for their own sakes and for the sakes of everyone else.

Individuals matter and communities matter. We can't have one without the other. If we begin with the idea that the community God wants is a potluck, where the poor are not only fed but also bring a plate, then that will shape the entirety of our economic lives. Putting this chapter together with the last one, we can say that our economic lives should be fundamentally oriented toward worshiping God and welcoming our neighbor.

> Our economic lives should be fundamentally oriented toward worshiping God and welcoming our neighbor.

In chapters 5 and 7, we'll look specifically at how Scripture calls God's people to address some of the issues that so often prevent people from participating in the King Jesus potluck. But in this chapter, we want to explore in more depth how Scripture calls us to aim our lives at the community. In the next chapter, we'll share stories and practices of how God's people are beginning to move, like New Prospect, from the "us"/ "them" of the soup kitchen to the "we" of the potlucking people of God.

"So That He Can Continue to Live among You"

In the Old Testament, the Lord gave Israel an astonishing array of economic legislation designed to protect poor widows, visiting immigrants, orphans, and just plain poor folk. Sabbath days created rest for workers, Sabbath years provided release for people in debt slavery, gleaning laws created opportunities for work for the unemployed, tithes provided for the needy, and more. We will look at many of these provisions in later chapters. For now, notice that the Lord constantly put constraints on what the well-off were allowed to do at work and with their stuff to protect the prospects of the marginalized.

All this culminated in the famous Year of Jubilee in Leviticus 25, when control of the family farm returned to those families who had been forced to sell it or otherwise lost control of it. Each provision in Leviticus 25 was designed to preserve an economy in which households and families were never permanently alienated from God's promised land.[7] Such an economy required families and neighbors to be ready to sacrifice in a variety of ways depending on their struggling neighbor's situation.

The goal of all this, though, wasn't simply to ensure that all Israelites could get food, shelter, and clothing. God's goals went far beyond that. Moses instructed the Israelites to follow the Jubilee regulations so their fellow Israelites could continue to live among them (see Lev. 25:35). In other words, the Jubilee "aimed to restore social dignity and participation to families through maintaining or restoring their economic viability."[8] Israel's economic policies served God's vision for community life, in which every member of the community could be a full participant. The Lord's goal in Israel was to create nothing less than a people whose life together embodied his design for the world. And that meant every Israelite's economic life had to be aimed at the community rather than their own self-interest or individual well-being.

Yahweh, it turns out, cares more about every single family being able to bring a plate to the potluck than he does about any one family's right to eat and store up as much as they can. God put constraints on individual Israelites' economic freedom to ensure that *every* Israelite could be a full participant in the community. Each family and clan within Israel had responsibilities both to their own farm and family *and* the larger community. Economic practices that threatened togetherness couldn't be tolerated.

> Yahweh, it turns out, cares more about every single family being able to bring a plate to the potluck than he does about any one family's right to eat and store up as much as they can.

Woe to Those Whose Wealth Wrecks the Neighborhood!

God must have known his people would have trouble with all this. While the Jubilee or debt forgiveness (see Deut. 15:1–18) sounded like good news to the debtors, Yahweh must have known it would seem pretty tough on those hardworking farmers who'd now never get back their expected return on investment. But for God, an economy aimed at togetherness wasn't an option; it was a command. And when his people forgot that, he sent prophets to set them straight.

That's why Isaiah pronounced, "Woe to you who add house to house and join field to field till no space is left and you live alone in the land" (Isa. 5:8). Apparently, Isaiah was confronting rich Israelites who used their social and economic power to push the poor off the land, acquiring more and more farms and fields and ignoring all God's laws ensuring every

Israelite had a place to stand within the community. Isaiah recognized that their actions:

- Created economic hardship for poor Israelites.
- Left the rich alone in the land.

Violating the Year of Jubilee and its intention to keep Israel together, those wealthy Israelites pushed the poor out of the neighborhood.

But Yahweh heard the cries of the oppressed and brought judgment on those wealthy Israelites. The Lord hit them where it hurt—at the very place where they'd tried to build up their little economic kingdoms. The beautiful mansions they'd acquired were devastated and left empty. Their big, shiny new vineyards produced no fruit (see Isa. 5:9–10).

When You Give a Feast . . .

Like the Israelites, though, most of us struggle to avoid idolatry and self-centeredness, even when we know it's against God's design, even when we know it's bad for us. The problem for the Israelites wasn't knowing what the Lord wanted; the problem was doing it. In fact, Moses repeatedly warned the people that when they prospered economically in the land, they would be tempted to forget the Lord and instead declare: "*My* power and the might of *my* hand have gotten *me* this wealth" (Deut. 8:17 ESV, emphasis added). Such forgetting leads to disobedience bound up in a self-centered "my, my, me" pattern that most of us relate to all too well.

So the question facing the Israelites on the borders of the promised land as they listened to Moses spell out his five-point plan for kingdom economics was how to become people who could follow the plan, who could experience economic abundance without becoming consumed by selfishness and pride.

The Lord had thought of this, and he had an answer. Moses instructed the people with the following:

> When you come into the land . . . take some of the first of all the fruit of the ground, . . . and you shall put it in a basket, and you shall go to the place that the LORD your God will choose, to make his name to dwell there. And you

shall go to the priest who is in office at that time and say to him, "I declare today to the LORD your God that I have come into the land that the LORD swore to our fathers to give us. . . . A wandering Aramean was my father. And he went down into Egypt and sojourned there, few in number, and there he became a nation, great, mighty, and populous. And the Egyptians treated us harshly and humiliated us and laid on us hard labor. Then we cried to the LORD, the God of our fathers, and the LORD heard our voice and saw our affliction, our toil, and our oppression. And the LORD brought us out of Egypt with a mighty hand and an outstretched arm, with great deeds of terror, with signs and wonders. And he brought us into this place and gave us this land, a land flowing with milk and honey. And behold, now I bring the first of the fruit of the ground, which you, O LORD, have given me." And you shall set it down before the LORD your God and worship before the LORD your God. And you shall rejoice in all the good that the LORD your God has given to you and to your house, you, and the Levite, and the sojourner who is among you. (Deut. 26:1–11 ESV)

This is the only place in all the first five books of the Old Testament where ordinary folks were given precise words with which to address the Lord in a worship setting.[9] Every Israelite farmer was to declare openly that their ancestors were wandering nobodies and oppressed slaves, that the only reason they weren't back on Pharaoh's never-ending assembly line was the lavish grace of a God who rescues his people in might and power. Here, on holy ground, every economically successful Israelite participated in a visible, ritual reminder that the abundance they experienced was all God's gift. Participation in such worship called on the worshiper to declare before the Lord that, despite experiencing his abundance in the land, "I have not turned aside from your commands nor have I forgotten any of them" (Deut. 26:13).

Such worship, though, culminated in joy-filled feasting with the community (see Deut. 26:11). These meals—eaten before God and shared with neighbors—forged "an inclusive and celebrative community, in light of the generosity of God."[10] Over and over again, Yahweh commanded Israel to party hard before him in nationwide feasts. Moses told the Israelites to take their tithe of grain, wine, meat, and oil that *they owed God* and *eat it together in his presence*. In a culture in which meat was consumed only on rare occasions, God was telling them to go above and beyond, to pull out all the stops.[11]

Indeed, if the way was too long for them to carry their tithes with them, the Lord allowed them to convert their crops and herds and grapes into money and buy whatever they desired (see Deut. 14:24–26). God even refused to leave any festival food item to the imagination, spelling out that steak dinner, wine, "strong drink" (often elsewhere forbidden or discouraged), and "whatever your appetite craves" can and should be included. "Come and feast with me," Yahweh declared to the people, "and rejoice, you and your household." God was so serious about people feasting with joy that throughout Deuteronomy he didn't expect, recommend, or anticipate festive joy . . . he *commanded* it.[12]

> God was so serious about people feasting with joy that throughout Deuteronomy he didn't expect, recommend, or anticipate festive joy . . . he *commanded* it.

This feast becomes even more incredible when we realize that everywhere else in the ancient world, a tithe was a tax that went to pay for priests and kings. But when Yahweh is on the throne, God gives back to us even those gifts we offer up to him! Feasting together with such a generous King shaped the Israelites' desires, drawing their hearts toward love of God and neighbor.

Party Planning for Pilgrims

Besides this command to rejoice, though, Deuteronomy offers few concrete stipulations about how the feasts were conducted. But there's one major exception. For while Yahweh held off on getting into the specifics of other aspects of the party planning, he never tired of giving strict instructions on the guest list.[13]

And you shall *rejoice* before the LORD your God, you and your sons and your daughters, your male servants and your female servants, and the Levite that is within your towns, since he has no portion or inheritance with you. (Deut. 12:12 ESV, emphasis added)

And the Levite, because he has no portion or inheritance with you, and the sojourner, the fatherless, and the widow, who are within your towns, shall come and eat and be filled. (Deut. 14:29 ESV)

And you shall *rejoice* before the LORD your God, you and your son and your daughter, your male servant and your female servant, the Levite who is within your towns, the sojourner, the fatherless, and the widow who are among you. (Deut. 16:11 ESV, emphasis added)

You shall *rejoice* in your feast, you and your son and your daughter, your male and your female servant, the Levite, the sojourner, the fatherless, and the widow who are within your towns. (v. 14 ESV, emphasis added)

And you shall *rejoice* in all the good that the LORD your God has given to you and to your house, you, and the Levite, and the sojourner who is among you. (Deut. 26:11 ESV, emphasis added)

Over and over again, the feast that God required was the joyous festival celebrated alongside the economically marginalized within the community. Once we realize that several of these feasts were part of annual pilgrimages to the central sanctuary, the community-shaping economics of this law become even clearer.

Imagine: you're a moderately successful farmer who depends on rain and good weather for your economic success. You hire immigrants who are passing through Israel to help out on the farm, and you have servants who also work your fields because last season you made loans to them they couldn't repay. Your children and spouse work alongside you. And several times a year, the Lord not only requires *you* to stop work, to take your eyes off the family business on which your livelihood depends, but he also commands you to take everybody in the village with you, including your servants and entry-level employees, the disinherited widows and orphans who live next door, and even the immigrant who lives in your neighborhood. No, Mr. Everyday Israelite, you aren't allowed to come represent the family at this important religious ceremony and leave the workers behind to keep grinding it out. This feast is for everyone.

And so everyone comes. There before Yahweh, every Israelite is reminded that they are a sojourner and debt slave to God, that all their abundance is a sheer gift from him. As they feast together, the wealthy remember their dependence, and the debt slave, the orphan, the widow, the disinherited remember that it won't always be this way. The Year of Jubilee is coming. Liberation from economic indebtedness is on the way.

All across the ancient world, shared meals created community, form-ing the sorts of social bonds that determined who people were, who be-longed, who was an insider, and who was an outsider. In the feasts of Deuteronomy, Yahweh gave his people a joyful ritual of belonging that reoriented them toward worshiping God and welcoming neighbor. At the feast, class barriers broke down, differ-ences disappeared.[14] All were dependent and all were participants. "Deliverance from homeless slavery 'into place' [for the wealthier Israelites] . . . [brought] with it the responsibility to draw the homeless fully into the experience and celebration of rooted belonging."[15] The festival played a critical role in shaping all Israelites, rich and poor, to seek such a community.

> The festival played a critical role in shaping all Israelites, rich and poor, to seek such a community.

Economist Bob Goudzwaard once said that the feast was the horizon, the goal of the entire Israelite economic arrangement. Because the feast was made up of God's good gifts given to his people who then gave those gifts back to him and to one another in worship (see Deut. 16:16), this feast that stood as the target of Israel's economy wasn't a soup kitchen. It was a potluck. At these meals, the community feasted simultaneously because of God's gratuitous gift *and* because all the festival participants labored together in God's land to put food on the table. "We know that God is good," an Israelite immigrant, landowner, or widow might have said, "because *our* work *together* has provided enough for *everyone* to have full glasses of wine and juicy ribeye steak."[16]

This potluck, with its requirement that every landowning Israelite regu-larly leave the farm in the hands of God and set off on the long, dusty pilgrim trail with all their poor neighbors and hired hands, shaped the economic imagination of every Israelite toward the inclusive, abundant economy of Yahweh.[17] God didn't just require the Israelites to aim their economic lives at "us" rather than "me." He created a new us through the regular require-ment that everyone, even the immigrants and outcasts, feast together in celebration of God's good gifts. The creation of that new us didn't just stay at the banqueting table though. It flowed out into a community where debts were forgiven, slaves were set free, and everybody was empowered to provide for themselves and contribute to the community.

The Son of Man Came "Eating and Drinking"

When Jesus came on the scene, his own dinner parties reflected the inclusive pilgrim feasts of the Old Testament. Tax collectors, prostitutes, sinners—all were welcomed at the table of our King. Not only socially and economically marginalized people but also spiritually and morally questionable folks found a place and a plate beside Jesus.

Of course, he caught a lot of flak for feasting with folks the Pharisees didn't consider "polite company." Indeed, they even called him "a glutton and a drunkard, a friend of tax collectors and sinners!" (Luke 7:34). But the Son of Man came "eating and drinking," embodying the gracious community of welcome that characterizes his kingdom.

Such feasts were part of Jesus's strategy for creating a new family among his followers. Such a family was to transcend boundaries of rich and poor, pure and impure, social insiders and social outsiders. Feasting fostered economic practices aimed at such a community. So Zacchaeus made it clear that he was truly part of this new family when, at a feast filled with tax collectors and sinners, he committed to giving half of his goods to the poor (see Luke 19:1–10). New Testament scholar Joel Green argues that, in a first-century context, such "conversionary behavior" presents a picture of Zacchaeus behaving "toward the poor and maltreated as if they were his friends, his neighbors, his kin."[18]

Indeed, when we pay attention to the meals and teaching of Jesus in Luke, we find that the Lord of the Feast constantly called his people to repentance, which includes a new economic way of life oriented toward the community. Jesus told his people to throw parties for "the poor, the crippled, the lame, and the blind," all folks who could never return the invitation (Luke 14:12–14). Unjust mammon vies for our worship, but according to Jesus, can be used to "gain friends" in the new community that God is creating, ostensibly by sharing generously with those who are in need (Luke 16:9). When Jesus told the story of a rich fool, he painted a picture of a man almost comically self-obsessed with his own economic well-being. Just listen to the guy!

> And he reasoned *to himself* saying: What shall *I* do, because *I* do not have anywhere to store *my* crops? And he said "This is what *I* will do. *I* will tear down *my* barns, and *I* will build bigger ones, and *I* will store all *my* grain and goods." Then *I* will say *to myself*, "*Self*, you have many good things laid

up for many years: relax, eat, drink, celebrate." (Luke 12:16–19, author's paraphrase)

But while wealth tempted this rich man to an economic way of life characterized by isolated individualism, Jesus assured Peter and the rest of his disciples that anybody who had given up relationships and possessions to follow Jesus would find themselves welcomed into a new community in which they would receive "many times as much in this age, and in the age to come eternal life" (Luke 18:28–30).[19]

In short, Jesus, in his teaching and table manners, called people to enter a new family and a new kingdom

- formed through a feast with their King at which all were welcomed, and
- solidified through economic practices aimed at a potlucking community of generous sharing.

Goods—What Are They Good For?

God's intention to create an economy aimed at community continues throughout the New Testament. Indeed, this theme is so pervasive that we can't possibly explore all the ways it shows up. Incredibly, the primary difference between the Old Testament economy and the New Testament economy is that the New Testament's version is even more inclusive. Nowhere is this clearer than in the famous passages in Acts 2 and 4.

> So those who received his word were baptized, and there were added that day about three thousand souls. And they devoted themselves to the apostles' teaching and the fellowship, to the breaking of bread and the prayers. And awe came upon every soul, and many wonders and signs were being done through the apostles. And all who believed were together and had all things in common. And they were selling their possessions and belongings and distributing the proceeds to all, as any had need. And day by day, attending the temple together and breaking bread in their homes, they received their food with glad and generous hearts, praising God and having favor with all the people. And the Lord added to their number day by day those who were being saved. (Acts 2:41–47 ESV)

Now the full number of those who believed were of one heart and soul, and no one said that any of the things that belonged to him was his own, but they had everything in common. And with great power the apostles were giving their testimony to the resurrection of the Lord Jesus, and great grace was upon them all. There was not a needy person among them, for as many as were owners of lands or houses sold them and brought the proceeds of what was sold and laid it at the apostles' feet, and it was distributed to each as any had need. (Acts 4:32–35 ESV)

In chapter 7, we'll consider some of the practicalities of these passages. At this point, though, just bask for a minute in the beautiful description of a group of people whose economic lives were aimed at the congregation. These first believers gathered for common meals, prayer, worship, and teaching. Life in Jerusalem during their time would have been tough, with many, many people barely able to survive. But day after day, they came into the community, carrying the fruits of their labor with them, sharing and feasting and watching God work miracles.

One of those miracles, of course, was the community itself. Survival for all Jerusalemites depended on belonging to a community, a "kin group, from which [the members] derived their identity" and through which they negotiated the harsh economic realities of their world.[20] Members of one's group were willing to open their homes and their wallets to make sure everyone's needs were met.[21]

But not everyone had stable membership in a group. Peasants driven off their land, younger sons lacking an inheritance, children sold into slavery, women no longer eligible for marriage due to sexual assault, widows and divorced wives, orphans, and others would all potentially experience exclusion or marginalization from their kin groups.[22] One possibility for such people was to enter into *fictive* kinship groups, groups that acted like family even though the members weren't blood relatives. Seen in this light, "the story of the beginning of the church in Jerusalem is the story of disparate people being melded into one family."[23]

The economic lives of the members of such a group, then, were aimed at the establishment, at great economic cost, of a community in which nobody in the group was in need (see Acts 4:34). This economic arrangement worked only because their lives were so oriented toward the group that they didn't even consider their possessions their own but "had everything in common" (Acts 4:32 ESV). While this probably didn't mean a one-time divestment of every single piece of individual property into a common fund, it absolutely meant people sold land and houses to share with the group. These Christians believed that since God owns everything, all we have is "ours" rather than "mine." "The goods I have are good," these early Christians might have said, "inasmuch as they become good for the community."

Once again, we find a feast in the middle of this countercultural economic experiment. Celebrating the Lord's Supper as a communal meal, the early church formed a new family and cared for the poor in their midst through the feast of God.[24] These meals were one aspect of the early church's devotion to *koinonia*, the Greek word often translated "fellowship," but which in the first century included the physical sharing of goods. In other words, shared meals enacted justice and mercy, as bread and wine were given and received among poor peasants, struggling merchants, vulnerable orphans, and despised tax collectors, some of whom probably depended on this meal for literal sustenance. At the same time, shared meals also shaped the hearts of those who participated in these unusual dinners to seek justice and mercy in every aspect of their lives.[25]

We find such communal meals in many New Testament passages. These meals provided opportunities for not only the marginalized to eat but also the entire community to reorient their lives toward worship of Christ and welcome of neighbor. These feasts, like those in Deuteronomy, probably worked at least partially like potlucks, in the sense that everybody contributed to them, either through working together within households, sharing apartment space or homes for meeting places, assisting in preparation, or contributing food or money.

Indeed, that may be partially what was behind Paul's famous instruction in 2 Thessalonians 3:10 concerning the one who didn't want to work. "Let him not eat!" Paul writes. But while we often read this as a commonsense statement of fact about the importance of individual self-sufficiency, Paul's words actually take the form of a command. In other religious and cultural groups of Paul's day, barring a person from the communal meal was a form of community discipline, and in any case, the command to not *let* a person eat only makes good sense in the context of a community in which people are contributing to a common meal.[26] In other words, Paul recognized how precarious the Thessalonians' potluck was and made it clear that everyone must contribute. To refuse to do so was to aim one's economic life at oneself rather than the community. Paul wasn't telling the Thessalonians that each person must pull themselves up by their individual bootstraps; he was instructing them that each person must do their part in preparing the potluck.

In fact, that's almost exactly what Paul says in 1 Thessalonians 4:10–12. (As you read, keep in mind that the "you" and "your" below are *plural* pronouns; if Paul had been a Southerner, he'd have said "y'all"!)

> Yet we urge you, brothers and sisters, to do so more and more, and to make it your ambition to lead a quiet life: You should mind your own business and work with your hands, just as we told you, so that your [PLURAL!] daily life may win the respect of outsiders and so that you [PLURAL!] will not be dependent on anybody.[27]

Paul was confronting a problem well-known to any group whose economic survival depends on the contributions of others: What happens if people slack off? Apparently some in Thessalonica weren't doing their part, and Paul told them God demanded they do so. But the point isn't to work hard to achieve individual independence, as seen by the plural pronouns. The point is to work hard to become the *inter*dependent people of God before the watching world.

Gathering for the Worse

Of course, the church often fell short of its lofty goal of becoming an interdependent people. Community creates vulnerability, and people sometimes take advantage of it. That's what was happening with the folks in Thessalonica who refused to work. That's what was happening with Ananias and Sapphira, who thought they could hustle the Spirit and gain street cred in the congregation without really sacrificing (see Acts 5). That's what was happening with the widows who tried to get on the welfare rolls who ought instead to have been finding ways to serve the church (see 1 Tim. 5:3–16). In short, a community whose economic life embodies the potluck is hard to come by.

We learn of one community's deepest failure to embody such an economic life in Paul's famous description of the Lord's Supper at Corinth. Paul came at the Corinthians with guns blazing:

I have no praise for you . . . (1 Cor. 11:17)

You don't gather together as the church for the better, but for the worse . . . (v. 17)

For when you come together in the church, it is not the Lord's Supper you eat . . . (v. 20)

Each one goes ahead with his own meal. One goes hungry, another gets drunk . . . (v. 21 ESV)

Do you despise God's church and shame those who have nothing? (v. 22)[28]

Even from a quick reading of the text, we can tell that, whatever the details, the Corinthian church's Lord's Supper did not please the apostle. In an effort to understand what exactly was going on at this disastrous meal, Bible scholars have studied both archaeology and ancient writing on meals. The picture they paint isn't pretty.[29]

Imagine you are a poor worker in Corinth invited to a meal with your religious group, one of any number around town. You might be glad to get an invitation from the wealthy guy who lives in the big house on top of the hill, especially since the fridge at home doesn't have much food in it. You head on over after work, but when you arrive, you come into a crowded hallway where most of the other poor guests are standing about, waiting for some food. Through a door, though, you can see that people on the homeowner's VIP list are kicking it in their own special lounge, reclining on couches and being served by servants. You can smell the tasty scent of steak and potatoes floating from the room, mixed with the aroma of fine wine. You wait a long time for the party to make its way out to where you are, your mouth watering and your stomach grumbling after a long day of backbreaking manual labor. But by the time the food gets out to you and the rest of the poor guests, all you get is a bit of dry bread and maybe some water with a few drops of wine mixed in to serve as food coloring.[30]

Even if you get into the VIP lounge, the host will make clear to you where you stand in the social pecking order. The most important guests recline close to him, and they get seconds on the beef and strong wine too. Everything about the meal, from the seating arrangements to the food portions to the quality of the cocktails, communicates to each and every person exactly where they stand in the hierarchy.

Apparently the Corinthian church had adopted some such cultural practices in their celebration of the Lord's Supper. Of course, everything described in this imaginary scene would have been normal, culturally acceptable behavior in Corinth. "It's just the way things are," the Corinthians might have said. "After all, Mr. Wealthy Corinthian did pay for everything."

For Paul, though, such socially stratified feasts couldn't be called the Supper that belongs to the Lord. For Paul, the purpose of the meal was corporate fellowship with King Jesus, *who creates the family of God among folks who would otherwise be enemies.* All kinds of meals create community, but the Lord's Supper is the particular feast at which Jesus presides as the host. "You can't do it this way," Paul was essentially saying. "This meal is making you worse."

Paul got ticked because such a community and such a meal stands in striking contrast to the original Lord's Supper that Jesus himself presided over as host. That's why Paul reminded them of what he'd been taught and had passed on to them: in the wine and bread of that feast, Jesus had given his very body and blood, declaring he would be given for them, that the meal would confirm the new covenant and a new covenant community, sealed in his own blood. To gather together as the one people of God, on equal ground at the foot of the cross, to eat and drink as one family across lines of both ethnicity and class, is to proclaim the Lord's death until he comes (see 1 Cor. 11:23–26).

To celebrate the Lord's Supper like a bunch of snobby Corinthians more concerned about honor and status than anything else . . . that, however, brings nothing but judgment. Such a meal solidifies each member in their own socioeconomic competition for individual acclaim. That's not the meal Jesus demands.

Paul's solution was for the Corinthians to examine themselves to make sure they were recognizing the body of Christ that is the church in the way they celebrated the Lord's Supper.[31] The point wasn't to stir up a bunch of hidden sin in the quietness of their hearts before they took the bread and wine; the point was to make sure the Supper that shaped the church's entire life truly embodied God's equally generous welcome to all who came, including the outcast and the poor. While many translations describe Paul as exhorting the church to "wait for one another" (1 Cor. 11:33 ESV), the word there is often used in meal contexts for welcoming. The meal that makes a community a community, that creates the economy of the kingdom, is a meal that welcomes the poor and marginalized as full participants in ways that make no sense to the surrounding culture.[32]

Why, then, did Paul, in verse 34, seem to permit the wealthy Christians to do what they pleased in their own homes? Academics often throw their hands up in the air at this point or suggest maybe Paul was just making a compromise regarding the wealthy's bigotry, perhaps buying himself some time to fix the problem fully when he came to visit. But just like in Deuteronomy, what was actually going on was far more profound. Gordon Fee states it beautifully:

> As with the issue of slavery in Philemon, Paul attacks the system indirectly to be sure, but at its very core. Be a true Christian at the table, and the care for the needy, a matter that is always close to Paul's heart . . . will likewise become part and parcel of one's life.[33]

Paul emphasized getting the Lord's Supper right because he believed the impact of that meal in the sacred space of the house-turned-church would ripple out into every aspect of the Corinthians' lives. He believed a renewed Lord's Supper practice would, by God's grace, form believers into people who would live lives of solidarity with the marginalized, show love for their neighbors, and embody generosity toward the "have-nots."

Embodying such virtues would stand their culture's competitive socio-economic hierarchy on its head. How long would economic distinctions be able to last among believers in daily life once they were removed from the Lord's Supper meal? How long could the wealthy continue to serve their slaves meager meatless portions and watered-down wine in a different room of their homes when, the evening before, they had both shared in the one meal, the one bread, the one cup given to them equally by the *Lord himself*? How long could any individual home embody a social world dominated by the haves against the have-nots when both parties participated in the enacted story of the upside-down kingdom, in which greater honor is given to the dishonorable parts and the foolishness of God overturns the wisdom of the world?[34]

> Paul was writing to a church whose Lord's Supper had become more Corinthian than Christian.

"Meals indicate social status," Tim Chester writes, "and they thereby allow us to transform social status. They're a microcosm of social reality that we can manipulate."[35] Paul was writing to a church whose Lord's Supper had become more Corinthian than Christian. But because Paul believed the Corinthian believers were new creations in Christ, his solution was for them to practice their Lord's Supper meal so that it reflected what God has done in Christ. Such a meal would reshape their social lives in the image of Jesus rather than in the image of Corinth.

The Lord's Supper feast made the kingdom of God, with its economy aimed at we and us rather than me and mine, *habitable*.[36] When rich and poor walked into the sacred space of that church, they didn't just taste the bread and wine. They tasted a new way of living, a new way of being human. Once you've entered the kingdom around that table, you'll never be the same.

Manna and the Potluck of Grace[37]

Paul's letters to the Corinthians give us concrete pictures of what he expected people transformed by the Lord's Supper feast to be like. Nowhere do we see this more clearly than in his fund-raising efforts among Gentile Corinthians on behalf of the poor in Jerusalem. Right after grounding his appeal to the Corinthians in the sacrifice of King Jesus, who "though he was rich, yet for your sake he became poor, so that you through his poverty might become rich" (2 Cor. 8:9), Paul gave the Corinthians a further glimpse into God's economy. "For I do not say this so there would be relief for others and suffering for you, but as a matter of equality," Paul told the Corinthians, who probably thought they had enough economic issues of their own, thank you very much. "At the present time, your abundance will meet their need, so that one day their abundance may also meet your need, and thus there may be equality" (2 Cor. 8:13–14 NET).

Did you catch that? Paul's vision was for the Corinthians to have their economic lives so shaped by Jesus's self-impoverishing death on their behalf, so oriented toward the entire church, that they were free to share radically and sacrificially with the Jerusalem Christians. Indeed, part of the reason the Corinthians could afford such risky giving for the Jerusalem saints was that they could depend on similar support *from* the Jerusalem saints at a later date, should they need it.

This shatters our own contemporary economic ways of thinking. Stewardship for Paul didn't mean making sure you were secure and then giving generously from what's left. We are free to take risks in sharing with others because we can depend on God's provision, not least as that provision comes through the commitment of God's people to share with one another.[38]

Later in this letter, Paul asserts that God will make the Corinthians rich in every way just so they might be generous on every occasion, to the glory of God and the good of his people (see 2 Cor. 9:11). Taken together, the almost unbelievable message Paul is giving us is that God has not given to each one enough for their needs. He's given *us* what *we all* need for *our* needs. Experiencing his economy depends in part on our willingness to participate in the "circulation of grace"[39] through concrete economic practices that flow from the wounds of Christ himself (see 2 Cor. 1:5; Col. 1:24–28; and Phil. 2:25–30). Embracing such practices requires us to recognize that God provides for the struggles of one part of the body by giving a shareable abundance to another part.

Sharing in the community is the Spirit-filled, God-given oil that makes God's economic engine run. Just three hundred years after Jesus's death, Basil the Great declared:

The bread in your cupboard belongs to the hungry; the coat unused in your closet belongs to the one who needs it; the shoes rotting in your closet belong to the one who has no shoes; the money which you hoard up belongs to the poor.[40]

What Corinthians makes clear is that this isn't true because we necessarily take the coat from the poor person's closet or that the needy have some sort of abstract right to our possessions. It's because the economy God is creating is a potluck. God has given us the abundance in our closets, cupboards, and bank accounts in part so we might have the incredible grace and privilege of sharing our excess with others. Indeed, we have freedom to do so in part because we can depend on the community to care for us in our need in similar ways.

Such almost unimaginable economic investment and dependence on the community is, believe it or not, good news. At least it was to those first Christians. For them, membership in such a community was expensive at first, but in the long run it was quite a "bargain."

Because the church asked much of its members, it was thereby possessed of the resources to *give* much . . . because Christians were expected to aid the less fortunate, many of them received such aid, and all could feel greater security against bad times. . . . Christianity greatly mitigated relations among social classes—at the very time when the gap between rich and poor was growing.[41]

In our own day, most of us middle-class Christians would be horrified by the idea of depending on the local congregation for our needs. But giving and receiving in risky ways was the norm for the early church. Their example invites us to take risks in caring *for* God's people, in part because God has promised to care for us *through* his people. God invites us into a mutually dignifying interdependence within the community in which we rely on *God's* grace given through his body, the church.

The feast of God embodied in the Lord's Supper created a community of sharing and solidarity in that first century that quite literally changed the world. The feast that God requires, the potluck where everyone *gives* and *receives*, launches a new way of being human, a way that welcomes all to the abundant hospitality of Jesus.

A Caveat: The Festival and Lament

The emphasis on the joy of the potluck, though, risks missing another practice that is central for any economy aimed at the community: lament. Lament is a "cry directed to God,"[42] whether by the broken and oppressed of our world or by those who would "mourn with those who mourn." Laments are prevalent in Scripture, comprising 40 percent of the Psalms and running through the poetry of Lamentations and Jeremiah right through Jesus's lament over Jerusalem. But what do they have to do with the joyful potluck of God? A lot.

For instance, one of the biggest threats to truly becoming the multicultural, multiethnic, multiclass party of Jesus is the temptation to settle for happy-clappy togetherness rather than the deep joy and hope that can only emerge once the truth has been named concerning our failures and our brokenness, our shame and our sin. (Keep in mind that the Corinthian church Paul scolded for their Lord's Supper was a multicultural, multiethnic, multiclass church. They had a diverse group of people in the room, but their gathering still fell so far short of God's standard that Paul said they gathered "for the worse" rather than for the better!)

Let's consider one specific example of how a particular brokenness can keep us from the potluck if we don't embrace lament: race relations in the United States. I recognize that this may feel like a bit of a detour from our general interest in economic issues throughout this book, but I think it is an illuminating example of how refusing lament can keep us from the potluck.

I'm convinced one reason we haven't become the potlucking people of God *across racial lines* is simply that white people like me aren't willing to enter the pain and complexity of racism with our brothers and sisters through lament. When a young, unarmed black man is killed by the police, we white evangelicals often respond by explaining it away, defending the system, or suggesting that it is an isolated, tragic instance. Meanwhile, police officers and their families (of all ethnicities) sit in our pews, often carrying unimaginable fear and pain regarding the turmoil in our streets. Again, God's people respond primarily with silence.

In the face of such tragedies, Bible-believing Christians are called first to lament and mourn the brokenness of our world, the injustice of our society, and the pain of our black friends who see in the one killed their own faces and the faces of their sons. "Tears are a way of solidarity in pain when no other form of solidarity remains."[43] We have no solutions that are not grounded in the lamenting, honest acknowledgment of pain. No amount of gospel music, diverse leadership, or fog machines and lasers in church can bring true racial reconciliation and solidarity if we aren't willing to hear the pain of our neighbors and join them in their grief. And processing such grief can't occur first and foremost on social media. It will occur together before God . . . or not at all.

As Soong-Chan Rah writes, "The power of Lamentations is that the voices of those who have actually suffered are not missing."[44] Too often, though, the actual voices of suffering among ethnic minorities and low-income believers are simply not tolerated by majority culture Christians like myself. Instead of the worship service being the place where the community of God expresses "the full extent of our trauma," working out *our* pain *together* with *our* King, we whitewash the pain of our fellow worshipers' experiences and try to fake our way through the diverse church party. But "hope expressed without knowledge of and participation in grief is likely to be false hope," incapable of reaching the depths of our neighbors' despair.[45] No shortcut around lament exists on the road to becoming the potlucking people of Jesus. If we want to share in the economy of the King aimed at the community of his kingdom, we're going to have to learn the language of lament.[46] We are going to have to practice mourning with those who mourn (see Rom. 12:15).

Perhaps that's why lament played a role in even the joyful biblical feasts, why even in the midst of rejoicing, the community rehearsed the memory of seasons of pain. Indeed, rehearsal of the suffering of slavery was often the pregame for the party (see Deut. 26), and the festivities included the commemoration of the Egyptian enslavement (see Deut. 16:12). During the Festival of Booths, the Israelites actually had to live in tents to help them really remember—mind, body, and soul—that their ancestors were slaves and sojourners. Even the words spoken over the Lord's Supper remind worshipers week in and week out that the joy of the Lord's Supper looks back to the night Jesus was betrayed to death by one of his closest friends.[47]

Such laments train the hearts of children, new members, and those who have not known suffering to recognize that the only way to become the people of God is to learn to mourn together with those who are mourning. The good news is that, while the lament of death at work in us may be painful, the life of resurrection and the wedding feast of the Lamb are the opposite.

The Community Key in Scripture: Summary

The Community Key reminds us that we are not merely a collection of individuals looking for the best way for each of us to get what we desire. As Christians, we belong to the body of Christ, and our King calls us to aim our economic lives at the community. Thus God's economic program enshrined in his law was designed to make sure that each and every Israelite family remained secure in the community. God's economy, then, isn't simply a soup kitchen where everyone gets fed; it's a potluck where everyone brings a plate to share.

Feasting together with God and neighbor has always been one of Yahweh's best strategies for shaping hearts that love God and neighbor. In the Old and New Testaments, such feasts always required that those most likely to be left off the guest list get welcomed as full participants. These feasts ultimately pointed to The Feast, the Lord's Supper, at which Christ created a new community for himself across all social and economic divisions. Participating in such feasts requires us honestly to name and lament our brokenness, sufferings, injustices, and sins. When we do, though, we find ourselves welcomed to a festival community that participates in the circulation of grace, a potluck party in which each member shares their best plate with everyone else.

THE COMMUNITY KEY TODAY

STORIES AND PRACTICES FOR THE POTLUCK

Paltry Potlucks

From the earliest days, the gospel created a community that welcomed everyone. In the process of becoming a community across all lines, few practices were as essential as the shared meal. The early church father Tertullian wrote that whatever the church spent on their feasts was "gain," since with the good things of the feast they "benefitted the needy."[1]

But our communities and our feasts in the twenty-first-century West seem to have undergone a deep impoverishment, both inside and outside the church. In his famous book *Bowling Alone*, Robert Putnam tracks a 33 percent decline in family meals over three decades and a 45 percent decline in entertaining friends in homes over the same period.[2] Moreover, for a variety of reasons, US citizens are increasingly likely to live in all-poor or all-rich neighborhoods and much less likely to live in communities where they would ever even have the chance of becoming friends with someone from a different class. If Deuteronomic feasts called the whole faith community, rich and poor, to journey to the sanctuary together, such festival pilgrimages today would face the added challenge that rich Christians and poor Christians quite simply do not know one another. From this perspective, in most middle-class churches, poor urban Christians in America "are no longer with us."[3]

Meanwhile, the Lord's Supper celebration in most churches in the United States seems to consist of consuming tasteless crackers and shots of grape juice grabbed from a passing plate or taken in single file lines that resemble a drive-thru more than they do the feasts of old. These Lord's Suppers are usually consumed by worshipers in culturally and economically homogenous churches. Sunday morning remains the most segregated hour of the week, with many church memberships failing to represent the ethnic and economic diversity of their neighborhoods. Such social realities undermine the community-creating function such meals so clearly had in both the Old and New Testaments. Paul believed the life of the church would make known the mystery of God to the rulers and authorities in the heavenly realms simply by becoming a community across ethnic lines (see Eph. 2:13–3:10). But our witness, our communities, our way of being in the world, and yes, even our economic lives suffer from our unwillingness to become the potlucking community of God. In our individualism and isolation, we fail to proclaim the good news of the kingdom or enjoy the Lord's Supper feast with our King. It's obvious we've fallen short of God's design for our lives. But what can we do?

The answer begins with embracing God's establishment of a potlucking people in his church through concrete practices of loving God and loving one another. While this may seem like the least "economic" chapter in the book in some ways, the more obviously economic practices of the later chapters depend on communities of believers radically committed to loving one another and welcoming all to the potluck of God.

Preparing the Potluck in South Memphis

Marlon Foster, an African American pastor and nonprofit leader who lives, works, and worships in the low-income South Memphis neighborhood my family also calls home, will tell you straight up: "I ran from being a pastor." Marlon had already chosen to stay in his neighborhood and raise a family rather than run for economically greener pastures. He'd already started a highly successful nonprofit that serves hundreds of at-risk youth in three sites all along the central street of the neighborhood he grew up in. He had every reason to resist more responsibility. You'd think God would have let him off the hook with the whole pastor thing.

God, and the pastor of the church Marlon was currently attending, had other plans. The church was changing buildings, but Marlon's pastor wanted him to start a new church at the old location. The pastor reminded Marlon that Marlon's own grandfather had helped establish the congregation nearly seventy years prior, and it would be a shame to see it without a worshiping community. Marlon reluctantly agreed to start a Sunday school and planned to stay a member of the relocating church. But when nineteen people joined during their second Sunday of worshiping, he finally accepted that "pastor" was one more hat he was going to have to get used to wearing.

Marlon was committed to leading Christ Quest to be a church that fully included the economically poor and represented the diversity of his community. But how? Marlon was also committed to pursuing the King's economy, where everybody is able to use their gifts to provide for themselves, care for their families, and participate in and serve the broader community. But how, in an economically impoverished community, do you actually begin to move toward such an economy? The answers for Marlon, like the answers for Moses in the Old Testament, included *food*.

"It all started because my family had to get here so early on Sundays that we ended up cooking breakfast at the church," Marlon explains. Soon, though, the Foster family was welcoming anybody in the neighborhood who wanted to come to breakfast. Today, more than twelve years later, Christ Quest still has a community breakfast before every service. Homeless folks, addicts coming down from their latest high, middle-class teachers, and older retirees all sit down together to eat at a table that becomes, each and every Sunday, a symbol and sign of the reign of Jesus in the heart of the neighborhood.

The breakfasts aren't the only important meals, though. Like the churches of old, Christ Quest celebrates with a big potluck lunch after their monthly communion services. Marlon knew that to be a church that welcomed the poor, they had to have a "come as you are" dress code, but this became complicated when one of his poorer congregants told him he'd always loved getting to wear his one suit to church. The only problem? This meant that he would only come to church about once a month because he also couldn't afford to have that one suit cleaned any more regularly. So the congregation decided they'd follow the come as you are dress code most of the time and then dress up once a month for Lord's Supper Sundays. That gentleman with the one suit soon started coming every week.

In beautiful and creative ways, Christ Quest's breakfasts and lunches embody the community-wide potlucking party Jesus created at meals wherever he went and at the Lord's Supper. This special Lord's Supper celebration binds Christ followers to one another across lines of economic status.

> Creating community comes down to questions like "Who do we eat with?" and "Who's welcome to eat, not *from* your table, but *at* your table?"

I once heard Marlon speak to a bunch of young ministry guys. They asked him what it took to lead a church that truly welcomes the poor. He said creating community comes down to questions like "Who do we eat with?" and "Who's welcome to eat, not *from* your table, but *at* your table?" Christ Quest's meal practices create a community that radically reshapes participants' understanding of who is welcome, who matters, who belongs in God's family.

Then he told the story of "John." John was homeless and mentally ill, and as a result, he had some serious body odor issues. "When I say he smelled bad," Marlon recalls, "I mean I was feeling nauseous in the pulpit while I was preaching. I mean I had most of the congregation sitting on the other side of the church." But Marlon made it clear to everybody that they were a church for John. He risked running members off rather than making John feel uncomfortable. Eventually, some church members let John use the showers at their homes. Today John is still a part of the church family.

These stories demonstrate the power of congregations that become oriented toward true community. They also effectively portray the role meals can play in shaping our hearts and minds to aim the whole of our lives at the family of God rather than at our own agendas and security. For the rest of this section, we'll tell stories of communities that have gone out of their way to welcome everybody, including those on the margins. And we'll highlight the way meals often serve as a key practice in creating and sustaining such communities.

Episcopal Community Services (ECS) in Kansas City runs the world's strangest soup kitchen.[4] Each day, homeless patrons eat alongside doctors, police officers, college kids, and anybody else who wants to eat meals such as "roast leg of lamb with red currant gravy, pilaf, steamed broccoli, fresh bread and fruit."[5] Oh yeah, and it's all free. For anybody. And you get served by volunteer waitstaff who treat you like you're in a restaurant, which is what this unusual soup kitchen looks like.

ECS doesn't stop there. They recognize that homeless patrons, like those at New Prospect, don't want to be just recipients. So the Culinary Cornerstones' six-month training program prepares men and women to succeed in the culinary industry. Participants in the program apply what they learn by beginning to cook, serve, and help run the restaurant.

The result? A place where people from all backgrounds can feast together. A place where those who typically aren't invited to bring a plate to the potluck get a chance to learn how to do just that. A place where one homeless patron said, "They're treating me good, like they don't know I'm homeless."[6]

For two years, Rebecca and I worshiped at New City Fellowship in Nairobi, Kenya, while serving as missionaries there. Planted by Joe and Elfi Mutuuki, New City is perhaps the most diverse group of people of which I've ever been a part. Each week, young twentysomethings from the slums, Gujarati shopkeepers from India, white missionaries from the United States and Germany, a family of Congolese refugees, fourth-generation Indian Kenyans, and a smattering of other folks from every corner of the globe gathered in a school cafeteria to sing in six different languages and learn to love Jesus and one another. Tribalism among black Kenyans is serious business and ethnic violence is a regular reality. Further complicating matters, black Kenyans and Indian immigrants often do not get along, but our church had plenty of both. You can imagine the kinds of cultural, linguistic, and interpersonal conflict and misunderstanding that made up a part of our life as a community.

But if you've never been there, you may not be able to imagine the sound of one hundred people singing "How Great Thou Art," each in their own language, all at the same time. You may not be able to imagine what it means to see upper-middle-class Indians wearing traditional African shirts and black Kenyans wearing Indian saris as they circled up to share the Lord's Supper together. And I'm confident you *cannot imagine* the food.

The smells of the potluck were overwhelming as we streamed out of the church. It was a foretaste of the party Jesus will throw when he comes, with the kings of the earth offering their tasty treasures to the kingdom, each of them bringing a dish to the party (see Rev. 21:26). Everybody brought something to share. The only way we could eat was if everyone was willing to give to, and receive from, everyone else.

Indeed, wherever we went in Kenya, we experienced the generous hospitality of God's people in the form of cups of shared chai tea, tables covered with small vegetarian Indian plates offered up in homes, and heaps of beef stew served to us by African farmers who could not afford to be so generous. Every bite was a reminder, if we had eyes to see, that God is calling his people to become a family the likes of which we simply cannot fathom.

Food could also be divisive at New City. Going to an upscale Indian club was a great way to reach out to unbelieving Indians, but the price tag kept Kenyan men from the slums from being able to attend (or forced them to be recipients of charity in the community). At first I was surprised by how hard it was for our church to navigate all this. Then I realized New City was the first church I'd ever been to in my twenty-two years as a Christian that had a substantial number of members who were economically poor, who came as full participants rather than objects of charity, who called out to be recognized as eyes or toes or thumbs of the body of Christ rather than simply as folks with empty bowls on the other side of the soup kitchen line. Sharing meals together forced us to figure out how to be the body of Christ reconciled across racial, ethnic, and class lines. And those same meals forced us to reckon with just how far communities have to go if they're truly committed to the potluck. New City's commitment to creating just such a community utterly transformed my family's view of God's kingdom and God's church.

Back here in the United States, when pastor Jimmy Dorrell started befriending homeless men and women under a bridge, he recognized just how much work it would take if he wanted to be part of a community that authentically welcomed the homeless.[7] Today the appropriately named Church Under the Bridge (CUB) is a thriving congregation that still meets under the same overpass where Dorrell started. The church has made welcoming those on the margins one of the main if not the key prism for evaluating what the church must look like. Dorrell and CUB bear witness to the reality that if you want to create the kingdom potluck at the margins, you must relentlessly pursue the sort of community that makes it possible for the marginalized to "bring a plate." For CUB, that often includes thinking creatively about how to incorporate the mentally ill as full participants in the congregation.

"Let's face it," Dorrell says, "the church has done a lousy job of dealing with the mentally ill. And we have to be confessional about that. . . . We don't tell them they can't be there, but there are certain guidelines that tell us there isn't a place for them."

Getting rid of those unspoken guidelines required CUB to get creative when Frank, a man with a serious undiagnosed mental illness that causes him to be frenetic and mumble awkwardly, made it clear he wanted to be on the worship team. Never mind that Frank doesn't have a typical singing voice nor can he play an instrument! The first week, Dorrell had him play the bongos, since they were in need of a bongo player. He hit them so hard they fell off the trailer. The next week they drew a box on the stage and said, "Frank, you have to stay inside your box." That didn't work either. Eventually, Frank got an electric guitar (unplugged) and began singing and playing at the front of the worship band. "But what has happened," Dorrell explains, "is he is part of our worship team." Frank is part of the potluck.

Ben, who has a significant mental disability, has also become part of the team. He sings "Jesus Loves Me" every week, despite also not having what you might call a traditional singing voice. "It will make you cry," Dorrell says. For him, all this is about creating a community, "a bunch of people who all feel included. It's a little piece of the kingdom of God."

When members of Zion Lutheran Church in Iowa began to encounter the refugee communities around them, they caught a similar vision for becoming a church as diverse as the kingdom and felt particularly called to meet the needs of those refugees' children.[8] This historic church of 1,900 has gone from 98 percent white to nearly 50 percent nonwhite in a matter of years. "We worship in four languages and pray in twelve," says Pastor John Kline. The church's radical commitment to welcoming the world has led to reconciliation between enemies, specifically the Hutus and Tutsis, the rival tribes in the Rwandan civil war in which millions were killed. Both worship together at Zion.

The late Glen Kehrein, a veteran in the Christian Community Development Association, wrote in *Restoring At-Risk Communities* of the lengths his church had to go to in order to experience true racial reconciliation between white and black worshipers. Having been through a devastating racial split in a church that had sought reconciliation and solidarity but ultimately only achieved temporarily getting people in the same room, Kehrein and the church's pastor, Raleigh Washington, knew they had to commit to becoming a family together. Kehrein writes:

> Struggles abound when Black and White folks get together! Soon we realized that we must become preventive, dealing with problems before they arose, rather than merely prescriptive, dealing with the problem after it had exploded. [Pastor Raleigh Washington], in his inimitable style, came up with a plan—chocolate and vanilla meetings. Once each quarter the church has a marathon Sunday. During the Sunday school hour all the Blacks get together—the chocolate meeting—and talk about the church from the Black perspective. After church, the Whites get together—the vanilla meeting—and talk from their perspective. Then both groups get together and open up all the issues. The goal is to get issues out on the table and address them proactively. And it works! Much racial tension comes from ignorance and assumptions. This forum gives the opportunity to address issues, answering questions (even "dumb" ones), and brings understanding. This one practice (now in operation nearly eight years) does more to instill the values and practice of racial reconciliation than any I have ever seen anywhere.[9]

It is no surprise that another high point of the church's work in their low-income community was a Harvest Festival feast, which included a week of luncheons with old-fashioned revival meetings and a Saturday carnival and BBQ. Thousands attended the festival, and the church welcomed hundreds each year into the potlucking family of Jesus.[10]

Some years back, my family and some friends of ours were inspired by the festivals of Deuteronomy, which combined worship, partying, fellowship, and mission into one enormous act of celebration. We realized that in our contemporary church, each of these elements was isolated and separated from the other. How many of us have hurried out of a Sunday evening Christmas service to get to the real party afterward being held somewhere else?

So at our church (Downtown Church), we began to throw what we call "liturgical feasts." We alternated between enormous parties and home-based festivals centered on the ancient church calendar to build into our communities a rhythm of feasting that brought together rich food and drink, Scripture reading, foot-stomping singing for which everybody's invited to bring an instrument or at least a homemade shaker, and, when possible, the celebration of the Lord's Supper as part of a full meal. (For how this works in light of our tradition's practice of "fencing the table," see pg. 123.)

Eventually, some folks from nearby Neighborhood Church attended Advent Extravaganza, one of our annual feasts. Their fellowship had celebrated Advent Conspiracy, the movement of churches committed to celebrating Christ's birth by spending less, giving more, and worshiping fully, which we discussed in chapter 2. They had been raising money for clean water and wondered if we could combine our efforts. Today more than a hundred Christians cram into an Irish pub in downtown Memphis every year to sing raucous Christmas carols in public and raise thousands of dollars to fund the digging of wells in parts of the world that desperately need clean water. People who don't know Jesus, who just showed up for a drink, hear us read the story of the King's arrival, listen to us shout "His power and glory evermore proclaim," and then watch God's people embody the economy of the kingdom through generosity to the global poor.

Patterned after the biblical meals, our liturgical feasts have always tried to embody a concern for welcoming the marginalized and lamenting injustice in the world. At Advent, we take turns ritually extinguishing the candlelight as we name places of brokenness that make us long for Christ's second advent. I will never forget watching my cousin, recently diagnosed with life-threatening cancer, blow out the candle that had kept out the darkness as he named the disease threatening to end his life and widow his young bride.

Into that darkness, we start our celebration with these ancient words:

O come, O come, Emmanuel
and ransom captive Israel,
that mourns in lonely exile here,
until the Son of God appear.

This sort of thing happens at all the feasts. At Epiphany, we celebrate the arrival of the Magi and ask God to continue calling the nations to Christ in words they can hear, just as he did in providing a wandering star to a bunch of pagan astrologers practicing an illicit religion. At our Maundy Thursday gathering, we celebrate an extended Lord's Supper meal that includes remembering and reciting the story of Israel's exodus from the land of Egypt and Jesus's new exodus out of the land of slavery and death. At Easter, we celebrate Jesus's kingship by hearing worshipers name their idols one by one: "Money is not king." "Sex is not king." "My work is not king." Calling out "Jesus Christ is King" in unison in response to every named idol.

Our feasts, though, have never captured the full economic and racial diversity of those biblical festivals. We have remained more symbolically representative of the diversity of God's kingdom than an actual foretaste of that kingdom. That one fact has long kept us from being able to trust these meals to be able to bind us together truly as the family of God. We have not yet become the potluck God wants us to be.

But we're making progress. Recently, our church cohosted several liturgical feasts. We celebrated the Lord's Supper as a full meal that actually fed folks in our church who really do wonder where their next meal might come from. For the first time, our church feasted at a potluck that included the symbols of the body of Christ in the form of bread and wine brought by the worshipers. God's gifts to each of us as individuals became God's gift of himself to the church. God provided a meal for us by providing his church with the gifts and abilities necessary to bring a potluck to life.

Such practices are also part of our church's recognition that we can't only talk about injustice. We have to hear the lamenting cry of the victims of injustice. In talks about reconciliation and solidarity across racial lines in the church, we often hear people say, "We need to change our dinner tables." But if the pain of those at the table remains unnamed, our dinner tables can't create true community.

We held our first ever impromptu service of lament after a week in which several unarmed black men had been killed in police encounters and several police officers had been killed in response. It wasn't until I saw adult African American men, one after another, weeping in public over this latest tragedy and naming the anger that threatened to overwhelm them, wasn't until we wept and prayed together, that I truly began to realize what it really costs to create the potluck God wants for his people. But I also have never been more convinced that the potluck is worth the cost.

"Life in the kingdom . . . demands that we adopt a new set of table manners, and as we observe this etiquette, we become increasingly civilized according to the codes of the city of God."[11] In other words, Christians feast differently, and as we feast differently, we grow more and more into the kingdom people of God. The kingdom becomes more and more our true home as the will of our Father becomes evident in our hearts, homes, and dinner tables.

And yet so many of our churches cannot adopt such table manners because all the people showing up to the table look like us. Pastor and theologian Tim Chester, in his outstanding book *A Meal with Jesus*, poignantly asks: "If your church stopped celebrating communion, what difference would it make to your life?"[12] The answer I'm afraid most of us would give is, "Not much."

But there is hope, so much hope. Our communities and feasts fall short, but in Christ they occur in the shadow of the banquet that is on the way. Isaiah 25 tells us that in that day, Jesus will welcome all nations to a festival of well-aged wine and rich food. In that day, he will swallow up death forever, including the death that lingers in our racism and poverty and segregation. He will wipe away every tear from every feaster's eyes. It will be said at that feast, "Behold, this is our God; we have waited for him, that he might save us. This is the LORD; we have waited for him; let us be glad and rejoice in his salvation" (Isa. 25:9 ESV). It is against this glorious background that Luke tells us that the "Son of Man came eating and drinking" (Luke 7:34); when King Jesus arrived, his kingdom came in the form of a feast. And ever since, Christians have lived, worked, worshiped, and, yes, feasted in the shadow of that coming kingdom banquet when our Lord will return.

Practicing the Feast

In many ways, this chapter and this practice may seem the least "economic." After all, we don't often think about the makeup of our communities or the meals of our churches as economic issues. I am convinced, however, that the more obvious economic practices of the next chapters have the power to make God's economy encounterable in the present *only if* they flow out of communities radically committed to loving one another and welcoming all to the potluck of God.

That's why the practice we're advocating for the Community Key is simply feasting. Feasts give us an easy-to-begin yet essential starting point for becoming a community capable of potlucking with the community of God. Feasts of all sorts among friends and neighbors, as well as the church's special celebration of the Lord's Supper, provide opportunities for all of us to become people whose lives are oriented toward God and neighbor.

Making sure everybody can bring a plate will require the rest of the practices in this book. But unless we're fostering the sorts of communities capable of setting the table, that work will leave God's people all dressed up with nowhere to go. As Ed Loring, an advocate and activist for the homeless, says, "Justice is important, but supper is essential."[13] So without further ado, here are some ideas about how to begin practicing King Jesus feasts today.

Feasting at Church

Consider: How and when does your church eat together? Who comes? Who contributes? Who only receives? How could your church gatherings become places where everyone gives, everyone receives, and everyone is welcome? What would that require?

Some ideas for feasting at church include:

- *Regularly practicing the Lord's Supper as a full meal that includes low-income and marginalized people as participants.* If economically poor people are already part of your church, this might be relatively easy. If not, this might require you to partner with a church in a struggling part of town or even with a ministry committed to alleviating poverty in your community. In either case, consider ways everybody can participate. Can people who can't afford to buy food help prepare it? Help serve it? Help set up the room? How can every person participate in giving gifts back to God, who will in turn give them to his people in the feast of the Lord's Supper?

Many churches understand the Lord's Supper as being only for baptized believers and thus "fence the table" (i.e., offer the Lord's Supper only to those who've committed to following Jesus). Celebrating the Lord's Supper in the context of feasts that are open to unbelievers therefore does require some creative thinking. But it can be done! There's no reason why the ritual portions of bread and wine can't be separated and shared only with believers in the midst of a meal at which all are welcome. Indeed, because all three of us are part of church traditions that do fence the table, all our experiments with Lord's Supper meals have required some creativity.

- *Consider celebrating feasts according to the church calendar to help you observe the Lord's Supper as a full potluck meal.* Robby's church has celebrated the Lord's Supper at Maundy Thursday services (the Thursday before Easter) held in homes across Chattanooga (with the help of their church's elders and the approval of their session). Michael has participated in similar Lord's Supper meals, both in individual homes and throwing big potluck feasts including the whole church.

- *Bend your food ministries toward potlucking, community building, and sharing, and away from one-sided soup kitchen giving.* Wherever possible, find ways to share with one another that allow everybody to bring a plate. Make potluck meals a centerpiece of your community groups. Include those who are food insecure in helping to prepare food for church meals. Host enormous Thanksgiving parties for the family of God rather than handing out turkeys. Use food distribution to train low-income people for work or empower them to use their gifts.

Feasting in the Family

Consider: Who is welcome at your family's dinner table? What do your meals communicate about God's kingdom?

Below are some ideas for feasting at home:

- *Throw potluck feasts that welcome the marginalized as part of your family's life.* Invite people to your home for Thanksgiving, Christmas, and Easter meals. Practice the liturgical feasts described above in your own home. Consider having a regular meal (once a week or twice a month) in your home at which you welcome people who are struggling economically or who are from a different ethnic background. Invite them to bring food to share or help you cook. Invite refugees or immigrants and ask them to teach you how to cook some of their traditional food. Find ways to hear their struggles and experiences.

  Having lived in South Memphis for more than six years, I can tell you one of my struggles is to unlearn my desire to provide all the food at gatherings. Slowly, gradually, I've realized that my neighbors *want* to bring a plate, *want* to man the grill, *want* to help me clean up after the party is over. Too often in my white, middle-class culture, hospitality is just a high-end soup kitchen: come into our home, sit back, and let us serve you. But what if hospitality was more about welcoming others into the family? Then our hospitality would help us begin to envision the potlucking economy of God.

Of course, I recognize that many of us don't have relationships with folks across racial and/or socioeconomic lines yet. Even if we want a meal that looks like the kingdom, we don't have any names on our potential guest list who don't look like us. But that's part of the beauty of the practice of feasting. If you sit down to prepare your family's potluck and don't have anybody on your guest list who doesn't look like you, you're going to have to do some homework before you can even get started.

Find an organization in your city that does empowering community development work along the lines of what is encouraged in *When Helping Hurts*—and then volunteer. Go talk to the neighbor across the street whose name you don't know. Ask yourself where those parts of the body of Christ who don't look like you hang out and figure out how to encounter them. Do what it takes to feast in ways that allow the meal to become a foretaste of the great kingdom potluck that's already on its way.

Start Practicing

Before moving on, take a moment and consider where to begin practicing feasting in your own life. Where are your easiest first steps? Consider: Are there communities that you're a part of in which feasting makes sense? People who feast well who you could come alongside? Places where you have connections that could be strengthened through practicing the feast? Ask Jesus to open your eyes to new ways of feasting and new friends with whom to feast. Before finishing this chapter, identify how you, individually or with a group, can participate in a feast that feels like God's potluck within the next month.

Within the next month, I can practice feasting by . . .

_____

_____

_____

_____

The Community Key: Conclusion

In this chapter, we've made two audacious claims:

1. God calls each of us as individuals to aim our economic lives at the potlucking community, where everyone gives and everyone receives.
2. God gives us feasts to which everyone is welcome as one of the key practices to begin creating such a community.

The activists and doers among us are probably pretty unsatisfied by this. Feasting together doesn't feel like actual work. Just getting people gathered together and sharing food, stories, and life doesn't sound like economic justice. But the Bible makes clear that the practice of feasting together creates a community capable of caring for the marginalized and embodying just economics.

During World War II, Christians in Le Chambon, France, turned their town into a refuge for Jews facing the horrors of the Nazis. At great personal cost, they risked their lives to welcome the most marginalized into their homes and community. But their heroism, according to those who have chronicled it, began with everyday acts of hospitality, of sharing daily necessities. Such acts led the Chambonnais to become the sort of people who simply could not imagine doing anything other than risking their lives for the sake of the suffering. "We fail to understand what happened in Le Chambon if we think that *for them* their actions were complex and difficult," one scholar writes. They practiced the economy of the kingdom in everyday mundane acts of hospitality, such as sharing food with the Jewish refugees. Having done so, when the refugees knocked on their doors, they opened them and said, naturally, "Come in, and come in."[14]

> Every road to the economy of the kingdom runs through the creation of community.

Finding a way to welcome those who are poor and broken and ethnically different from us to the potluck feast shapes us to become people capable of welcoming the economy of God in all its justice, righteousness, and peace. Every road to the economy of the kingdom runs through the creation of community. Thankfully, Jesus gives us just such a community and welcomes us to embrace it through concrete practices of togetherness, including the feast.

Jean Vanier writes that "God is a family of three; three persons in communion with one another, giving themselves totally one to another, each one relative to the other."[15] I was working on this chapter and read those lines shortly before putting my kids to bed one night. My boys, Isaiah and Ames, four and two at the time, were in their bunk beds. But our daughter Nova, just barely one year old, crawled into the room and up onto Ames's bed. As I followed behind, Ames said, "Novey wants to sleep with me, Daddy. I love her. You sleep with me too. I love you, Daddy." I crawled into the bed, and then Ames said, "Put your arm around Novey, Daddy, so she doesn't fall. I'll put my arm around her, Daddy."

I teared up right there lying in the bed, realizing what a parable of God's invitation to a community of love Jesus had given me. The love between

Rebecca and me, like the love of the Triune God, brought these people into the world. And now they are in love with us—and more in love with one another. Community is nothing more than responding in childlike prayer to the God who first loved us: "Come be with me, Jesus. Watch out for my friend. I love her. I'll watch out for her too." Community flows into us and through us, straight from the love of the Father, Son, and Holy Spirit. This truth lies at the heart of the King's economy. May we enter into it with joy.

"WORK AND WAGES, GLEANING AND GIVING"

THE WORK KEY IN SCRIPTURE

Six years into our global data collection effort, we may have already found the single most searing, clarifying, helpful, world-altering fact. What the whole world wants is a good job. This is one of the most important discoveries Gallup has ever made.

Jim Clifton, CEO of Gallup

I grew up hearing over and over, to the point of tedium, that "hard work" was the secret of success: "Work hard and you'll get ahead." . . . No one ever said that you could work hard—harder than you ever thought possible—and still find yourself sinking ever deeper into poverty and debt.

Barbara Ehrenreich

Anyone who has been stealing must steal no longer, but must work, doing something useful with their own hands, that they may have something to share with those in need.

Ephesians 4:28

Wes Gardner and Prime Trailer Leasing's Story[1]

"There came a point in my business career," Prime Trailer founder and serial entrepreneur Wes Gardner says, "when I realized that business could be a platform for serving my neighbor." Wes, whose story we first encountered in chapter 2, had already begun practicing cross-shaped giving. But when he read the conclusions of the Gallup study quoted at the head of this chapter—that what everybody wants is a good job—he realized that as a business owner, he had a special opportunity to serve. In 2011, Prime Trailer began the Career Partner Program (CPP). Through this program, Prime hires unlikely job candidates through partner ministries and provides them with above-market wages for at least twelve months, while investing in them personally and professionally.

Lauren was living at Hope House, a home for teenage mothers, when she got hired by Prime through their CPP program. Through the program she became a full-time permanent employee and outstanding contributor to Prime. But that's not how things got started. "My mom was a teen mom," Lauren says. "My dad joined the military, my mom was homeless, so we lacked stability." When she was sixteen, Lauren became pregnant herself. "I remember thinking, *Oh my gosh, even when I'm trying to do something, I'm not really getting anywhere.*

"The first six months at Prime were extremely rocky," Lauren says. "I struggled so much. I was like, *I don't want to let anybody in. People just leave, and they'll just abandon me, or if things get too tough, I'll just be out on the streets.* But this company is nothing like that." Prime's willingness to welcome Laura and love her along the way allowed her to contribute to the company and her community.

Through work, Lauren is able to provide for her daughter. "She's three and a half, and she's sassy, but she has stability I never really had even at that age," Lauren says. "This company has done so many things for me. The reason I come into work every day and want to work my butt off for this place is that they provided me with an opportunity that I wouldn't have gotten anywhere else."

Wes and the team at Prime, like most of us, wanted to do something about poverty. They had given generously to charities and charitable causes.

But through their CPP program, they went further: they sacrificially adjusted their hiring practices to focus on marginalized workers such as Lauren. This didn't mean they became a nonprofit or stopped making money. They still value profit-making as a core part of their business. But they adopted a new way of looking at their work when they began bending their business toward folks like Lauren.

For instance, Prime no longer views what they pay workers simply as a cost to be controlled. "I look at our payroll as profit," says Wes. "I look at that line in my financial statements that shows how much we spend on wages and I think, *Look how much money we've made*."[2] Prime has created a real, dignifying, life-changing chance for people to work. The company's story gives us a glimpse of how God's people can bend their marketplace activities toward the King's economy.

> "I look at that line in my financial statements that shows how much we spend on wages and I think, *Look how much money we've made*."
>
> —Wes Gardner

Why Work?

Let's start with a question: Why do *you* work? What difference does work make in your life? In your family? What would you do without work? Gallup recently announced that the number one thing people across the globe want is a good job. But why is work such a big deal?

Paul offers a glimpse of how he would have answered these questions. He challenged the Christians in Ephesus to cast aside their old ways of life and "put on the new self, created after the likeness of God" (Eph. 4:24 ESV). Paul then turned to those in the community who were stealing. "Anyone who has been stealing must steal no longer," he writes, "but must work, doing something useful with their own hands, that they may have something to share with those in need" (v. 28).

In that one verse, we get an indication of why work matters for any of us. Work empowers us to

1. do something good,
2. provide for ourselves and our families,[3] and
3. have something to share with those who are in need.

Clearly, Paul saw work as allowing workers to produce something good. Understanding what Scripture considers "good work," though, requires us to go all the way back to the Genesis description of humans as made in God's image and given the task of coruling his world. This idea of humanity's "vocation" includes coruling with God by preserving and protecting the physical world (which we'll discuss as part of the Creation Care Key), as well as imitating our thoughtful Creator God in designing culture and unpacking the potential of God's good gift of the world.

At the same time, numbers 2 and 3 on the list point to Paul's belief that work enables people to provide for themselves and to contribute to the community. Paul saw these latter two points as absolutely essential to understanding why we work.

When Paul gives his last in-person speech to the Ephesians, as recorded in Acts, he reiterates his convictions about work by declaring that *he himself* has worked hard with his own hands to provide for himself and those who were with him (see Acts 20:34). Indeed, Paul declares that in all his "hard work,"[4] he had shown them that "by working hard in this way we must help the weak" (v. 35 ESV).

But in Ephesians 4:28, Paul isn't talking to just anybody. He's talking to *thieves*. He's talking to folks whose mug shots show up on the five-o'clock news. And Paul declares that work ought to be the means by which even they can contribute to their neighborhoods and have something to share with their neighbors.

It is interesting what Paul does not say. He doesn't say thieves should start working so they can get off welfare rolls or achieve the ancient world's version of the American Dream of middle-class independence. Paul says they should work *so that they can have something to share*.

The apostle Paul cared about work at least partially because he believed in communities where every single person, made in God's image and endowed with unique gifts and abilities, contributes to the life of the community. And in the community of faith, the community where we are being re-formed into the image of God through Christ, that means even community destroyers can become community philanthropists through work.[5]

In other words, Paul believed in the potluck.

From Genesis to Revelation, the Bible reflects Paul's concern about work and reveals God's heart for work as one of humanity's highest callings. Indeed, as we saw in the introduction, work was part of God's original creation, and though our work is broken by the fall, in Christ our work becomes part of how we live as coworkers with God (see 1 Cor. 3:9).

When Work Doesn't Work

But what happens when someone *wants* work but can't find it? What happens when the thief wants to become a philanthropist but can't get a job? What happens when thieves find work that is so temporary, unsteady, or poorly paid that they can't get off food stamps, much less have something left over to share?

In the United States today, these questions aren't theoretical. Let's look at some numbers:

- *75 percent.* Unemployment rates among ex-felons in their first year out of incarceration have recently been as high as 75 percent.[6]
- *60 percent.* Number of employers in one multicity study who said they would "probably not" or "definitely not" hire somebody with a criminal record.[7]
- *10–20 percent.* The reduction in wages caused by incarceration.[8]

Nor are former offenders the only ones struggling.

- 40 percent of *all* workers in the United States are in temporary, contract, or nontraditional employment.[9]
- In the neighborhood I (Michael) live in, a historic neighborhood of concentrated poverty, roughly 70 percent of adult residents are not working.[10]
- A high proportion of the jobs that have come back since the 2008 recession have been in low-wage sectors, leading many individuals and families across the nation to enter the ranks of the "working poor."[11]

- By some estimates, over half of those who receive food aid in America have at least one person in the home who is working.[12]
- Nearly 25 percent of working Americans earn less than $10 per hour.[13]

We started out by talking about how thieves may struggle to find work. But it's crucial to recognize that folks with criminal records aren't the only ones who struggle to find good work. Minorities, those failed by our education systems, people with disabilities, Native American populations, and people who grow up in neighborhoods of concentrated poverty all struggle to find jobs that pay wages high enough to allow them to achieve anything like financial stability. Furthermore, evidence shows that such struggles with employment are partially the result of systemic racism in the workplace. Consider, for instance, the following two stats from studies on race and work:

- The exact same résumé was 50 percent more likely to receive a callback from a potential employer if it had a "white name" (Brendan) versus a "black name" (Jemal).
- In one study, African American applicants with no criminal record were offered jobs at a rate as low as white applicants who had criminal records.[14]

In other words, not only those who commit injustices against society through theft struggle to find work. *Victims of injustice in our society also struggle to find jobs and thrive at work.*

In addition, in a fallen world, broken economic systems can prevent people from working even if nobody is intentionally discriminating against them (although that certainly happens). For example, a host of factors can cause an economic recession, putting millions of people out of work even when nobody meant them any harm.

As another example, a good friend of ours owned an auto-mechanic shop for many years. While he ran the business, he essentially hired *only* people with criminal records. All of them had been with him for many years and all were outstanding employees. But when he sold his business to a national chain, they immediately fired all these outstanding employees because of their criminal records (even though all their offenses were more than seven years old). This exemplifies one of the many ways our economic system is broken; the people who made the decision to fire these workers were likely compelled by a complex set of policies at the national level that are shaped by all sorts of liability concerns and insurance issues. In short, the economic and social systems of our world are broken in ways that often put the marginalized at a particular disadvantage.

> Our biggest problem may not be that people don't want to work. Our biggest problem may be that for too many of our neighbors, work just doesn't seem to work anymore.

What we're saying is that we might typically be tempted to think of lack of work as having to do with unemployed people being *sinners* (or at least not very talented). But in a world marred by the fall, we must recognize that many struggle with unemployment at least in part because they've been *sinned against* and/or simply work within broken and unjust economic systems. Indeed, our biggest problem may not be that people don't want to work. Our biggest problem may be that for too many of our neighbors, work just doesn't seem to work anymore.

Of course, people ask many big-picture, systemic questions when it comes to how to help everyone, including former thieves, contribute to the community and provide for themselves through work. Often we jump straight to questions about how markets work best or how governments can intervene on behalf of the poor. But for all the reasons we discussed in the introduction, we want to explore what Scripture calls God's people to do together to address unemployment. We'll start our journey by taking a look at a seemingly obscure bit of legislation from way back in the Old Testament: the gleaning laws.

"When You Reap Your Harvest": The Gleaning Laws

When Yahweh wrote the HR manual for his chosen people, he instituted a strange employee policy that affected every Israelite firm.

> When you reap your harvest in your field and forget a sheaf in the field, you shall not go back to get it. It shall be for the sojourner, the fatherless, and

the widow, that the LORD your God may bless you in all the work of your hands. (Deut. 24:19 ESV)

Old Testament gleaning laws required that Israelite landowners leave the edges of their fields unharvested so that the most vulnerable people in the land could provide for themselves by harvesting these leftovers. Once we remember that Israel was an agrarian economy in which the family farm was the family business, we can see just how radical this commandment was.

Imagine what these gleaning laws required from Israelite landowners. After each small business owner had invested in his business and worked his field throughout the growing season, he was ready to gather the fruits of his labor.[15] Even though he had taken responsibility for all the work and investment, he wasn't allowed to gather all the profits. Instead, God called him to create opportunities for work for the orphan, the widow, the immigrant, and the poor by leaving some of his own profits in the field. While the marginalized had to work in his field to gather these profits, their work didn't contribute anything to the landowner's business. The gleaning laws required every Israelite landowner to create access to work for others by accepting lower profits for themselves.

The gleaning laws provide the church with a paradigm that is vastly different from our own approaches to work and poverty alleviation. Using our usual economic logic, it would seem far more practical for God to simply let the business owners maximize profits, gather every last scrap of their harvest, and then redistribute a portion of it through taxation. But in the gleaning laws, God gives us something altogether different. Let's consider at least three ways the gleaning laws defy our contemporary expectations.

- *The gleaning laws provided work for, and required work from, the marginalized.* Contemporary charity often overlooks and sometimes even discourages work. Many people argue that this is a serious problem with government-run safety nets, and it certainly can be. But the truth is, Christian nonprofits and churches are often every bit as bad or even worse. For instance, research suggests that only 2 percent of all churches have any work-related ministry.[16]

- *The gleaning laws required Israelite business owners to create work by sacrificially leaving profits in the field.* God cared more about every poor person in Israel being able to provide for themselves through work than he did about any particular Israelite landowner's "right" to maximize the profits from their enterprise. In Israel's God-ordained economy, what ensured that each person had access to at least their daily bread was neither a robust economy nor a redistributionist government policy;[17] it was the willingness of Israelite farmers to leave profits in their own fields to create opportunities for the marginalized to work.

> God cared more about every poor person in Israel being able to provide for themselves through work than he did about any particular Israelite landowner's "right" to maximize the profits from their enterprise.

Make no mistake: unless these Israelite farmers continued to be "profitable," there would be nothing for them to eat or for the gleaners to glean. Neither the gleaning laws nor the authors of this book are against profits themselves. In fact, many of the solutions we suggest next are about how profits and social impact can go together. What the gleaning laws did, though, was make *profit maximizing* no longer tenable as the ultimate goal. Profits were part of the puzzle for Israelite farmers following the gleaning laws, but they couldn't be the only priority.

- *The gleaning laws made each and every "family business" the place where economic justice happened.* Don't miss one of the "by-products" of the gleaning laws: the working poor and the landed Israelite found themselves laboring in the same field. The landowner's sacrifice for the marginalized in the gleaning laws wasn't sent in the mail to a charity run by professionals; it was collected by the marginalized on the edges of the landowner's property. This made every Israelite's farm a place of personal encounter and economic transformation. And while elsewhere God did call Israel to tithe to a centralized system of charity to provide food aid for the poor, God *also* called for a work-based system that occurred on each and every Israelite farm. (Simply put, it's not either giving to charity or creating opportunities in our own "fields"; it's both/and.)

Every bit as important as the legal commandment itself is God's own explanation of *why* the Israelites had to leave profits in the field to be gathered by the immigrant, the fatherless, and the widow: "You shall remember that you were a slave in the land of Egypt," said Yahweh, "therefore I command you to do this" (Deut. 24:22 ESV). The gleaning laws served as reminders to the Israelites that they themselves had experienced deep economic oppression and that Yahweh had liberated them because of his love for them. In Egypt, the slave state stole the fruits of Israel's labor. In Israel, God called his people to leave some of the fruits of their labor in the field so that everyone might be able to work. The gleaning laws thus institutionalized the economic liberation of the exodus and enshrined that liberation in the law of the promised land.

Furthermore, the Israelites' history in the wilderness reminded them that *every Israelite* ultimately enjoyed the fruit of their labor *only* because of God's provision. Israel's work only worked because of God's work. As we'll see in chapter 7, the first economy Israel entered after the exodus wasn't the economy of the promised land. It was the economy of the wilderness. In that wilderness economy, God miraculously provided the daily bread of manna. One scholar points out that the Hebrew word used for "gathering" in the manna story is the same Hebrew word used in the Levitical gleaning laws and in the story of Ruth's gleaning.[18] The connection is clear: the Israelites allowed the poor to glean in their own fields because they themselves were but gleaners in the fields of Yahweh himself. That Yahweh liberated the Israelites from generational slavery, rained down manna for them to "glean" in the wilderness, and allowed them to labor on his promised land as tenants (see Lev. 25:23, 55) reminded them that Yahweh had the right to require them to leave some of their profits in the field for the marginalized to gather. Without Yahweh's ongoing provision, the wealthiest Israelite farmer never would have made it out of Egypt; how then could any landed Israelite possibly deny others the opportunity to participate in the community through work?

The Gleaning Laws in Action

In addition to the command for Israel to follow these laws, God also gave us a narrative of economic and spiritual redemption that depends, in part, on the gleaning laws: the book of Ruth. Ruth tells the story of Elimelech and Naomi, an Israelite couple who moved to Moab during a famine. While there, their sons married Moabite women, and then, in a series of almost unimaginable tragedies, all the men died. So Naomi decided to go back to Israel and send her Moabite daughters-in-law back to their own families. One of them, Ruth, refused to return. In one of the most memorable speeches in Scripture, Ruth declares to Naomi: "Where you go I will go, and where you lodge I will lodge. Your people shall be my people, and your God my God. Where you die I will die, and there will I be buried" (Ruth 1:16–17 ESV).

This remarkable confession, which amounts to a conversion to faith in Israel's God, is all the more remarkable when we remember that in the Old Testament, the Moabites were the bad guys. When Israel came out of Egypt, the Moabites stood against them and even hired a prophet to curse them (see Num. 22:4–6). Because of the Moabites' enmity with Israel, God actually declared that no Moabite could ever enter the "assembly of the LORD" (Deut. 23:3), even after ten generations.

Ruth wasn't just the wrong ethnicity, though. She was wrong on every count! Childless, husbandless, a woman in a patriarchal "man's world," Ruth had absolutely nothing going for her in the eyes of her Israelite neighbors. And yet this outcast foreigner went out to glean in the field of a righteous Israelite named Boaz, whose willingness to obey the gleaning laws created the opportunity for Ruth to provide for herself and Naomi.

Moreover, because the gleaning system gave Ruth an opportunity to work, she inspired her entire neighborhood. That's why Boaz told her that he had gotten a full report of all she had done for Naomi (see Ruth 2:11). That's why when Ruth married Boaz and bore him a son who would be the forefather of David the king, the women declared, in the midst of their patriarchal society, that Ruth was worth more to Naomi than seven Israelite sons (see Ruth 4:15).

The gleaning laws allowed even Ruth—the childless, husbandless widow from the wrong ethnicity, gender, and religion—to provide for herself, have something to give to her family, and become a full member of the neighborhood in Israel. Ruth experienced what Paul writes work would give even the thieves in the community: the opportunity to bring a plate to the potluck (see Eph. 4:28).

When we meet Ruth, she's a nobody of nobodies. At the end of the story, she's Jesus's great-great-grandmother! Ruth's full inclusion in the community and as a heroine in the faith depends in part on Boaz's obedience to the gleaning laws. If Boaz doesn't leave profits in the fields, Ruth remains an outsider, disenfranchised from the community, unable to give her gifts to the neighborhood, and potentially starving alone with her mother-in-law. And without Christians today intentionally creating work opportunities for the jobless, we too would miss out on the God-given gifts of those marginalized workers who long to bring a plate to the potluck but whose joblessness prevents them from doing so fully.

Just Work Elsewhere in Scripture

God's passion for work is not confined to the gleaning laws, of course. Consider a few other biblical themes related to the Work Key.

First, work allows us to fulfill our God-given vocation of creatively unpacking creation's potential. This happens in all God-honoring work, from designing hospitals to sweeping hospital floors, from marine biology to building bridges, from writing a song to working on a car engine. Moreover, doing good work well isn't just part of the cultural mandate given to us in the Garden; it's part of what it means for us to participate with Jesus in his reconciliation of all things. Theologian Al Wolters says it well:

> In the name of Christ, distortion must be opposed everywhere—in the kitchen and the bedroom, in city councils and corporate boardrooms, on the stage and on the air, in the classroom and in the workshop. Everywhere creation calls for the honoring of God's standards. Everywhere humanity's sinfulness disrupts and deforms. Everywhere Christ's victory is pregnant with the defeat of sin and the recovery of creation.[19]

All work that honors God and aims at participating in his renewing work in the world allows us to take up our task as people who bear God's image. (For this aspect of faith and work in particular, we highly recommend Amy Sherman's *Kingdom Calling* and Tim Keller's *Every Good Endeavor*.)

Second, work is the normal, appropriate means by which people ought to provide for themselves. The Bible recognizes the dignity of all kinds of work, including types of work that many cultures, including our own, often deem "undignified." So, for instance, God described the craftsmen who worked on the tabernacle as Spirit-filled (see Exod. 31:1–11), and Paul's apostleship never led him to abandon his tent-making trade (see Acts 18:3). Paul exhorted the Thessalonians to aspire to live quiet lives, working with their hands (see 1 Thess. 4:11–12), and declared that anybody who was unwilling to work shouldn't eat (see 2 Thess. 3:10). In short, work is good, people ought to work if they can, and refusing to work to provide for oneself is sin.

Third, however, the Bible testifies that injustice often corrupts work by oppressing workers. We see this in the laws of the Pentateuch designed to protect workers by requiring employers to pay fair wages in a timely manner (see Deut. 24:14–15) and in the damning critique of the prophets who declared that Israel failed miserably to treat their workers justly. Thus, Yahweh declared through the prophets that he would "draw near" in judgment "against those who oppress the hired worker in his wages, the widow and the fatherless, against those who thrust aside the sojourner and do not fear me" (Mal. 3:5 ESV). In this passage, Yahweh puts those who oppress workers in the same category as adulterers and sorcerers, both of whom were subject to the death penalty in the Old Testament. Mistreating employees is serious business.

Jeremiah railed against those who built their houses "by unrighteousness" and their "upper rooms by injustice, who makes his neighbor serve him for nothing and does not give him his wages" (Jer. 22:13 ESV). In the New Testament, James picks up this prophetic critique, declaring that the unpaid wages of the poor are crying out against the rich. Their oppression has allowed them to live "on earth in luxury and self-indulgence" (James 5:5), but their rotten mammon will "eat [their] flesh like fire" (v. 3).

We cannot be certain exactly how James or Jeremiah would have defined "just wages," so we will not try to offer a precise definition of what a just wage is in our own day either. What's abundantly clear, however, is that wage injustice is often perpetrated on the poor by the faith community and that wage oppression is a serious offense.

Other forms of injustice that the Bible recognizes occur in the workplace include oppressive lending practices (see Exod. 22:25–27; Deut. 15:1–15; 24:17), forced labor (see 1 Sam. 8:11–18), and stealing assets and resources from the marginalized (see 1 Kings 21:1–26; Isa. 5:8–10). If we care about the relationship between faith and work, then we have to care about the ways that injustice deforms work for many of the world's workers.

Fourth, God's people are called to intentionally create opportunities for work for the marginalized. In the release of slaves in Israel every seventh year (see Deut. 15) and the return to the family farm every fifty years at the Year of Jubilee (see Lev. 25; see also chapter 7 in this book for a detailed discussion), God created laws that, if followed, would eliminate multigenerational poverty by ensuring opportunity for work. Jesus's miraculous healings of the lame, the leper, and the blind offered not only physical healing from disability but also economic restoration to the community.

Indeed, what sometimes gets lost in translation when we read 2 Thessalonians 3:10—"If anyone is not willing to work, let him not eat" (ESV)—is that Paul was criticizing people who do not *want to work* (the Greek word translated "willing" normally includes the idea of desiring). The idea isn't that people who can't find work should be allowed to starve but, rather, that people who do not desire to work ought not to be allowed to eat from the community's common table.[20]

In short, in a world where work is good for all but injustice and oppression often render work ineffective or unjust, God calls his people to create opportunities for the marginalized to provide for themselves through their own work.

When we think of our own context in the West, the Scripture around the Work Key ought to call us to deep repentance that leads to obedience in light of God's kingdom economy. Ask yourself:

- Have I squeezed all the profit out of my proverbial field? Have I treated people who work for me as labor costs to be controlled rather than as humans to be cared for?
- Have I failed to treat people who work for me (either directly or by making stuff I depend on) with the dignity that belongs to them as image bearers of God?

- Have I assumed that the only reason people couldn't find work was due to their own poor choices and sin?

The Work Key in Scripture: Summary

We are in a strange situation in the American church. Many of us have bought into an economic system in which we do not consider the wages we pay our workers or the availability of work for marginalized groups to be a moral issue. Many Christians believe it is legitimate to pay wages as low as a business can legally get away with. And then we shower the families of these same workers with turkeys at Thanksgiving and toys at Christmas! But the King's economy is one in which everybody can buy enough turkey to share some with their neighbors. Far too often we have assumed that our assets, profits, and income were ours to handle as we desired, rather than gifts from God that come with the obligation to leave profits in the field to create space for others to work.

To repent of these idolatrous sins is also to commit to a new way of being in the world. As soon as we try to live toward the King's economy in our own lives, though, we quickly find that there are some problems with trying to apply the gleaning laws and these other Bible passages today. Most of us no longer have fields. We no longer live in an agrarian economy. Nobody *wants* to glean in my measly front-yard garden. Moreover, at a theological level, we no longer live in a theocracy with God on the throne of our particular nation as king, lawgiver, and judge.

What do we do with this tension? Probably the most common option is simply to ignore the Old Testament. But Old Testament scholar Chris Wright argues for another option. Instead of simply trying to replicate the laws of the Old Testament, we ought to see the laws of Israel as a "paradigm" that can inspire us toward faithful, creative action in our very different context.[21] To live toward the Work Key, then, requires all Christ followers to bend their economic lives toward the marginalized, creatively and sacrificially leaving some of our own profits in the field to create opportunities for struggling workers in our societies. Fortunately, as we'll see in the next chapter, Christians across the country are finding creative ways to do just that.

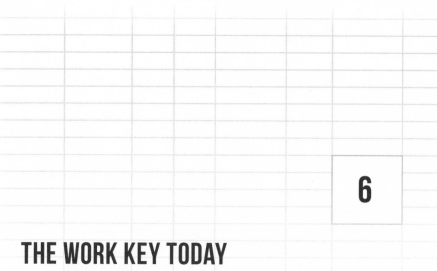

THE WORK KEY TODAY

STORIES AND PRACTICES OF GLEANING JOB CREATION

What does it look like for God's people to leave profits in the field to create opportunities for others? How can churches, families, and businesses begin to live toward the King's economy in light of the Work Key? While this is very new terrain for many of us, God's people are embodying his kingdom economy in creative ways all across our country and world.

Kingdom-Minded Business

Traditional businesses are beginning to look for ways to creatively and sacrificially create opportunities for the marginalized to provide for themselves through work. Wes Gardner, whose story you heard in chapter 5, is part of that movement. But he's not alone.

Since 1999, Cascade Engineering has helped more than eight hundred individuals move off welfare and into meaningful careers within the company. To accomplish this, Cascade began educating its entire management team on the realities rather than the stereotypes of who the working poor are and what barriers they face. The company also provides in-house training to new hires and has a social worker on-site to help employees work through common problems, such as transportation and childcare.[1]

Or consider the story of Barnhart Crane and Rigging, whose owners' generosity we explored in chapter 2. Barnhart not only creates opportunity for others externally by giving millions of dollars away every year, but they also create opportunity in-house by partnering with local nonprofits to bring in ex-felons to work and receive training.

Broetje Orchards, one of the largest and most successful privately owned orchards in the country, is another example of a business that has sought to leave profits in the fields on behalf of workers. Having seen the toll put on the children of seasonal agricultural workers, the family that owns the orchard sought to create full-time, year-round employment for the majority of their employees and built a preschool to support child wellness.[2]

Please note: Broetje Orchards is a business, and a good one at that. But the Broetje family's perspective is markedly different from the norm. "Sure, we have to make money or we'd have to shut the doors," says Cheryl Broetje, "but profit isn't our main motive."[3] Because of the company's commitment to Jesus and the family's countercultural perspective, Broetje has looked for ways to care for and create opportunities for workers, often by willingly accepting lower (or riskier) profits for the sake of their employees.

In 2006, for instance, the family faced a major decision when hail wiped out 70 percent of their apples. Insurance would pay only if they agreed to do no more harvesting for the season. While this would have recouped some of the losses, it also would have put hundreds of workers out of a job. So the Broetje family decided to keep their workers and keep picking the fruit, letting the insurance company keep their money. The company didn't lay off a single employee and still managed to break even that season.[4]

Or consider Broetje's approach to technology. When the leadership identified the need for new technology in 2004, they considered how to make such changes without having to get rid of workers. In the end, they did upgrade their technology but chose a slightly less efficient capital investment that allowed them to hire thirty-five new workers.[5]

Other traditional businesses partner with nonprofits to hire unlikely employees or even outsource work to nonprofits dedicated to job training. One such example is the partnership between National Guard Products (NGP) and Advance Memphis, which began in 2007. Advance, where I worked for five years, serves our South Memphis neighborhood, which struggles with the highest rates of economic poverty in all of Tennessee. But through their Work Life job readiness program, whose curriculum was copublished with the Chalmers Center and Jobs for Life, Advance has helped hundreds of formerly unemployed neighbors find jobs and flourish at work. NGP, a local manufacturer, partners with Advance by hiring Work Life graduates and outsourcing some of their production to Advance.

Through the outsourcing partnership, Work Life graduates work in their own community, surrounded by people they trust. This has proved particularly important for graduates who grapple with unique challenges to employment. Advance's outsourcing program allows those who've struggled in other jobs to receive job coaching in a positive environment. Folks between jobs have been able to bridge the gap between the last job and the next one through a few shifts at Advance. Folks who have been fired elsewhere can get a second shot. Pregnant mothers and individuals with moderate disabilities have been able to earn some money close to home through a job that accommodates their unique situations. In 2014, forty-one South Memphis neighbors did at least some work through Advance's outsourcing program, primarily through the partnership with NGP.

Since 2007, NGP has done more than $280,000 worth of business with Advance. They've hired dozens of Advance's graduates in full-time positions. As NGP has partnered with Advance in kingdom ministry, they've connected with some incredible employees as well. One employee, a friend of mine from my time at Advance, came to NGP after serving ten years in federal prison, having been shot eleven times, and recovering from a serious drug addiction. In approximately two years, that man has seen his wages go up 300 percent. And because of his God-given abilities, his desire to work and provide a better life for his family, and NGP's willingness to partner with Advance, today he manages more than fifty employees.[6]

Advance's outsourcing program has grown from one customer whose work was completed in a hallway at Advance's office to, at the time of this writing, six customers being served in the 24,000-square-foot, formerly abandoned warehouse that Advance recently took ownership of and renovated. Work in this warehouse generated $38,000 in wages for Advance graduates between October 2015 and December 2016. Advance anticipates this part of their program will create eight full-time positions by 2018.

Barnhart Crane and Rigging, Broetje Orchards, Cascade Engineering, and NGP and their partnership with Advance Memphis are just a few of the examples of kingdom-minded businesses that are making conscious and often costly decisions to create opportunities for marginalized workers. Each of these examples shows how regular for-profit businesses can leave some of their profits in the field. And each of these examples reminds us of the opportunity for businesses to bend their marketplace activities toward the potluck.

The Social Enterprise Movement

Another creative opportunity to bend our marketplace lives toward the marginalized can be found in the social enterprise movement. This movement has mobilized an army of entrepreneurs who join together the "social mission of a non-profit . . . with the market-driven approach of a business."[7] The resulting enterprises generate revenue in the market to fulfill their primary purpose of creating jobs or bringing services to at-risk communities. Social enterprises such as ThriftSmart in Nashville have created dozens of jobs in struggling neighborhoods that pay above-market wages and provide on-the-job training. ThriftSmart even shares profits every month with both full- and part-time workers, literally allowing unlikely employees to glean profits left over in the fields.[8]

Justin Beene's experiences growing up in a low-income, biracial family in Grand Rapids, Michigan, which was recently named one of the worst cities in America for African Americans, drove him to seek holistic and sustainable empowerment for his community. But while working on his master's degree in social work management, he became increasingly frustrated one summer by a rash of homicides, many of which were connected to his brother's caseload as a probation officer. In response, Beene and his brother began hiring local youth to pick up trash in their communities.

Beene is now a serial social entrepreneur working on his doctorate in entrepreneurial transformational leadership. When Beene got hired by a nonprofit to find jobs for area youth at the height of the economic downturn in 2008, he developed the trash pickup gig into Building Bridges Professional Services, a business that hires low-income youth to do landscape maintenance. Today the company maintains more than five hundred properties, providing residential and commercial landscape design and installation and snow removal in the Grand Rapids area. In addition to becoming a self-sustaining enterprise with annual revenues of more than $600,000, Building Bridges is now beginning to share the profits with its young employees.

Beene also founded Rising Grinds Café, an urban café that ethically sources its coffee products and provides jobs to local residents, and Coco-Works!, a developing for-profit social enterprise that seeks to source coconut oil products from a partner social entrepreneur in Guatemala who shares Beene's vision for global transformational impact. All this relentless innovation is driven by Beene and his community's desire to "disrupt poverty" through sustainable business models.[9]

Or consider the astounding story of Autonomy Works, a business built specifically to provide employment for people struggling with autism. Since many people with autism "possess exceptional attention to detail, excel at repetitive tasks and are extremely at ease in working with facts and figures,"[10] Autonomy Works has been able to create real market opportunities for people with autism by creating a work environment conducive to helping autistic workers cope with some of the more difficult parts of the workplace.

David Dunavant, a Memphian with a son on the autism spectrum, received some life-altering advice from his pastor. "After hearing my story," David says, "my pastor suggested that maybe I should find a way to be an advocate for young people on the autism spectrum, creating ways for them to have meaning, work, and purpose. He even thought this could possibly be my legacy."

In mid-2016, David launched GiveGood (www.givegoodco.com), a registered benefit corporation (B-Corp)[11] that sells toffee and healthy energy bars, which hires millennials on the autism spectrum. Given that millennials on the autism spectrum experience an unemployment rate of 84 percent in their twenties, GiveGood provides an excellent product while empowering adults who are often marginalized in the workforce. Within their first twelve months, GiveGood hired six part-time workers and got their products in twenty stores across Memphis.

The There's a Better Way program, run by St. Martin's Hospitality Center in partnership with the city of Albuquerque, New Mexico, embodies the gleaning laws by giving homeless men and women the opportunity to work for five hours a day for $9 an hour. The There's a Better Way van simply drives around looking for potential workers, who are also fed lunch and given access to programs designed for the homeless (including emergency shelter) at the end of the workday. "In less than a year since its start, the program has given out 932 jobs clearing 69,601 pounds of litter and weeds from 196 city blocks. And more than 100 people have been connected to permanent employment."[12]

Father Rusty of St. Martin's sees this program as an alternative for folks for whom a typical full-time, forty-hours-a-week job may not be a reality, particularly those suffering from mental illness. "If you're dealing with mental health issues," he says, "often one to three days is all you can do." Such programs are easily replicable and would fit many existing homeless-oriented ministries. Meanwhile, in Memphis, the Hospitality Hub's Work Local program provided 1,040 daily jobs to homeless men and women, eighty of whom went on to find permanent positions, in its first year alone.[13]

Another outstanding example of social enterprise is Advance Memphis Staffing. In 2009, after many years of referring graduates for jobs in the marketplace, Advance launched AM Staffing, a social enterprise staffing service that sends employees who've graduated from the Work Life program to logistics and manufacturing companies around Memphis. AM Staffing has helped hundreds find work and paid millions of dollars in wages to workers from the economically poorest urban zip code in the state. It also covers the costs of the staff who operate it and often generates profits that help support Advance Memphis's other ministry programs.

One worker who got help through AM Staffing is Donald Jenkins. Donald used to live on the street, addicted to drugs. He cleaned up after Lemar Walker, a heroic pastor from the community, brought him to faith in Jesus. Donald became a new creation in Christ, passionate about sharing his faith with others. But he also found himself looking for work.

After graduating from Advance, Donald landed his first real job in a lower-wage, temporary assignment through the staffing service. Because of his own fear of failure, Donald turned down his first opportunities for a promotion. The Advance staff kept working with him, though, and eventually got him to take a full-time, permanent job with benefits that *also* came with a lot more responsibility and work. Juanita Johnson, director of employment support at Advance, recalls that she met with Donald almost daily just to keep him from quitting. He didn't think he could handle the responsibility of the new job.

But Donald thrived for years, received a promotion, and eventually trained others. Today he works for Advance, supervising other folks who are getting their first job through the Advance program. What his story reveals is that sometimes workers appear to be unwilling to work, when in reality they simply do not believe they can do the job. Others may lack the talent and persistence to succeed at work initially but can gain both skills and commitment through opportunities to work. You can't learn to ride a bike without falling off a few times, and for individuals from communities of concentrated poverty or with serious barriers to work, learning to succeed on the job will entail some failure. Through social enterprises such as Advance Memphis Staffing, God's people can create the context for folks like Donald to find jobs and flourish at work.

Gleaning Goes to Church . . . and Comes Back Home

But the Work Key isn't just for business people; all of us can leave some of our profits in the fields to create opportunity for work. Many churches have done this simply by creating "gleaning jobs" within the church itself. My (Michael's) church, Downtown Church (DC), has hired people with criminal records or those struggling to make ends meet to set up chairs, break down the nursery, and help out around the church office. Like many other churches, DC has also encouraged members to hire those who are in need of extra cash to do odd jobs around the house, cook meals for events, help with a move, or assist an elderly neighbor with their yard. Our deacons even surveyed our congregation to identify members who would be willing to hire people to do odd jobs or who oversee hiring in their workplaces so the diaconate can help people who are struggling find work.

When gleaning comes home to our families and churches, we see how embodying the gleaning paradigm can reconcile relationships between people and put cash in struggling neighbors' pockets. In one of DC's first deacon meetings, the diaconate received a request from Sarah, a woman living in government housing and dealing with some health issues. Sarah needed help with a predatory rent-to-own furniture debt she'd incurred when she replaced her apartment furniture after a bedbug episode. The church connected her with our community group Bible study, which meets near her home, and with a mentor, Jane, who also has had some health problems. DC had already paid Sarah to clean the church offices, and when a deacon asked her if she had any ideas about how to gain some extra income, Sarah said she loved to clean and would love to clean more homes each month. In God's incredible providence, Jane, because of her own health issues, needed some extra help cleaning her house. So she began hiring Sarah twice a month to help out around the house.

By bending her economic life toward Sarah and leaving some of her family's profits in the field, Jane created the opportunity not only for Sarah to provide for herself but also for Sarah to give back to Jane. Jane, the "helper," all of a sudden became the "helped." By embodying the gleaning paradigm, reconciliation between two people from different races and economic classes began to happen. *And* as soon as Sarah paid off her debt (with the help of the deacons and her new extra income), she began bringing food to her community group Bible study. Work became the means by which Sarah did something good, provided for herself, and brought a plate to share to the King Jesus potluck. Hallelujah!

Other churches have turned ministries aimed primarily at giving stuff away (turkeys at Thanksgiving and toys at Christmas, for instance) into thrift stores and holiday markets that allow parents to purchase goods at reduced prices or even earn credit by working in the store. Bob Lupton led the charge in this shift after he first saw how defeated the dads looked when his church from the other side of town showed up with gifts for the kids of those working-poor fathers.[14] The Pride for Parents Christmas Store has allowed parents in the community to experience the joy of providing gifts for their kids and has created sales revenue to help them start an employment training program.

Practicing Gleaning Job Creation

These contemporary stories give us targets at which to aim. By leaving our own profits in the field and bending our economic activities toward the unemployed, we can create opportunities for the marginalized to provide for themselves. But how do *we* begin to *practice* the Work Key? We encourage you to embrace the practice of gleaning job creation. This spiritual economic discipline challenges us to find ways to create work opportunities for others by leaving some of our own profits in the field.

Gleaning Job Creation at Work

Consider: Do you have influence at your workplace? How could your workplace and coworkers bend your business or workplace toward the marginalized?

Some ideas for practicing gleaning job creation at your workplace include the following:

- *Partner with a nonprofit to hire marginalized job seekers.* These job seekers include the long-term unemployed, people with disabilities, people with criminal records, those with low education who may require more on-the-job training, and many more. Pay them more than the market requires. Consider working with a nonprofit to outsource some work to that ministry.

- *Create a paid internship or apprenticeship program for youth from low-income communities.* An eight-week paid summer jobs program for disadvantaged teenagers from Chicago resulted in a 43 percent decrease in juvenile delinquency for participants over an eighteen-month period.[15] That makes hiring at-risk youth for a summer job one of the most successful community development initiatives ever! Nearly every business could find ways to welcome a teen or two into its workforce.

- *Change your hiring policies.* Allow people with criminal records to access at least some jobs. Provide more on-the-job training to allow the undereducated and lower-skilled workers access to work in your company.

- *Start a social enterprise.* Tap into your inner entrepreneur to create opportunities for others. Most social enterprises require a team of people, often bringing together younger, entrepreneurial risk-takers with committed, more experienced business folks. We hope this chapter in particular inspires many conversations between young and old; nonprofits, for-profits, and hybrids; investors and entrepreneurs; and many more.

Gleaning Job Creation at Church

Consider: What opportunities exist for your church to pay somebody to do something meaningful that would also help the church? Do you have a group of business owners who could help job seekers find work in their own businesses or within their network? Are there other ways to create opportunities for paid work within the congregation?

Some ideas for practicing gleaning job creation at church include the following:

- *Pay people struggling financially to do odd jobs.* Strong caveat: it is far, far better to approach this conversation with a job seeker with a question such as, "Is there any skill you've used to gain some money on the side when things were tight in the past?" or "What sort of work have you enjoyed doing in the past to make ends meet?" This ensures that the gleaning jobs created are dignifying for the person who does them. This is particularly important in light of the context of America's racial history. For instance, for many years black Americans were confined to certain types of work (housecleaning, for example) that have acquired negative connotations as a result.
- *Connect job seekers with members who are gatekeepers to jobs in the community.* Consider doing this in partnership with a Work Life program or start one of your own (for details on how to do so, go to www.chalmers.org). Encourage your members who are gatekeepers to employment to consider the gleaning job creation practices above.
- *Turn your Christmas giveaway/food pantry/clothes closet into a Christmas/thrift store that allows low-income parents to earn store*

credit.[16] So often our handouts hurt rather than help (which is why you should read *When Helping Hurts* if you haven't already!). But many Christian community development organizations have found that converting these giveaway ministries into thrift stores or holiday stores empowers parents to provide for their kids and equips those who earn store credit with job skills.

- *Organize your members to begin practicing gleaning job creation in their own families* (see below).

Gleaning Job Creation at Home

Consider: Where could your family create opportunities for work within your own sphere of influence?

Some ideas for practicing gleaning job creation at home include the following:

- *Pay people struggling financially to do odd jobs.* My family has personally embraced this practice over the years in the community we call home. In the past six years, I have hired neighbors to help me build one fence, tear down another one, detail our cars, install a flower bed, break into my car to get a key that was locked on the inside, floor parts of our attic, cook meals for parties, give me a haircut, BBQ at our community group, deep clean our home, and mow our yard. This has worked both when we have intentionally hired new entrepreneurs from our neighborhood's entrepreneurship program and when people have asked us for money. When people do good work, we refer them to others. When they don't do good work, we try to help them improve.

  Ironically, embracing this practice has forced us to give up some of our conventional morality from our middle-class culture, namely that good Christians should mow their own lawns. To be frank, at our income level, all else equal, we would. However, we have found that embracing this gleaning job creation practice has shifted our relationship with struggling neighbors from one-way charity to a more empowering relationship of giving and receiving. (Note that the strong caveat mentioned on page 154 applies here as well.)

- *Participate in your church's efforts to help the unemployed through the gleaning job creation practices mentioned above.* Just think about it: if ten families in your church decided they would be willing to have someone in need of work cut their grass or clean their homes twice a month, you could provide a job for somebody every workday of the year.

Start Practicing

Before moving on, take a moment to consider where to begin practicing gleaning job creation in your own life. What are your easiest first steps? Consider: What's the local job market like in your community? Are there nonprofits or churches engaged with job seekers that might be potential partners for you in pursuing gleaning job creation? Before finishing this chapter, identify how you, individually or with a group, can create a work opportunity within the next month for someone struggling financially.

I will practice gleaning job creation in my life within the next month by . . .

_____

_____

_____

_____

The Work Key: Conclusion

We could certainly write much more about how best to help the unemployed and underemployed. Gleaning job creation gets messy and can take a lot of work. One African American inner-city pastor told me a heartbreaking story: A suburban congregation had been doing a Christmas toy giveaway for many years at his church. This pastor was happy for his congregants' kids to get gifts, but he was heartbroken by how harmful the process was to the parents' self-esteem, especially as the gifts were given away publicly with members of the suburban church present. After a while, the pastor took a risk and asked the suburban church to help him set up a Christmas toy store instead. The suburban church turned him down. They were too used to charity as usual.

But while gleaning job creation is messy, as Wes Gardner reminds us, "It's worth it." This is because it allows people to move from simply getting fed to bringing a plate to the potluck. In our churches, workplaces, and homes, we can leave profits in the fields to create opportunities for others to participate in the life of the community through work.

Beyond gleaning job creation, though, a full answer to how to make sure everybody, including thieves, can give their gifts to the community through work will require tremendous dedication, wisdom, Holy Spirit guidance, a deep understanding of economic realities, and real relationships with those who are struggling to find work. Only God knows all the ways his people might embody the Work Key if we were to truly follow him with our whole lives, bending our economic activity toward those on the margins.

But by practicing the King's economy through gleaning job creation, we believe your church, family, and workplace can begin to create opportunities for the marginalized and, at the same time, invite God to transform you and your community, orienting your hearts toward his economy and his people. In other words, doing gleaning job creation will help you discover what God has next for you in his kingdom economic journey and become a person capable of coworking with him in that economy.

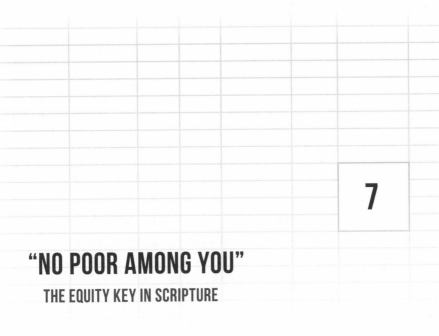

"NO POOR AMONG YOU"
THE EQUITY KEY IN SCRIPTURE

The broad purpose of [the OT Jubilee and debt forgiveness laws] was to preserve families as participating members in the economic and social community, and thereby to preserve their place within the covenant community as well.

Christopher J. H. Wright

The Exodus was a journey from the scarcity of slavery to the abundance of neighborly bread, a prospect impossible in Egypt, but possible in the wilderness.

Walter Brueggemann

But the jubilee . . . offers a term to the situation of inequality. . . . Division of YHWH's people into sellers and buyers, patrons and clients, masters and servants marks the period between jubilees; at the jubilee each one returns, takes up his holding and the nation once more becomes equal. At that point the poor cease from the land.

Walter J. Houston

But they shall sit every man under his vine and under his fig tree, and no one shall make them afraid, for the mouth of the LORD of hosts has spoken.

Micah 4:4 ESV

Donald Jenkins, the formerly homeless and drug-addicted man mentioned in the previous chapter, didn't stop once he got that living-wage job through Advance Memphis's staffing service. Having started to cut grass on the weekends to earn some extra cash, he jumped at the opportunity to take a class Advance adapted from LAUNCH Chattanooga, an organization that helps people from marginalized neighborhoods start or improve their own businesses.

For ten weeks, Donald and his wife, Jean, attended the LAUNCH class. Between classes they talked to potential customers, worked on their financial numbers, and prayed. On pitch night, a very nervous Donald fumbled his way through a sales pitch for Jenkins Lawn Care and Tree Removal. Toward the end of the pitch, his wife interrupted and said, "Donald, tell them about the jobs!"

Immediately, Donald went from self-conscious salesman to prophetic pastor. "I want to start this business," he said, "because I want to create one hundred jobs for young men like me, who didn't feel like they had any choice but drugs. I want to create opportunities for them."

Donald used a matched-savings program through Advance to buy a truck, saved up for a zero-turn mower, and then won a small business grant to buy a trailer. He services customers all across the city. In 2016, Jenkins Lawn Care brought in around $23,000 in revenue (in addition to what Donald earns from his full-time job). He's more financially stable and can give more to the neighborhood church he attends, whose pastor brought him to faith many years ago.

Maybe best of all for Donald is when I look out the window and see him working on my street, he's often got somebody working with him, somebody who likely wouldn't have gotten a shot anywhere else. In a neighborhood where upwards of 70 percent of working-age adults aren't employed, kids see few examples of good work. But Donald gives the kids on our street a vision of possibility (I know because my two sons, Isaiah and Ames, often dress up like Donald and pretend they're mowing lawns). Becoming an entrepreneur has given Donald greater stability and empowered him to bring a better plate to the potluck.

What makes a person or family economically secure and allows them to give their gifts to others? We know that ultimately there is no security, economic or otherwise, apart from God. In this chapter, though, we'll discuss how part of the way that God has designed people to experience security in his world is through having an economic stake in the neighborhood.

"No One Will Make Them Afraid"

The prophet Micah looked forward to the great day of the Lord, when Yahweh will judge the nations and God's people will melt down their swords and spears and turn them into gardening tools. He also prophesied that in that day everyone will sit under their own vine and fig tree, and "no one will make them afraid" (Mic. 4:4). Micah saw that when God's kingdom is fully established, each person will have an economic stake, an economic place to stand, an economic portion to steward.

> Micah saw that when God's kingdom is fully established, each person will have an economic stake, an economic place to stand, an economic portion to steward.

This won't be some scrappy subsistence garden used for survival; vineyards and fig trees will be used to create wine and delicious food that can be sold or shared or used for celebrations. The result of everyone having such equity in the community will be nothing short of revolutionary: no one will make them afraid. Micah grasped deep in his bones that the King's peace will be not only an end to violence but also the establishment of an equitable community in which every person has access to the factors of production, the stuff that makes stuff in the economy.

Micah's prophetic vision wasn't some sort of left-wing innovation. His end-time vision of everybody having access to ownership in the community has roots that run all the way back to Mount Sinai. And to understand Sinai, we have to go back even further, back to the "house of slavery."

Out of the House of Slavery

It's easy for us to forget that Israel was enslaved to the economic superpower of its day. Since Pharaoh believed he was god, he also believed he owned everything. His hierarchical political economy combined with Egypt's incredible natural resources created unprecedented wealth. This wealth, though, went mostly to the very rich and was created on the backs of Israelite slaves. The god of Egypt required the sweat of the Israelites' brows and the blood of their children.

The early chapters of Exodus give us a picture of a contest between this would-be god, Pharaoh, and Yahweh, the God of Abraham, Isaac, and Jacob (see Exod. 3:6). Up through the plagues and the crossing of the Red Sea, this contest was pretty straightforward: Yahweh heard the cries of his people groaning under Pharaoh and responded by rescuing them in might and power and glory. Yahweh lifted up the good guys and zapped the bad guys. What could be simpler?

Once Israel left Egypt and entered the wilderness, though, Yahweh battled not so much with the king of Egypt on his throne as with the Egyptian way of being enshrined in his peoples' hearts. Apparently, even slaves got occasional access to the "pots of meat" created by Pharaoh's empire (Exod. 16:3). So while it's likely that the Israelites only ever enjoyed the meager scraps from the Egyptian economic table, almost as soon as God got them out of Egypt, *they wanted to go back!*

> They said to Moses, "Was it because there were no graves in Egypt that you brought us to the desert to die? What have you done to us by bringing us out of Egypt?" (Exod. 14:11)

> The Israelites said . . . "If only we had died by the LORD's hand in Egypt! There we sat around pots of meat and ate all the food we wanted." (Exod. 16:3)

> They said, "Why did you bring us up out of Egypt to make us and our children and livestock die of thirst?" (Exod. 17:3)

As the old saying goes, "It only took a day to get Israel out of Egypt, but it took forty years to get Egypt out of Israel." Even after their bodies were liberated from Egyptian slavery, the Israelites' economic imaginations carried "Egypt's disease."[1]

The Wilderness School of Economics

Yahweh responded to his people's sickness by welcoming them into his Wilderness School of Economics. In this school, manna was Econ 101. In response to Israel's longing for the flesh pots of Egypt, the Lord rained down bread from heaven so that the community would "know that the LORD [had] brought [them] out of the land of Egypt" and to test whether the Israelites would obey his commandments (Exod. 16:4–6 NET).

Yahweh's manna lecture worked on two levels: first, they would know that *the Lord* brought them out of Egypt. In other words, their experience with manna would tell them something important about the heart of their God: Yahweh was a God who rescued his people from slavery and welcomed them into the promised land. But second, they would also learn that they *had been brought out* of the land of Egypt. Manna shaped not only Israel's view of God but also their view of the world. Manna taught Israel that they were in new territory now. Egyptian rules didn't apply on Yahweh's turf.

Yahweh instructed the Israelites to gather only enough bread for their daily needs Sunday through Thursday. On Friday, the sixth day, they got to collect enough for both Friday and the Saturday Sabbath day of rest. Of course, some Israelites broke both rules. When they tried to store up manna overnight during the week, the manna was full of maggots in the morning, and the Israelites who went out on the Sabbath found none to collect. Wilderness School of Economics Lesson #1: God's economic gifts rot when hoarded, and workaholism gets you nowhere.

Wilderness School of Economics Lesson #1: God's economic gifts rot when hoarded and workaholism gets you nowhere.

Each morning, the Israelites went out and worked for their daily bread. Some gathered more, some less. But when it got to quitting time and they tallied up their take for the day, "the one who gathered much had nothing left over, and the one who gathered little lacked nothing" (Exod. 16:18 NET). Wilderness School of Economics Lesson #2: When God gives, he provides enough for everybody. In Egypt, there was economic excess—pots of meat and bread in full (see v. 3)—because Pharaoh took control, grabbed up all the land, and squeezed every cent out of his slave labor. In the wilderness,

Yahweh's abundance came in the form of daily bread equally available to all and absolutely impossible to hoard. "This surely is bread from an economy Israel did not know or understand, bread given and not planned, received and not coerced, bread on someone else's terms."[2]

Wilderness School of Economics Lesson #2: When God gives, he provides enough for everybody.

These wilderness economy[3] lessons challenged every assumption Israel held about economic security. But because Pharaoh, the chief economist of Egypt, claimed to be god, Exodus economics isn't just "A Tale of Two Economies." It's "A Tale of Two Gods." Experiencing God's manna economy gave the Israelites a glimpse of the character of the Lord of heaven and earth, reminded them they were no longer in Egypt, and invited them to embrace a new economic kingdom (see vv. 4–6).

Establishing the Manna Economy in the Promised Land

Of course, the Israelites weren't supposed to stay in the wilderness forever. When they arrived at Mount Sinai, Yahweh gave them laws for entering the promised land. These laws were designed to help Israel become a "kingdom of priests" among the nations. They were to show the world what life looks like with Yahweh on the throne.[4]

Not surprisingly, then, these laws included a road map for establishing the manna economy in the land. No, bread would no longer fall from heaven. Nevertheless, God gave the Israelites rules for receiving and managing land that would embody the manna economy's dependence on God and commitment to everyone having enough, so long as they were willing to work. Indeed, Yahweh provided Israel with a one-two punch designed to prevent multigenerational poverty by creating an equitable economy for all.

First, Yahweh told Israel they were to divide up the land among families, giving each clan roughly the same amount (see Num. 33:54). Second, Yahweh outlawed the permanent sale of these ancestral lands. If all this wasn't enough, he also required Israel to push a giant economic reset button every fifty years. This "reset button" came in the form of a yearlong blowout party: the Year of Jubilee. "Consecrate the fiftieth year and proclaim liberty throughout the land to all its inhabitants. It shall be a jubilee for you; each of you is to return to your family property and to your own clan" (Lev. 25:10).

To understand the Jubilee, we have to keep reminding ourselves of two important pieces of background information. First, Israel's economy was built on agriculture. It's almost impossible for us to imagine in our day, but in Israel, basically everyone's primary occupation was farmer. If Israel had a second-grade classroom, when the teachers asked their students what they wanted to be when they grew up, everybody in the class would have said basically the same thing: I'm going to be a farmer.

Because agriculture so dominated Israel's economy, a family's survival depended on their being able to control land for farming. Without access to farmable land, a family literally would have had no place to stand, economically or socially. If a person lost their land, they couldn't get a decent job waiting tables or working in IT. They became a landless peasant, often sucked into an oppressive sharecropping cycle somewhat similar to the situation facing people in the American South in the early twentieth century. Job paints a truly horrifying picture of the plight of the landless poor in the ancient world:

> The poor are pushed off the path;
>> the needy must hide together for safety.
> Like wild donkeys in the wilderness,
>> the poor must spend all their time looking for food,
>> searching even in the desert for food for their children.
> They harvest a field they do not own,
>> and they glean in the vineyards of the wicked.
> All night they lie naked in the cold,
>> without clothing or covering.
> They are soaked by mountain showers,
>> and they huddle against the rocks for want of a home.
> The wicked snatch a widow's child from her breast,
>> taking the baby as security for a loan.
> The poor must go about naked, without any clothing.
>> They harvest food for others while they themselves are starving.
> They press out olive oil without being allowed to taste it,
>> and they tread in the winepress as they suffer from thirst.
>
> (Job 24:4–11 NLT)

Poverty in the ancient world was brutal. If you wanted to avoid it, land was practically everything.

Second, though, to understand the Jubilee, we need to understand that Yahweh's land policy completely overturned the land policies of Egypt and the Canaanite city-states that existed in the promised land before Israel's arrival. In these Canaanite city-states, the king owned all the land and everyone else worked it as a tax-paying peasant at the mercy of the ruler.[5] Kings, priests, and members of the elite used debt bondage, tenant farming, forced labor, heavy taxes, and outright theft to force the agrarian economy to serve their endless desire for power and luxury. The "city-states of Canaan, then, were responsible for the creation of poverty among their citizens."[6]

This economic system was shored up by Canaanite theology. "The gods of Canaan sustained the political, social, and economic status quo,"[7] because, of course, they had given the Canaanite kings ownership of everything. In most of the ancient Near East's theology textbooks, it wasn't *humanity* that was made in God's image; it was the *king*.[8] That theology justified the king doing basically whatever he wanted with the land. The social, theological, and economic structures systematically dispossessed the average person from land, leaving many destitute.

But in the wilderness, Israel had learned that Yahweh, Lord of heaven and earth, did not act like these other gods. Nowhere do we see this more clearly than in the Year of Jubilee in Leviticus 25. The entire chapter provides a series of laws that prevented any Israelite family from being permanently disenfranchised from their family farm. The long and short of it is that if you, the reader, worked hard, saved, acquired access to new farms and fields, essentially spending forty-nine years being the Proverbs 31 woman, while I spent that same period getting drunk and gambling and losing my land in the process, when the Jubilee trumpet sounded, those ancestral lands of mine that you acquired by your thrift got returned to my children. For one giant yearlong party, everyone in Israel feasted off what the land produced, and then every Israelite family got a fresh start.

You see, as we've witnessed time and again, Yahweh cares infinitely more about *every family* having the opportunity to provide for themselves and participate in the economy than he does about *any one family's* "right" to acquire more and more, whether through thrift or theft. When King Yahweh wrote the land-use policy in Israel, the primary goal was to ensure that every family had an economic place to stand. The Year of Jubilee, when implemented, allowed every family in the community whose members were willing to work to escape multigenerational poverty by ensuring that every family had a stake in the community, equity in the economy. As with manna in the wilderness, the Jubilee invited the Israelites to embody an economy in which the one who has much doesn't have too much and the one who has little doesn't have too little.

It may seem that we've gone pretty far afield, getting into the intricacies of an ancient nation's bizarre land tenure system. But this journey into the heart of God's economic arrangement for Israel provides us with a priceless glimpse into the King's economy for today.

For instance, don't miss how different the Jubilee was from either of our typical modern-day "conservative" or "liberal" options. The Jubilee wasn't conservative, because it radically restricted the invisible hand of the market and undermined the effectiveness of economic incentives (by restricting the sale of land and thus placing some limits on people's ability to capitalize on investments). Nor did it treat the endless acquisition of personal property as a right.

But the Jubilee wasn't liberal either, because it didn't create equity by redistributing the results of the community's labor. It created equity by restoring the factors of production to Israel's equitable starting point, where each family had access to their own family farm.

> When King Yahweh wrote the land-use policy in Israel, the primary goal was to ensure that every family had an economic place to stand.

That such a complete reset occurred only every fifty years makes clear that individuals would have felt the effects of their decisions.

In chapter 5, we saw how the gleaning laws ensured that every Israelite could provide for themselves by their own work, even in times of crisis. But the Jubilee shows God going further; not only was every Israelite to be able to provide for their family's survival through their own work, every Israelite was to be able to eventually return to their plot in the promised land. The immediate availability of the gleaning laws allowed Israelite farmers to survive while they looked forward to a greater, fuller economic liberation at the end of every fifty years. All the charity and assistance in Israel's laws occurred in the shadow of the Jubilee. Israelites gleaned in the fields of others in the sure hope that they would be restored to the fields of their fathers. It was not enough for every Israelite to have access to work; when Yahweh was on the throne, every Israelite had equity in the economy.[9]

Clearly, this economy, like those of Egypt and Canaan, had a theological basis. No Israelite could claim the right to endless acquisition of land because *the land belonged to Yahweh* (see Lev. 25:23). You couldn't sell permanently what was never yours to begin with. Of course, the kings and pharaohs around Israel would have agreed that the land belonged to the gods. They just knew those gods gave it to the rich and powerful. In Israel, though, every Israelite, from king to peasant, was nothing more than an immigrant and tenant farmer working for Yahweh. When Yahweh owns the land, control doesn't go to the powerful. When Yahweh owns the land, everyone gets access to it. Yahweh's rule creates socioeconomic standing and security for all.

> Yahweh's rule creates socioeconomic standing and security for all.

Rejecting Yahweh's Economy

Of course, Israel ended up rejecting God and his economic policy. Fat in the land flowing with milk and honey, forgetful of the manna Yahweh fed them in the wilderness, the Israelites began to declare, "I have achieved this wealth with my own strength and energy" (see Deut. 8:14). They forgot the Lord of the Jubilee.

This rejection included a rejection of God's economy in favor of the economies of Canaan and Egypt. Indeed, Israel demanded that Samuel give them a king "like the nations," even after Samuel warned them that such a king "will take the best of your fields and vineyards and olive groves" (1 Sam. 8:14). The story of Solomon makes clear that idolatry to the gods of the nations went hand in hand with an economic policy that abandoned Yahweh's commitment to relative equity for all in favor of an economy of extravagance for the king and his crew, an economy of forced labor and dispossession (see 1 Kings 4:1–34; 12:1–33).

Nor is it a coincidence that when King Ahab turned to Baal worship to provide the rain, he turned to Baal land management to cheat Naboth out of his ancestral vineyard and kill him in the streets through a sham trial and false witnesses (see 1 Kings 21). This is part of the reason why, as we saw in chapter 3, Isaiah and the other prophets declared exile and punishment for the Israelites on account of their oppression of the poor. This oppression included adding "house to house and field to field," rejecting Yahweh's equitable economy and driving neighbors from their ancestral lands (Isa. 5:8–10). But even after the return from exile, some Israelites forced other Israelites off their fields through taxes and predatory loans (see Neh. 5:1–8). The manna economy, it turned out, was hard to live by.

The Jubilee of Jesus

We might expect, then, that such a strange and difficult piece of land legislation as the Jubilee would get left behind in the New Testament. We would be wrong. In fact, Jesus referred to the Jubilee in his first sermon in Luke 4:16–21.

> [Jesus] went to Nazareth, where he had been brought up, and on the Sabbath day he went into the synagogue, as was his custom. He stood up to read, and the scroll of the prophet Isaiah was handed to him. Unrolling it, he found the place where it is written: "The Spirit of the Lord is on me, because he has anointed me to proclaim good news to the poor. He has sent me to proclaim freedom for the prisoners and recovery of sight for the blind, to set the oppressed free, to proclaim the year of the Lord's favor." Then he rolled up the scroll, gave it back to the attendant and sat down. The eyes of everyone in the synagogue were fastened on him. He began by saying to them, "Today this scripture is fulfilled in your hearing."

Scholars recognize that in Jesus's day, "the year of the Lord's favor" was another name for the Jubilee. Incredibly, Jesus declared that the Jubilee is fulfilled in his own person. His presence creates the Jubilee.

Of course, living under Roman occupation, Jesus's listeners did not and probably could not have instituted a literal Jubilee return to property. Indeed, Isaiah had already used the Jubilee as a symbol of the social, spiritual, and economic liberation of God's people in exile rather than as a literal land policy. It is this holistic symbol use that Jesus picked up on in his sermon. That's why everywhere in Luke and Acts we see people restored physically, socially, economically, and spiritually. It's also why Jesus so often talked about forgiving sins *and* forgiving debts. Freedom from individual sin and freedom from oppressive economic relationships go together. Jesus brings the greater Jubilee!

But this newer, greater Jubilee doesn't leave behind God's concern for economic equity within the community as a means to ensuring everyone can participate in the potluck. In fact, I suggest we can find the Jubilee's influence in two of the Bible's most controversial economic passages.

Jubilee Church

In the first chapters of Acts, we encounter a fledgling church in Jerusalem facing enormous crises. Jerusalem was under occupation by hostile powers, revolution was in the air, and the majority of the people struggled just to avoid abject poverty. As discussed in chapter 3, families survived by working with extended family and community networks that labored together and took care of one another.

But when three thousand Jews from all over the place came to faith in the crucified and risen Jesus in Jerusalem, many of them stuck around. The twelve disciples suddenly found themselves in the midst of a new group of people, numbering in the thousands, many with families who may have rejected them because of their strange new worship of Jesus, all crowded into Jerusalem and wondering how to survive. How did they?

Luke tells us straightaway:

> They devoted themselves to the apostles' teaching and the fellowship, to the breaking of bread and the prayers. And awe came upon every soul, and many wonders and signs were being done through the apostles. And all who believed were together and had all things in common. And they were selling their possessions and belongings and distributing the proceeds to all, as any had need. And day by day, attending the temple together and breaking bread in their homes, they received their food with glad and generous hearts,

praising God and having favor with all the people. And the Lord added to their number day by day those who were being saved. (Acts 2:42–47 ESV)

All the believers were one in heart and mind. No one claimed that any of their possessions was their own, but they shared everything they had. With great power the apostles continued to testify to the resurrection of the Lord Jesus. And God's grace was so powerfully at work in them all that there were no needy persons among them. For from time to time those who owned land or houses sold them, brought the money from the sales and put it at the apostles' feet, and it was distributed to anyone who had need. (Acts 4:32–35)

In other words, the new believers became a *family*. As a family, they took care of one another, no matter anyone's economic class or geographic origin. Through worship, prayer, and sharing possessions, they became a new community capable of caring for all.

It's very easy for us to treat this familiar passage as if these folks were sitting around selling stuff and just eating off the proceeds, like a bunch of Communists who didn't understand the factors of production or something. (In fact, some scholars declare that this "experiment" didn't work, even though Luke clearly rejoiced in the early church's behavior, essentially repeating the story twice to make sure we've gotten the memo.)[10] Scholar Reta Halteman Finger reminds us that this is incredibly unlikely because what was happening was this group of people was becoming *family*—and *families* in the ancient world didn't just consume together, they also produced together. Men might have gone out together to tend flocks, work as fishermen, or try to get hired as day laborers, while women might have tended small kitchen gardens and run home-based businesses, spinning wool or making tents. Children contributed to the work of preparing meals and much else. The revenue, tools, social connections, and even living and work spaces required to pull all this off were shared within large family networks like the one the early church became.[11]

So the picture we should have is probably not of Christians selling their homes and eating off the proceeds, but of Christians doing whatever it took to get everybody in the family contributing so everybody in the family could eat. We should picture them, perhaps, liquidating Barnabas's farm to purchase livestock in Jerusalem or tools for a new olive oil–press operation in the city. We should picture children working together in gardens and men working together in trades they shared through their connection to Christ. And we should picture all these nearly impoverished Christians coming home hot and sweaty at the end of the day to share in a little potluck meal called the Lord's Supper.

Through sharing possessions, the early church ensured that everyone had a stake in the community. According to Luke, "There were no needy persons among them" (Acts 4:34). Since this is a deliberate quote from the regulation in Deuteronomy 15 concerning sabbatical years, what we have here is a Jubilee-esque allusion to Israel's practice of debt forgiveness and land return in describing the early church's practices of sharing possessions. Luke has already given us a Jesus who declares the Jubilee; here he gives us a church that embodies it in new, creative ways. Rather than rejecting the commitment to equity, inclusion, and the potlucking party of God found in Israel's laws, the early church figured out how to live out the Jubilee in fresh ways under different circumstances. The result? No poverty among them, a church of "one heart and mind" (Acts 4:32 NET), the favor of the outside world, and the Lord adding to their number daily.

Remember in chapter 3 when we looked at Paul's words in 2 Corinthians 8:14? We saw that Paul invited the Corinthians to share their abundance "at the present time" with the struggling Jerusalem church because the church's abundance could take care of the Corinthians when the shoe was on the other foot. The very next thing Paul writes is this: "Thus there may be equality, as it is written: 'The one who gathered much did not have too much, and the one who gathered little did not have too little'" (vv. 14–15 NET). That last phrase, of course, is a reference to the miracle of manna. What Paul told the Corinthians, then, and what we see throughout the New Testament, is that Jesus invites his people to participate in the manna miracle by embodying an equitable economy in which everyone has a place to stand and a portion to steward.

The Equity Key in Scripture: Summary

Scripture shows us that in God's economy, everyone has a stake in the community. The Israelites were introduced to this economy in the wilderness, and God gave them laws like the Jubilee to establish and protect that economy when they entered the promised land. When Jesus came on the scene, he adapted the Jubilee as a metaphor of the physical, social, spiritual, and economic liberation that he came to announce in his own life, death, and resurrection. The church took up this commitment, finding creative ways to embody the Jubilee in their life together, especially in the earliest days we read about in Acts 2 and 4.

Jesus invites his people to participate in the manna miracle by embodying an equitable economy in which everyone has a place to stand and a portion to steward.

Of course, throughout history, the church, like Israel, has fallen short. But the prophets remind us that the day when everyone shall sit under their own vine and fig tree is still ahead. Isaiah's vision of the new heavens and the new earth included an economy where God's people would no longer build houses only for others to live in them or plant vineyards only to watch others eat their fruit. "They will build houses and dwell in them," declared Yahweh. "They will plant vineyards and eat their fruit. . . . My chosen ones will long enjoy the work of their hands" (Isa. 65:21–22). One day, Yahweh's rule will be universally recognized, his glory covering all creation as the waters cover the sea. In that day, everybody will again have an economic place to stand, an economic portion to steward.

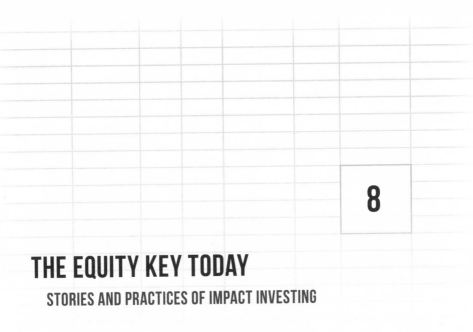

THE EQUITY KEY TODAY
STORIES AND PRACTICES OF IMPACT INVESTING

In chapters 5 and 6, we saw that businesses, churches, and families can bend their economic lives toward those on the margins through gleaning job creation. By leaving profits in the fields, God's people create opportunities for work and empower the economically poor to bring a plate to the potluck.

The Equity Key takes us further, challenging us to creatively imagine how we can bend our economic lives toward more equitable communities. The Equity Key tasks us with pursuing Micah 4:4 neighborhoods, in which everyone sits under their own vine and fig tree and nobody needs to be afraid. The Equity Key reminds us that God's economy demands that we ask tough questions about what it would mean for the marginalized to be *re-enfranchised* into the community, empowered to steward their gifts and abilities, and restored to economic standing in society. Zechariah caught this vision, prophesying that when God brought his kingdom, everyone would invite their neighbor to sit under their vine and fig tree (see Zech. 3:10). But you can't invite your friends to join you under vines and fig trees you ain't got. The potlucking party of Jesus depends on a community willing to commit to pursuing Jubilee equity for all.

Our Sins and the Sins of Our Fathers

When we consider our communities' histories, the challenge and need for the Equity Key becomes even clearer. This is because our nation has a long history of disenfranchising minorities and other groups, intentionally denying them equity in society. Like the wealthy of Isaiah's day, white Americans in particular have often been guilty of "adding house to house and field to field" until we dwell alone in the land—at least in terms of owning the land and its wealth. What's worse is that just as with the Canaanite and Egyptian kings we discussed earlier, a long history of American theology *supports this inequity.*

Before we get to concrete examples, though, I want to anticipate a common criticism of this line of thinking. "That was a long time ago," some say. "I wasn't there, and I can't be held responsible. More importantly, people need to just get over stuff from hundreds of years ago."

In response, consider two counterpoints. First, many of the injustices we describe weren't all that long ago; some extend to the present, and most have had demonstrable impacts over long periods of time. Think about it: Does what your grandparents did affect you? Are you inspired and shaped by their work ethic, their immigrant story, their patriotism in this or that war? Of course our grandparents' experiences affect us! Many of the injustices we discuss below were in full swing less than one hundred years ago.

Second, and more importantly, in contrast to what we sometimes hear even in Christian circles, it is appropriate for us, as God's people, to confess and repent of our own sins *and* the sins of our fathers. When Nehemiah wept before the Lord, confessing his own sins and the sins of his "father's house," he was referring to evil and wickedness that had occurred before he was even born. That the sins occurred before Nehemiah's time didn't absolve him of the need for repentance born out in concrete acts of justice, mercy, and service.

Consider, then, just two examples of a long history of disenfranchisement.

First, ponder the case of Native Americans. Mark Charles, a Native American worshiper of Jesus, writes that fifteenth-century church doctrine in Europe actually encouraged Western Christians to systematically disenfranchise Native communities. Pope Nicholas V wrote in 1452 that European Christians had the full support of the church to

> invade, search out, capture, vanquish, and subdue all Saracens and pagans whatsoever, and other enemies of Christ wheresoever placed, and the kingdoms, dukedoms, principalities, dominions, possessions, and all movable and immovable goods whatsoever held and possessed by them and to reduce their persons to perpetual slavery, and to apply and appropriate to himself and his successors the kingdoms, dukedoms, counties, principalities, dominions, possessions, and goods, and to convert them to his and their use and profit.[1]

An 1823 US Supreme Court case enshrined this "Doctrine of Discovery" within US law, essentially arguing that "by stepping foot on North America, settlers had . . . the absolute right to the land on which they stood."[2] Pushing Native communities off their "vines and fig trees," a longstanding American tradition by 1823, was now recognized as fully legal and legitimate.

The Trail of Tears is just one example of what this wholesale rejection of the Equity Key looked like in practice. In 1838, the US government removed seventeen thousand Cherokee men, women, and children from their homes, forcing them to walk from the Southeastern United States to land west of the Mississippi River. Scholars estimate that more than half of them died as a result of this forced relocation.[3]

This is just one example of many. Indeed, in his book *American Holocaust*, David Stannard suggests that "the destruction of the Indians of the Americas was, far and away, the most massive act of genocide in the history of the world." Upwards of 95 percent of Native American populations were killed off.[4]

The intentional disenfranchisement of Native Americans has left serious wounds in many Native communities that last today. Native Americans living in Native communities have incomes that are less than half the general population and often experience unemployment rates many times higher than the rest of the country. The Blackfoot Reservation in Montana, for instance, has experienced unemployment rates as high as 69 percent.[5]

In 2000, "Native Americans' median wealth was equal to only 8.7 percent of the median wealth among all Americans," and Native communities experience "a significantly lower homeownership rate than whites." When

Native Americans do own homes, they tend to be worth much less than those of their white counterparts.[6] Since wealth and homeownership get at modern equivalents to vines and fig trees, we can see clearly that our nation's history of injustice against Native Americans has contributed to their disenfranchisement from the national neighborhood.

No wonder Randy Woodley, a Native American theologian and missiologist, says that when he's asked when Native Americans are going to "get over it," his response is simply, "When it's over."[7]

Second, consider the case of African Americans. Of course, the entire slave system deprived African Americans of the rewards of their labor, to say nothing of depriving them of the ability to gain wealth. Even more horrifying, the vast majority of written defenses of this slave system were written by white ministers.[8]

After the Civil War, racist policies and structures continued this pattern of disenfranchisement. Let's consider just a few points strictly related to the issue of housing (since homeownership represents one of the most significant sources of wealth in our contemporary economy).

- *African Americans were excluded from the Homestead Act, a government program enacted in 1862 whose impact can be directly traced to the present.* In 1862, the Homestead Act "permitted pioneers to purchase 160 acres of public land in the western US for a small fee after living on it for five years. A quarter of the current US population aged twenty-five and older has a legacy of property ownership and assets in their background that can be directly linked to this national policy."[9] Almost none of the 246 million acres sold went to African American families.

- *African Americans were shut out of our nation's largest wealth-building initiative: FHA-backed mortgages.*[10] African Americans were systematically excluded from Federal Housing Authority–backed mortgages from the 1930s through the 1960s; such mortgages represent the largest wealth-building initiative in US history, but black families were excluded because of the widespread practice of "redlining" (redlining refers to banks refusing to make loans in communities that had more than a few African Americans living in them).

- *Lack of access to FHA-backed mortgages exposed African Americans to vicious predatory lenders.*[11] Excluded from normal mortgages, African Americans often ended up buying houses "on contract." This practice allowed unscrupulous lenders to sell rent-to-own contracts to poor African American buyers, who unknowingly accepted all the responsibilities of homeownership while receiving none of the benefits. If these renters were late on even one payment, they could be evicted and denied any of the equity from their payments on the house. Like some used car lots today, which often depend on repossessing a car multiple times to make a profit, such housing practices were extremely predatory. (Keep in mind, many African Americans living today were victims of predatory contract house sales; indeed, when I teach on this at MCUTS, I regularly have students who personally experienced redlining or some other form of predatory lending in the housing market. This is most certainly not ancient history.)[12]

- *Racist government housing policies destroyed black homes and communities.* In my neighborhood, for instance, the white political machine labeled a working-class African American neighborhood with significant homeownership a slum in order to access federal slum clearance dollars.[13] The city used those dollars to raze those black-owned homes to the ground and replace them with a large, racially segregated government housing project that turned a mixed-income community into a neighborhood of multigenerational concentrated poverty. All this occurred within the last one hundred years, and the effects are obvious right outside the window of my house where I'm writing this sentence. And my neighborhood's story is just one of many.

- *Race-based predatory lending and redlining have continued into the present.* In Memphis, both Wells Fargo[14] and BancorpSouth[15] have paid multimillion dollar fines for practicing race-based predatory lending and redlining between the years 2000 and 2013. In one particularly disturbing episode, bank employees from one bank were recorded using racial epithets and laughing while considering whether to hire an African American.

- *Largely because of such injustices, median wealth among white families is roughly eleven times higher than that of black and Hispanic families.* The Pew Research Center reports that as of 2013, the median net worth of white households was $141,900, while the median net worth for black households was a mere $11,000 and that of Hispanic households $13,700.[16]

In short, we have to ground our attempts to pursue the Equity Key in a repentant recognition of our history. If we are to follow in Nehemiah's footsteps, repenting of our sins and the sins of our fathers, we must commit ourselves to costly, sacrificial action in pursuit of an equitable community. Such action is one part of what it means to "bear fruit in keeping with repentance" (Matt. 3:8 ESV).

The good news is that God's people are finding creative, imaginative ways to embody the Jubilee economy today, pursuing equity by bending their economic lives toward the disenfranchised. In the rest of this section, we'll consider some of their stories.

Building Wealth at Work

One creative approach to embodying the Equity Key is to allow workers to build wealth through their employment. Profit sharing, worker-owner cooperatives, and Employee Stock Ownership Programs (ESOPs) all allow employees to gain economic ownership in the business where they work.

In 1941, a young, socially conscious priest named José María Arizmendiarrieta arrived in a small town in Spain's Basque Country. Economically depressed and reeling from war, the region must have seemed like an unlikely place for the birth of anything remotely resembling the King's economy.[17] But under Arizmendiarrieta's leadership and beginning with the establishment of a cooperative technical college, the community began a journey that would lead to the establishment of the world's most successful worker-owner cooperative. Eventually, Mondragon was founded as an umbrella organization for worker-owner cooperatives committed to "one worker, one vote" decision-making, profit sharing, and cooperation across individual companies to avoid job loss. From humble beginnings, today Mondragon employs 800,000 people in more than 280 cooperatively owned businesses.[18] Mondragon provides jobs for unemployed workers in one of Spain's economically depressed regions and creates assets for workers through its commitment to making every long-term worker an owner.

While worker-owner cooperatives in the United States often look to Mondragon for inspiration, African American scholar Jessica Gordon Nembhard tells the story of the rich history of African American cooperatives, a history that reaches back into the early days of the post–Civil War era. Nembhard suggests that such cooperatives gave African Americans a strategy for resisting economic oppression, while also anchoring economic development within neighborhoods and facilitating the recirculation of money within the community. Cooperatives also provided meaningful jobs in depressed communities that not only paid decent wages but also invested in employees through significant employee training and education.[19] The Federation of Southern Cooperatives alone has created or supported more than two hundred cooperatives in ten states over its forty-five-year history.[20]

From its earliest days, the African American cooperative movement meant far more than better financial returns. In 1919, W. E. B. DuBois wrote the following concerning black cooperatives:

> The good results of co-operation among colored people do not lie alone in the return of savings. They show, also, new opportunities for the earning of a livelihood and in the chance offered our colored youth to become acquainted with business methods. . . . [They hire members of the community] Thus, in a larger and different sense, we have another form of co-operation. Colored people are furnishing their own with work and money for services received and the recipients are handing the money back for re-distribution to the original colored sources.[21]

In places where African Americans were excluded from a stake in the neighborhood, cooperatives created new vines and fig trees in the midst of an oppressive economy. They produced subversive potlucks, empowering people who had been systematically excluded from the party to bring plates.

The cooperative movement continues. Evergreen Cooperatives launched in 2008, seeking to create worker-owner cooperatives to help lower-income, inner-city workers in Cleveland not only get jobs but also become business owners.[22] Because of this commitment, Evergreen Cooperatives intentionally launched businesses that would be able to hire employees with limited education, experience, and occasionally, criminal records. To date, the cooperative's environmentally friendly laundromat and energy solutions businesses are now profitable, with a third, Green City Growers, set to break even in late 2017.[23] The company employs 120 people, many of whom would otherwise have a hard time finding work.

Another example of the power of worker-owner cooperatives is Prospera, a twenty-year-old nonprofit organization committed to launching worker-owned cooperatives that benefit low-income Latina women. As of 2014, Prospera's five co-ops sustained nearly one hundred high-quality jobs and provided ecofriendly housecleaning to more than two thousand customers annually, generating more than $3 million in sales each year. These Latina worker-owners have tripled their incomes on average and hold $9,000 in business equity. Given that the average program participant has a personal income of only $13,820 when they begin the program, Prospera's cooperative movement represents incredible life change for the women who work for, and own, these businesses.[24]

Lupita,[25] a founding member of one of Prospera's cooperatives, shares how her job in an orange-packing facility was unstable and did not provide sufficient wages for her to take care of her family. When Lupita found Prospera, she was able to get a better job as a housecleaner by becoming a worker-owner in one of their cooperatives. Because of the co-op's employee-oriented focus, Lupita was able to move up in the business and invest in her abilities as an employee. Four years later, Lupita took over the management of the co-op's operations; today, she speaks English, interacts with clients, uses QuickBooks, and has doubled her income. "I feel like I have accomplished a great deal," Lupita says, adding that her favorite part is the *apoyo mutuo*—the mutual support—she gives and receives from other worker-owners. Her involvement in the co-op has helped her family and made it possible for her children to go to college. Having gained access to "vines and fig trees" through worker-ownership, Lupita has been empowered to bring her proverbial plates to the potluck.

You don't have to be a cooperative to create equity at work, though. Many businesses have committed to sharing profits as a way to empower employees to gain an economic stake in the company and the community. ESOPs allow traditional businesses to offer workers the opportunity to own stock in the company. While ESOPs retain traditional management structures, those employed in companies with ESOPs "earn more in wages and retirement income than their counterparts in traditional firms." Furthermore, these companies are less likely to lay off workers during downturns and more likely to include workers in decision-making processes.[26]

Entrepreneurship Training and Support

But what if instead of sharing existing businesses, Christians helped those who are marginalized create new ones? That's LAUNCH Chattanooga's approach, which Advance Memphis offered to Donald Jenkins to ramp up his lawn care business. A few years back, Hal Bowling, cofounder and executive director of LAUNCH Chattanooga, recognized that too many in his city were being excluded from the opportunity for entrepreneurship. As an entrepreneur himself, he knew entrepreneurship could open doors to greater economic stability and community involvement. Hal, along with a team of entrepreneurs, pastors, and community leaders, started LAUNCH with a mission to empower underserved communities and individuals through starting businesses.

"Entrepreneurship is the way of the future. It's the way out of unemployment and poverty and the way to wealth building, job creation, and economic development," Hal says. "At LAUNCH, we believe entrepreneurs can come from unlikely places."

After only five years, the founders of LAUNCH have seen their vision become a reality. They've trained 270 entrepreneurs who've currently launched 168 businesses and created 207 jobs for themselves and others. LAUNCH's ten-week entrepreneurship class, a version of the Co.Starters curriculum,[27] is offered in some of the city's most economically challenged communities. Through the class, entrepreneurs learn the startup process and get their business idea out in front of potential customers. They also meet business owners like themselves and connect to a supportive community of consultants and service providers.

Robin Davis, a hardworking single mother, had been working at a local hospital for many years. As time went on, she began to notice that many of the hospital's patients came out of surgery or a procedure only to wait several more hours for someone to pick them up and take them home. That didn't seem right to her, so she began to dream about addressing this issue.

Through the LAUNCH program, Robin did the market research to determine how to start a nonemergency medical transportation service. Because she wanted to help precisely those patients who are least likely to be able to pay, she scoured the insurance policies of all the major insurance providers in the area to figure out every possible way to get reimbursed for trips. And after meeting with another business in town offering this service, she managed to negotiate a partnership with them to handle all the business they couldn't manage themselves.

Today Loving Hands Helping Hearts Transportation has a small fleet of vehicles and is providing greater financial security and opportunity for Robin and her family. Maybe most exciting of all, before graduating and going to college, Robin's daughter also participated in the LAUNCH program through her high school's entrepreneurship academy.

One reason LAUNCH works is that it invites God's people to share their own expertise and social capital with new entrepreneurs. When we brought LAUNCH's model to Advance Memphis, a graphic designer built websites and business logos at a much-reduced rate to help our entrepreneurs get in the game. Friends and supporters became some of our neighbors' first clients, hiring our graduates to DJ parties, cater business lunches, provide lawn care to office complexes, or clean their homes. Others provided mentoring and even financial investment in these enterprises.

Recently, a visitor to the LAUNCH class who works in commercial real estate committed to helping several entrepreneurs understand the commercial bidding process and has since hired one of their businesses to do work for his company. In all these ways and more, God's people bend their economic lives toward the Jubilee, sacrificially creating access to vines and fig trees for neighbors long excluded from such assets.

Prison Entrepreneurship Program (PEP) is another organization dedicated to nontraditional entrepreneurs. Their mission is to work with people who are incarcerated to secure the sorts of opportunities that will allow them to thrive when they get out of prison. Nearly 100 percent of the program's graduates find work within ninety days of leaving incarceration. But maybe more astoundingly, 20 percent of their graduates actually start their own businesses. Kevin Rainey is one of those whose relationship with PEP led him to launching his own enterprise.

"I lost everything as a result of my actions, including my son," Rainey says. "I thought prison was the hardest part of the journey, but it wasn't. It was just the beginning. The hardest part was getting out and having to learn how to live life." But when Kevin met the folks from PEP, he also found people who believed in him enough to invest in his life. That investment encouraged Kevin to persevere through not being able to see his son for more than a year after his release, to get a job within a week of leaving incarceration, and eventually to launch his own business, Uptown Transportation.

Kevin's hard work has paid off. He's financially stable and has been able to rebuild his relationship with his family. "I'm able to contribute to my son's college," Kevin says. "That's something I never thought I'd be a part of."[28]

Even churches are finding ways to support entrepreneurs, often by connecting church members who have gifts and experience in entrepreneurship with struggling individuals who want to start businesses. Through their Circles USA program, Fairhaven Church[29] came around Joy Barnhill, a woman in poverty struggling with a significant learning disability.[30] Joy got connected with mentors who became friends. Over the course of eighteen months, they helped Joy set goals and then achieve them. "But they also loved me for who I was," Joy says. "These people don't see me as just a poor person. They see me as Jesus sees me, someone worth dying for." While Joy was being loved on by these supporters, one of the pastors at Fairhaven Church led her to faith in Jesus. Today Joy is the proud owner of Joy-Full Cleaning. Empowered to bring her gifts to the potluck, she has also helped five others begin the Circles USA program at her church, including her mom.

More and more organizations and churches are finding ways to encourage microentrepreneurs, and we've included a variety of links on our website and in the Resources for Further Study section at the end of this book. As God's people bend their economic lives toward supporting entrepreneurship among those typically excluded from the economy, they're embracing the Jubilee and pursuing the Equity Key today.

Impact Investing

But how do Robin, Kevin, and entrepreneurs like them get investments for their businesses? For that matter, how do social enterprises like the ones we discussed in the last chapter find capital? Increasingly, the answer comes through one of the kingdom economy's coolest innovations: impact investing.

Impact investing (at least as we're using the phrase) refers to financial investments that accept a lower financial return in exchange for a higher social return.[31] Impact investing isn't charity and it isn't just good business. Instead, it represents a third space, yet another way God's people can practice the King's economy. Let's take a look at just a few of the ways impact investing is happening in our world.

Kiva

One of the easiest ways to participate is through Kiva. Kiva allows individuals to help crowdfund 0 percent loans for entrepreneurs who wouldn't be able to get financing from a traditional bank. Lenders can contribute as little as $25, making Kiva the easiest way to give impact investing a try. To date, Kiva has made loans to 2.2 million borrowers in eighty-two countries, with a 97.1 percent repayment rate.[32] Kevin and Robin are just two of the many who've received such loans.

Jonny Price, who runs Kiva's US branch, sees Kiva as giving everyday folks an opportunity to democratize finance and revolutionize entrepreneurship. "When conventional financial institutions step back, based on black-and-white underwriting criteria, and a desire to minimize risk and maximize profit," Price says, "a community of supporters steps up to democratically empower an entrepreneur."[33] Price points out that because Kiva is crowdfunded, investors also become cheerleaders and evangelists for these fledgling entrepreneurs, providing much-needed promotion and encouragement.

The "Friends and Family" Certificate of Deposit

Often, though, entrepreneurs may need access to larger loans. One cutting-edge effort to address this is the brand-new "friends and family" certificate of deposit (CD). Impact Hub Oakland, Neighborhood Economics, Self-Help Federal Credit Union, and others have come together to address one of the biggest hidden roadblocks for black and Hispanic entrepreneurs: the wealth gap.

When entrepreneurs go to a bank for a loan, they're almost always asked: "Have you asked your friends and family?"[34] This isn't surprising, since friends and family invest $60 billion every year in businesses (more than angel investors and venture capital combined). The problem is, as we discussed earlier, on average, black and Latino families have significantly less wealth than white families. There just aren't nearly as many friends and family dollars to go around in communities of color.

The friends and family CD seeks to change that. CDs are savings certificates with a fixed time period; a person buys a certificate and then the bank returns the money plus interest after a certain period of time (in this case five years). Selling these CDs will raise capital, which the Self-Help Credit Union will then loan out to black and Hispanic entrepreneurs. These entrepreneurs will receive loans with favorable interest rates "meant to replicate the kind of terms your rich uncle might give you, if you had one."[35] While this is a pilot program, if it works, it could be brought to communities around the country as a strategy to create equity through impact investing.

Donor-Advised Funds

Another frontier for impact investing is happening through donor-advised funds (DAFs), which are typically run through community foundations or similar organizations. Individuals make a donation to the fund, receive a tax credit for their donation, and then direct the fund to distribute that money to actual charitable causes at a later date. In the meantime, DAF money is invested in the market, so it's actually earning interest. The whole thing allows individuals to have their own mini-foundation of sorts.

But some DAFs have begun allowing donors to direct donations toward social impact investing. Mike Harris, former president of the Hope Community Foundation in Memphis, oversaw DAF impact-investing loans to finance real estate development owned by the Anglican Church in Rwanda, construct wind turbines in Asia, provide water filtration systems in Africa, and fund coffee grower cooperatives in Central and South America. Other DAFs are finding ways to make similar impact-investing loans in the United States.

Pitch Competitions

Yet another way to raise impact-investing funds is through pitch competitions. Randy White and the Center for Community Transformation (CCT) at Fresno Pacific University decided that what their economically depressed community needed was jobs, and social enterprise was a good strategy for individuals, churches, and nonprofits to try to create them. So CCT began hosting an annual summit on social enterprise where churches, nonprofits, and individuals can learn how to launch their own social enterprise. Then, several months after the summit, CCT hosts a pitch competition where participants can pitch their ideas in front of a big crowd and a panel of expert judges. Each year, CCT grants thousands of dollars in prize money to new social enterprises, with mentorship and support emerging from the competition as well. Winners include the following:

- Say Hello Advertising, a small business launched out of On Ramps Covenant Church that provides local marketing services by hiring unemployed neighbors.
- 5 Gals Cleaning, a social business that hires women from Evangel Home shelter to clean vacant homes being prepared for the real-estate market.
- Kings Cornerstone Recycling, LLC, a recycling business that provides revenue and employment opportunities for adults living in the Kings Gospel Mission, a nonprofit focused on empowering homeless men.

Individual Development Accounts

Individual development account (IDA) programs allow low-income neighbors who have gone through a financial literacy program, such as the Chalmers Center's *Faith & Finances* course, to open a savings account. Once opened, participants save each month toward the purchase of an asset, such as a house, small business capital, education, or a car. When these savers reach their savings goal over a period of months or years, an outside organization or church matches their savings 2:1 to help them obtain their asset. Such programs create a powerful opportunity for kingdom-minded investment in line with the Equity Key. Indeed, Donald Jenkins, who started the lawn care business we mentioned at the beginning of this chapter, used an IDA through Advance Memphis to purchase the truck for his business.

Churches across the country have also started leading *Faith & Finances* classes, and some have started offering IDAs within their churches.[36] Mark Bowers, the primary author of *Faith & Finances*, helped his church, New City East Lake, offer the class and IDAs. One program participant, Amber, used her IDA to go back to school. A team of supportive allies in the program met with Amber to help her understand credit, tuition, and school loans. "It was fun to meet monthly and see her understanding and her confidence grow," one of Amber's supporters in the program said. "She'll graduate this year, and we're going to have the biggest block party ever."

Meanwhile, in my own work at the Memphis Center for Urban Theological Studies and in partnership with the Memphis Leadership Foundation and Alcy Ball Development Corporation,[37] we've started a pilot program where we work with neighborhood churches to offer IDAs. We train our all-adult students to lead *Faith & Finances* ministries in their churches and then partner with those churches to offer IDAs to graduates from courses led by MCUTS students. As of July 2017, we have two IDAs open and have identified three to four more savers who will open accounts by September.

IDAs help address the wealth gap and inequity of our communities that we've explored throughout this chapter. As such, when we give to these programs, we enter the Jubilee movement of God, whereby our excess lands and fields create opportunities for others to establish themselves in the neighborhood.

Impact Investing: Choose Your Own Adventure!

All these are formal strategies and many more are accessible too. But impact investing can also be an informal strategy for folks wanting to get started in practicing the King's economy. While writing this book, my family committed to get more personally involved with impact investing. We were inspired by our friend Mark Bowers, who, apart from his day job, has helped six Latino families in his neighborhood become homeowners through his social enterprise, *Restablecer*. By structuring his tenants' agreements to allow them to purchase their homes over time while contributing sweat equity in the form of home repairs, he's helped his neighbors gain an economic place to stand in his neighborhood. Our intentional community members in South Memphis had long recognized that many of our African American neighbors struggled to become homeowners (no surprise, given my neighborhood's history, described previously in this chapter), and wondered if we could adopt Mark's model for our own neighborhood.

So we started New City Housing Strategies, LLC, a small, housing-oriented social enterprise.[38] Our first project involved purchasing a home on tax sale in our neighborhood, renovating it, and then renting it to our long-term friend and neighbor, Rhoda, who had been renting from a slumlord in a house with one functioning light, one functioning receptacle, and no heat through a cold winter. As part of the rent agreement, we set aside a portion of Rhoda's rent for her down payment. A few months ago, Rhoda was able to buy this property from us and become a homeowner (in part through an IDA at Advance Memphis!). Not only does this mean she will get a chance to benefit from owning an asset, but it also has allowed her to bring a plate to the potluck: she now regularly hosts our church's community group Bible study in her home. As of July 2017, New City has a second house under contract and is beginning to raise impact-investing dollars to expand our work.

Invest in Education

Finally, in a knowledge economy like the one most of us live in, part of the Jubilee equity that we must pursue includes helping our neighbors gain access to one of society's most essential assets: education. Churches and nonprofits have long recognized how tutoring programs, scholarship funds, investing in schools, and more can become strategies for pursuing Jubilee equity for our neighbors. Furthermore, many Christians are beginning to see teaching in a struggling school as a kingdom calling. My bride, Rebecca, went through and now works for the outstanding Memphis Teacher

Residency program, which equips and trains excellent teachers and then deploys them into struggling public schools.

Ground zero for empowering folks educationally also happens at GED programs like the one at Advance Memphis, especially since the median family income for those with a high school degree is $51,154 versus $32,214 for those without.[39] Such programs allow adults to turn back the clock on a decision they've regretted their whole lives: dropping out of school. Having taught in Advance's GED program for several years, I can say confidently I will never forget the joy on people's faces as they walked across the graduation stage. Earning a GED also immediately opens up significant economic and educational opportunities.

My former college roommate and current neighbor, Mike Shaw, oversees the GED program at Advance. He emphasizes that earning a GED is about not only job opportunities but also the way a person views themself. He tells the story of Jackson, who was awarded a certificate of completion in high school because he was diagnosed with a learning disability and placed in resource classes. For more than three years, Jackson attended GED classes at Advance to try to earn his diploma. In late 2016, he finally passed the test. "His whole demeanor has changed," Shaw says. "The other day he showed up wearing a tie and jacket because 'he felt good about himself.' Education, like work, does a lot to push people toward positive change simply through the dignity it provides." In spring 2017, Jackson enrolled in trade school.

Speaking of trade school—another lesser-known opportunity for helping those struggling economically comes in the form of vocational training. The United States has hundreds of thousands of job openings—with more opening up all the time—for employment in fields that require some training but not a traditional four-year college degree. Middle-class careers as electricians, advanced manufacturing machinists, radiology technicians, and more are open for the taking for those who get the appropriate training, either through on-the-job programs or, more likely, vocational colleges and technical programs often offered at community colleges and other local institutions.

In the past, many have viewed technical training as a "second-class path." Stats like the following tell a different story:[40]

- 36 percent of science, technology, engineering, and math (STEM) jobs require postsecondary credentials that can be obtained within two years of graduating high school.[41]
- Experts expect there to be two million unfilled jobs by 2025 due to the so-called "skills gap," with manufacturing to see the highest impact.[42]
- Graduates with technical or applied science associate degrees can outearn bachelor's degree holders by $11,000.[43]
- The skilled trades are among the fastest growing occupations in the United States.[44]

Given stats like these, God's people have a tremendous opportunity to promote technical training and skills acquisition, not least through partnering with and supporting community colleges and technical training centers.

Whether promoting early childhood education, postgraduate education, or anything in between, God's people can help equip folks with the educational vines and fig trees that will make flourishing in our current economy, and thus contributing more fully to the potluck, significantly easier.

Practicing Impact Investing

So how do we get started? Faced with the inequities of our world and the terrible realities of multigenerational poverty, God's people can practice the King's economy through impact investing. Don't get overwhelmed by all the options. Find somewhere to start and get moving. As we begin to bend our investments toward the Equity Key, God will use these practices to exercise our kingdom economics muscles, training us to create ever-greater expressions of God's economy in our world.

Impact Investing at Work

Consider: How could your business or workplace invest in everyone who has an economic stake in the community? How could you promote wealth building and equity among those often excluded from such economic ownership?

Some suggestions for impact investing at work include the following:

- *Share profits with employees.* Consider regularly sharing profits or even becoming an ESOP.

- *Intentionally hire minority-owned businesses and nontraditional entrepreneurs.* Hire an entrepreneur from a program such as LAUNCH to provide services to your company. Set standards to give a certain percentage of contracts to minority-owned businesses.

- *Invest your time, talent, products, and services in supporting nontraditional entrepreneurs.* Consider mentoring an entrepreneur through a program like LAUNCH. If your company can provide specific consulting (legal counsel, marketing advice, etc.) or services (web design, photography, etc.), consider offering these services at a reduced rate to entrepreneurs being trained by programs aimed at creating equity for all.

- *Invest in your employees' education and workforce development, both outside your company and through on-the-job training or apprenticeships.* In-house training and investment in education can help your employees gain the knowledge assets necessary to flourish economically.

Impact Investing at Church

Consider: How could your church create Jubilee opportunities for low-income neighbors to gain an economic stake in the community?

Suggestions for impact investing at church include the following:

- *Mobilize your congregation to invest their time and talents in wealth building and entrepreneurship.* Gather together the business owners in your church and pair them with members or neighbors who have shown an interest in entrepreneurship. Within most churches are business owners, lawyers, accountants, IT folks, and many more. Your congregation has all the human capital resources the average microbusiness startup needs. Your church could even run a pitch competition for your community. You could also learn about the existing infrastructure in your community for aspiring entrepreneurs and find out how to support those involved.

- *Organize church members to do impact investing in the community.* Folks in your church could do impact investing together. Gather a small group to study the Equity Key chapters and then invest as a group. The Criterion Institute's 1K Churches campaign provides a number of ideas along these lines, including:

  a. Loaning money to a business that can "repay" the loan through providing services to the community (i.e., lend $5,000 to an aspiring lawn care entrepreneur who "repays" the loan by providing lawn services to widows and the elderly in the community).

  b. Organizing lending clubs of "angel investors" or working together to invest in an entrepreneur through a Kiva campaign.

  c. Investing some percentage of the church's funds in a community development finance institution, credit union, or microloan fund.[45]

  (Keep in mind that whenever you're working with nontraditional entrepreneurs, it is essential to pursue a mutual relationship that does not take the business owner out of the driver's seat.)

  Or perhaps, like my friends and me, members of your congregation could join together to invest directly in social enterprises that promote a more equitable community.

- *Open your space to entrepreneurs.* Your church's commercial kitchen could give an aspiring caterer an opportunity to legally launch their business. A social enterprise coffee business could take over your church's coffee kiosk. Recruit food trucks to provide food for your church picnic or Wednesday night program. Some churches might have office space available to entrepreneurs in the startup phase, while some city-center churches might even have potential storefront or retail opportunities.

- *Start a* Faith & Finances *course and offer matched-savings Individual Development Accounts (IDAs) to graduates.* By giving to matched-savings programs that empower lower-income neighbors to gain assets, we embrace the Jubilee, in which our excess farms and fields are used to empower others to gain a stake in the community.

- *Support educational efforts among those often left behind by our educational system.* This could include running tutoring programs; raising scholarships for kids otherwise unable to attend college;

sponsoring, encouraging, or mentoring folks in vocational-technical education; or simply promoting teaching in under-resourced schools as a Christian calling. Support and celebrate the teachers in your congregation.

Impact Investing at Home

Consider: How could your family invest in Jubilee-style equity? Some suggestions for impact investing at home include the following:

- *Invest some of your money for social impact.* Make a loan on Kiva. Put your money in a community development financial institution or credit union. Angel invest in an aspiring entrepreneur either directly or through a donor-advised fund. Give to raise money for a local pitch competition. Invest in a larger-scale impact-investing fund. Invest in a social enterprise or social entrepreneur whose work aims at the Equity Key. Give to an IDA matched-savings program.
- *Invest your time and talent in nontraditional entrepreneurs.* Volunteer with an organization such as LAUNCH or help with your church's efforts to identify and encourage nontraditional entrepreneurs. Patronize their businesses, provide professional support if you have those skills, or simply be an advocate and encourager.
- *Get involved with education.* Volunteer at a tutoring program or other education initiative.

Start Practicing

Before moving on, take a moment and contemplate where to begin practicing impact investing in your own life. Where would it be easiest to take your first steps? Consider: What's going on in your city that's similar to the stories described in this chapter? Are folks involved with empowering entrepreneurs, impact investing, or education for underserved folks? Could some ministries that you're already involved with benefit from some of the strategies discussed here? Ask Jesus to show you ways to bend your economic life toward equity. Before finishing this chapter, identify how you, individually or with a group, can invest in Jubilee equity within the next month.

I will begin practicing impact investing in the next month by . . .

_____

_____

_____

_____

The Equity Key: Conclusion

Remember our discussion of Matthew 6:20–21 in chapter 1? Remember how Jesus said that where we store up our treasures determines, at least in part, what's going on in our hearts? I can tell you from my family's experience that this is *certainly* true when it comes to impact investing. Our investment in homeownership in South Memphis ignited our hearts for God's good and just economy, grew our understanding of how to contribute to that economy, and deepened our relationships with our neighbors in whom we've invested. In fact, I've never in my life felt more aware of how dependent I am on the gifts of my neighbors than when we all had our money and sweat equity invested together in our cooperative commitment to help a friend become a homeowner.

Contributing $25 to a loan for an aspiring barber may not seem like much. Then again, your first workout after being MIA from the gym for six years is usually equally unimpressive. The good news is, when we get to exercising, when we start practicing for the King's economy, God uses our efforts to create change in his world *and* in our hearts. Impact investing is one workout that we're confident will get your heart, head, and habits whipped into top shape for participation in God's economy. Let's get to it.

"THE HEAVENS DECLARE THE GLORY"
THE CREATION CARE KEY IN SCRIPTURE

The custody of the garden was given to Adam, to show that we possess the things which God has committed to our hands, on the condition, that being content with a frugal and moderate use of them, we should take care of what shall remain. . . . Let everyone regard himself as the steward of God in all things which he possesses. Then he will neither conduct himself dissolutely, nor corrupt by abuse those things which God requires to be preserved.

John Calvin

In sum, the politeia of ancient Israel communicates that neither economic expansion nor national security nor even personal economic viability is legitimate justification for the abuse of the land, the abuse of the poor, or the abuse of the domestic or wild creature. Rather all these laws of land, tree, and creature communicate a similar theme: Israel was a tenant on God's good land; a steward. The land, its produce, and its inhabitants belong to God, not humanity. . . . God takes pleasure in his creation. He has designed it, provided for it, and his expectation is that his people will respect and protect it.

Sandra Richter

The heart of Christian ethics is to relate to all creatures and all creation in a manner appropriate to their relationship with the Creator.

Noah Campbell

The creation itself will be set free from its bondage to corruption and obtain the freedom of the glory of the children of God.

Romans 8:21 ESV

The time has come for judging the dead,
    and for rewarding your servants the prophets,
and your people who revere your name,
    both great and small—
and for destroying those who destroy the earth.

Revelation 11:18

Farming after Eden

When the sun comes up on the EdenThistle farm, the light of the new day reveals horses, pigs, chickens, goats, quail, and other creatures happily munching on grass or pecking at grain. That's quite a lot of livestock on this small twenty-acre farm. But as a land stewardship company committed to treating animals with dignity and investing in the soil *while* generating profits from farming, EdenThistle depends on that diversity. Indeed, their entire model, as we'll see below, depends on cultivating an ecosystem, a community of creation even, in which each animal's eating, drinking, foraging, pooping, and moving contributes to the well-being of all the others *and* the land itself. "Our business," founder Marshall Teague emphasizes, "depends on stewarding this place in line with God's design. When we do our job well, the farm flourishes *and* the business flourishes."

This farm is a beautiful place, but take a second and ponder that beautiful name: *EdenThistle.* Two simple words that capture something of the promise and the problem of our lives in the world after humanity welcomed sin into God's good creation. We believe EdenThistle and the Scripture we unpack in this chapter capture an essential piece of the King's economy and even what it means to be human. We want to suggest that loving care for the physical world is a central aspect of both God's economy and our vocations.

But for most of us, this way of thinking is new territory. If we grew up going to church, our Sunday school flannel board did not include much about "creation care." Indeed, many Christians wonder whether worrying too much about the environment isn't actually unbiblical—just a bunch of tree-hugging, neo-pagan nonsense. Ann Coulter's understanding of the "biblical view of nature" as "rape the planet—it's yours"[1] may be over the top, but it captures something at the heart of many of our worldviews. "It's here for our use, after all," we might say. "And anyhow, it's going to get burned up in the end." From this perspective, worrying too much about creation in our economic lives might lead to economic costs that are simply unnecessary. Caring for creation could be an irresponsible distraction from our real economic work of *human* flourishing.

Other readers, whether or not they grew up in church, may find themselves on the other extreme. They wonder whether people aren't the problem in the first place and therefore Christianity, which gives humans a privileged place in the natural order, isn't guilty of causing the destruction and abuse of the world that folks in this camp identify as a major social issue of our day. Indeed, one author suggests that the idea that Christianity is guilty of causing widespread destruction of the natural world is an "established cliché" among those concerned about the environment.[2]

In the midst of all this, we want to explore how Christians can seek to practice the King's economy in relationship to the physical creation. This is no easy task; even if we agree that we ought to care for creation, how to do so is up for debate and hard to nail down. But as we'll see, this hard work is a core concern of Scripture that must drive us to find ever-better ways of living in the King's economy. In this chapter, we'll explore Scripture through the lens of God's creation and his people's role in relation to it. In the next chapter, we'll tell stories of folks seeking to experiment with economic practices that lead to creation and human flourishing. Once again, we'll have to go back to the beginning.

The Story of Creation and People As Stewards

As we discussed in the introduction, our generous God created the world and all that's in it. As he brought each new element of the world into existence, he looked at what he had made and declared it *good* (see Gen. 1).

Right here in the opening words of the Bible, we see that the goodness of rocks and trees, stars and suns and moons, flying fish and panda bears was announced by God even before he created Adam and Eve. Creation, it seems, isn't just good for people to use; it is good in and of itself.

> Creation, it seems, isn't just good for people to use; it is good in and of itself.

God places his "seal of divine approval on the whole universe," even apart from the incredible value that creation has for people. If our understanding of creation begins with the Bible, it doesn't start with how useful creation is to people and how we might run out of stuff to use if we aren't careful. It starts by recognizing that creation is good because God created it and loves it.[3]

Nevertheless, these opening chapters also show that the Creator King gives humanity the highest of callings as members of his royal family made to reflect his image and corule with him over vast regions of the rest of creation. God-the-Giver has endowed us richly indeed! We exist for God's glory—and we enjoy his glory as we engage his good creation in ways that fit his design. Genesis 1 gives us the thirty-thousand-foot view of God's good and wise creation order and our place in it.

Figure 9.1

God's Wise Creation Order

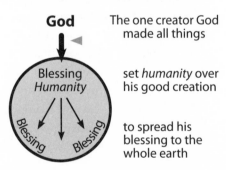

God	The one creator God made all things
Blessing / Humanity	set *humanity* over his good creation
	to spread his blessing to the whole earth

As God's image bearers, we are living emblems of his rule, living statues of his authority, members of his royal family who bear our Father's family resemblance. The whole creation is God's kingdom,[4] good because God loves it, and we are his chosen vice-regents. God has placed us here to rule in his name. Our basic, divinely given job description is to cultivate God's good creation in line with God's wisdom.

But for many of us, the *last* place we think to apply this call is the first place God called Adam and Eve to apply it: the literal creation itself. What does it mean to co-rule with God in relation to starfish and soil, tomatoes and tree frogs, the world and all who inhabit it? Contemporary pundit Ann Coulter says the following:

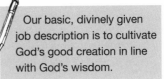

Our basic, divinely given job description is to cultivate God's good creation in line with God's wisdom.

> The ethic of conservation is the explicit abnegation of man's dominion over the Earth. The lower species are here for our use. God said so: Go forth, be fruitful, multiply, and rape the planet—it's yours. That's our job: drilling, mining and stripping. . . . Big gas-guzzling cars with phones and CD players and wet bars—that's the Biblical view.[5]

Is it?

Practicing Stewardship: The *How* of Our Royal Calling

Genesis 2 unpacks what humanity's rule over creation looks like. If Genesis 1 shows humanity enthroned on the sixth day, reflecting God's glory, Genesis 2:15 shows us *how* the Great Gardener King expects his vice-regents to express the authority he has delegated to us. (Note that we've left two of the central words untranslated in the translation below.)

> Yahweh God took the man and placed him in the Garden of Eden to *abad* it and to *shamar* it. (Gen. 2:15)

Those two crucial verbs—*abad* and *shamar*—summarize how God's image bearers are to practice ruling his creation. Let's look at some of the various ways they get translated:

> God placed Adam in the garden . . .
> "to work it and keep it"(ESV)
> "to tend and watch over it" (NLT)
> "to cultivate it and to keep it" (LEB)
> "to work it and take care of it"
> "to tend it and guard it" / "to tend it and protect it" (Sandra Richter)[6]

Often, though, *abad* can be translated "to serve," while *shamar* is frequently used to describe a watchful, careful keeping. So you could translate Genesis 2:15 in the following way:

> Yahweh God took the man and placed him in the Garden of Eden *to serve it and to care for it.*

In other words, part of Adam and Eve's job is to care for creation as humble servants, careful learners, and wise lovers of the good things placed under their care.[7] So long as they obeyed their Creator and walked in his ways, teaching their children to do likewise, Adam and Eve wouldn't simply use creation, they'd bless it and cause it to flourish. Humanity's high calling to rule *and* develop (see chapter 5) did not give them a free pass to use and abuse creation; it bound them to creation as its loving, wise caretakers (humble stewardship).

The Rebellion of the Stewards: Spreading the Wrong Stuff

Of course, as our pains and sorrows testify, Adam and Eve did not obey God. Rather than becoming ministers of *blessing* as co-rulers with God, they became conduits of *curses* through blatant rebellion. Because God had entrusted the created world to humanity, humanity's disobedience wreaked havoc throughout creation. The pain and curses that came out of Adam and Eve's sin included every key relationship (as outlined in *When Helping Hurts*);[8] even creation itself became subject to thorns, thistles, and the bondage of decay (see Gen. 3:16–19; Rom. 8:20–22). The catastrophe of human rebellion reverberated out into spiritual, personal, psychological, emotional, physical, relational, social, environmental, and economic brokenness.

But while God disciplined Adam and Eve, he did not jettison his plans for humanity to serve as his co-rulers over the world. At the same time, the Lord declared open war on the serpent who enticed Adam and Eve into idolatrous rebellion. God declared there would be war between the offspring of Eve and the offspring of the snake but that eventually a human child would win the ultimate victory. "He will crush your head," God said

Figure 9.2

God's Wise Creation Order Corrupted by Human Sin

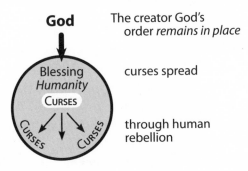

God — The creator God's order *remains in place*

curses spread

through human rebellion

to the serpent, "and you will strike his heel" (Gen. 3:15). Thus, the drama of Scripture is bound up in the conflict between humanity and the forces of sin, death, hell, and the devil, with humanity and creation's hope lying in a promised Son sent from God.

Many of us know this story. What we often are in danger of missing, though, is that God's salvation does not merely mean forgiveness for our sin. God's salvation also includes graciously restoring his image bearers as caretakers of the "rocks and trees, of skies and seas" of his created world.[9] The story of Scripture isn't just the drama of the creation, fall, and redemption of *humans*. It is also the drama of the rest of creation (the physical world). It is the story of God's rescue and renewal of "all things . . . in heaven and on earth, visible and invisible" (Col. 1:16 ESV). In the words of that glorious Christmas hymn:

> No more let sins and sorrows grow,
> Nor thorns infest the ground;
> He comes to make his blessings flow
> Far as the curse is found.[10]

That's why care for the created world is an essential aspect of the story of Scripture, the mission of God, and the economic lives of his people. How do we see God's plan to restore his people as stewards caring for the created world within the story as it unfolds in the Bible?

Stewardship Redeemed: Early Signs of the Creator's Plan to Rescue His Good Creation

Sign 1: People Longing for Relief

We don't have to wait long to see the people of God anxiously waiting for God to act to restore his created world and his people as stewards within it. Just a few generations after Adam, Lamech named his son Noah (meaning "comfort" or "rest"). "Out of the ground that [Yahweh] has cursed," Lamech declared as he signed the birth certificate, "this one shall bring us relief from our work and from the painful toil of our hands" (Gen. 5:29 ESV). Here we see God's people were looking for a special Son to come and heal their wounds *and the wounds of God's world* from the effects of humanity's temptation and rebellion.[11]

But Genesis 6:5 paints a bleak picture. Adam and Eve's rebellion extends to the whole of humanity, to the heart of every person—thoughts, motives, and all. Nevertheless, Noah, the hopeful son in the line of promise, "found favor [the Hebrew word for grace] in the eyes of the LORD" (Gen. 6:8).[12]

This grace showed up in Noah's life through the Lord's command to build an enormous boat. This infamous ark allowed Noah's family to escape the flood that devastated the earth and wiped out rebellious humanity. But the ark was also a vehicle of grace for the entire animal kingdom, because God made sure Noah left a seat open for at least two of every kind of creature. Don't let overfamiliarity with the flannel-board version of this story keep you from catching one of its major points: God actively worked to save the animals by raising up Noah as a faithful steward of God's creation.

After the flood, God promised Noah he would never again curse the ground or strike down every living creature, "even though every inclination of the human heart is evil from childhood" (Gen. 8:21). This should grab our attention like sirens from a fleet of fire trucks! God has wiped out *the effects* of human rebellion, while also choosing to limit his righteous judgment on

- his rebellious stewards and
- the created world that suffers as a result of their rebellion.

Even though the core problem—human rebellion—hasn't changed, God takes on the responsibility for maintaining his creation: "While the earth remains, seedtime and harvest, cold and heat, summer and winter, day and night, shall not cease" (v. 22 ESV).

Sign 2: Creatures Pulled into Covenant

After treating Noah like a new Adam, telling him twice to "be fruitful and multiply and fill the earth" (Gen. 9:1, 7 ESV), God spelled out a special covenant promise. This covenant is worth quoting in full:

> Then God said to Noah and to his sons with him, "Behold, I establish my covenant with you and your offspring after you, and with every living creature that is with you, the birds, the livestock, and every beast of the earth with you, as many as came out of the ark; it is for every beast of the earth. I establish my covenant with you, that *never again* shall all flesh be cut off by the waters of the flood, and *never again* shall there be a flood to destroy the earth." And God said, "This is *the sign* of the covenant that I make between me and you and every living creature that is with you, for all future generations: I have set my bow in the cloud, and it shall be *a sign* of the covenant between me and the earth. When I bring clouds over the earth and the bow is seen in the clouds, I will remember my covenant that is between me and you and every living creature of all flesh. And the waters shall *never again* become a flood to destroy all flesh. When the bow is in the clouds, I will see it and remember the everlasting covenant between God and every living creature of all flesh that is on the earth." God said to Noah, "This is *the sign* of the covenant that I have established between me and all flesh that is on the earth." (vv. 8–17 ESV, emphasis added)

Did you catch that? God didn't partner with only Noah and his descendants in this covenant of blessing and grace. God entered into a committed relationship with the following:

- Every living creature (see vv. 10, 12, 15, 16)
- The earth (see v. 14)
- All living creatures on the earth—"all flesh" (see vv. 11, 15, 16, 17)

This covenant is perpetual, giving us three promises:

- Never again shall *all flesh* be cut off by flood waters.
- Never again will *the earth* be destroyed by a flood.
- Never again will a flood destroy *all flesh*.[13]

The message couldn't be clearer: God will never give up on his world. He will preserve his good creation. He has given his promise.

God's covenant with Noah also shows us that God's creation order, with people as his chosen co-rulers, is still in place. God didn't "cut out the middle man," circumventing humanity in his relationship with the rest of creation (although Noah's covenant does remind us that God doesn't work *exclusively* through human stewards; he covenants directly with the created world).

It also makes clear that God's continuing intention to partner with humanity in stewarding creation is risky business. It leaves the created world at risk of corruption as long as the chief stewards remain corrupt (see Gen. 6:5; 8:21). Some Christians have seen the earth as a basically inexhaustible resource whose survival is guaranteed simply by its size and resilience. But the story of Noah reminds us that the ongoing existence of God's good world isn't a "built-in feature" so much as a "mark of divine forbearance, an expression of God's covenantal faithfulness."[14] Noah's story reminds us of God's love for creation, his commitment to humanity's place as stewards of it, and the need for another, better Noah who can bring redemption even to the wayward hearts of these broken stewards.

Israel and the Restoration of Creation and Its Caretakers

God's plan to rescue the world from the curse and restore humanity to their role as caretakers of it continues throughout the Old Testament. The Lord called Abraham to become a special family, a new people through whom God would bless all the nations of the world.[15] This would come about in part through Israel becoming a community that keeps "the way of the Lord by doing righteousness and justice" (Gen. 18:19 ESV). To accomplish this, after rescuing Israel from Egypt, Yahweh gave the Israelites laws as guidance for life in the promised land. If they followed Yahweh's guidance, the Israelites would become a picture of God's intention for humanity: just and righteous Israel would show the world what being in the image of God is all about. A flourishing promised land would remind the world of God's original garden.

We have explored in the previous chapters some of these just and righteous laws with respect to Yahweh's care for the poor. But many of these laws also invited Israel to practice justice and righteousness in caring for the earth and other creatures. These laws therefore give us a glimpse of God's heart for creation and his intention for his redeemed people to care for it.

> To describe the universe as "creation" is to claim that God's world has a shape we must discern if our work is to care for it rather than corrupt it. Our lives ought to go "with the grain of the universe." The creation care laws of the Old Testament instruct us on how to do just that.

They also give us insight into the way Yahweh has designed his universe and how that design should inform the way we treat his creation. A helpful image for this concept comes from the realm of carpentry. When cutting or sanding wood, it's essential to identify which direction the grain of the wood runs and to cut or sand along, rather than against the grain. Working against the grain is harder and often ruins the wood.

Similarly, to describe the universe as "creation" is to claim that God's world has a shape we must discern if our work is to care for it rather than corrupt it. Our lives ought to go "with the grain of the universe."[16] The creation care laws of the Old Testament instruct us on how to do just that.

Rest for Land and Animals Alike

As we'll explore in greater detail in chapter 11, Israel's calendar was structured by cycles of work and rest. Weekly Sabbaths, for instance, were central to keeping covenant with Yahweh. But this day of rest benefited not only humans:

> Six days you are to do your work, but on the seventh day you shall cease from labor so that your ox and your donkey may rest, and the son of your female slave, as well as your stranger, may refresh themselves. (Exod. 23:12 NASB)

Work and rest were structured to include rest for domestic animals and those who steward them (see also Deut. 5:14–15).

Indeed, God even included a yearlong break from planting and harvesting altogether. This could have been pretty hard to swallow for the average Israelite. Imagine being a peasant working a rain-dependent family farm in the ancient world. Life was hard enough, and now God wanted you to shut down the family business one year out of every seven? Why? Again and again, the Lord named the *ecological* beneficiaries of his righteous rule:

> The land is to have a year of sabbath rest, a sabbath to the LORD. . . . Whatever the land yields during the sabbath year will be food for you . . . as well as for your livestock and the wild animals in your land. (Lev. 25:4, 6–7)

> But during the seventh year . . . the wild animals may eat what is left. (Exod. 23:11)

Imagine! Yahweh shaped his kingdom economy around creating rest and provision for not only his people but also the land, domestic animals, and even the wild creatures that lived in Israel. Economic life lived with the grain of God's design doesn't just avoid destroying the created world; it blesses *all* the created world.

Before moving on, it's worth pointing out that the ecological and economic message of these Sabbath texts is built on Yahweh's insistence that he is, and remains, the Ultimate Owner. "The land is mine and you reside in my land as foreigners and strangers" (Lev. 25:23). In other words, humanity stewards creation on behalf of the God who owns it all. The Bible does not teach that we humans own the world and can use it how we like. The Bible declares that we manage creation on behalf of Yahweh and in ways that reflect his love for it.[17]

Protecting Creation: God's Responsibility and Ours

Yahweh gave the Israelites responsibility for protecting creation even when doing so would cost them something. Even war was no excuse to abuse creation, as God made clear in his command that they not destroy fruit-bearing trees when they attacked a city. "Are the trees in the field human," God almost sarcastically inquires, "that they should be besieged by you?" (Deut. 20:19 ESV). Of course the economic element is at play here, since they were allowed to use trees that weren't fruit-bearing (see v. 20). But the point remains: wise economic life includes protecting the productivity of God's good world.[18]

Indeed, the Lord seems to see domestic animals as deserving care and respect in part because they are humanity's coworkers. For instance, Israelites were not allowed to muzzle an ox while it worked in their grain fields (see Deut. 25:4). The ox, the partner-worker in the family business, had a right to eat of the fruits of the land while engaged in agricultural production. The economic implications of such care for one's animals becomes clearer when we realize that the cost of allowing an ox to feed while it worked would have been approximately "15,000,000 calories a year . . . an annual shortfall of 60 days per family."[19] The righteous person's care for the needs of their animals (see Prov. 12:10) isn't some quaint affection for pets; it's a serious, economically significant attempt to work in such a way that our economic lives *bless the land and all that depend on it.*

All these laws clearly demonstrate that God's economy is deeply and practically shaped by a concern that our economic activities reflect God's care for and blessing of land and animals alike. This isn't a "do no harm" ethic; it's a proactive commitment to bless the world by living economic lives that reflect the Lord's generous rule. Such commitments often, at least in the long-term, lead to more productive land and animals. This only makes sense, as these commands invite us to go with the grain of the universe.

But we can't miss that this long-term blessing must be received as an act of faith, because in the short term, caring for creation in ancient Israel looked like a shorter work week, higher costs, and lower profits for human owners. This economic life lived within the limits of creation reflected God's wise economic way of life. At times, though, I'm guessing it was a hard pill for the average Israelite farmer to swallow.

Perhaps that's why God reminded his people that if they *failed* to embody his wise stewardship by bending their economic lives toward the flourishing of his good creation, this disobedience would harm creation. That's why only one chapter after the Lord gave the Israelites the Jubilee, with its rest for land, humans, and animals, he declared that if they rejected his decrees (see Lev. 26:15), the result would be the overthrow of his good creation order: the rain would fail (see v. 19), the land would refuse to give its fruit (see v. 20), and wild animals would destroy Israel's livestock and even children (see v. 22). If the Israelites persisted in their disobedience, the ultimate end would be exile from the promised land itself.

Here again we see that when Yahweh's people failed to care for the creation, he stepped in to get the job done. Yahweh's ways are inviolable. If his rescued people failed to live like wise stewards in his good land, "then the land [would] enjoy its sabbath years all the time that it [laid] desolate ... then the land [would] rest and enjoy its sabbaths" (v. 34). When God's people rebelled against the call to be godly stewards, everything got flipped upside down. But God promised to intervene—and ensure the land got its vacation.

In short, Israel's laws don't make sense in light of our contemporary Western Christian idea that what God is doing is rescuing our souls from sin so that he can blast the earth and take us to strum harps on clouds. But these laws fit perfectly in the story we actually encounter in Scripture, the story that reveals

- the scope of human stewardship as co-caretakers with the God of the entire created world (see Gen. 1–2);
- the cosmic hope of redemption from sin and restoration to our job as stewards (see Gen. 3:15; 5:29); and
- the creation-preserving covenant (see Gen. 9:8–17) God made with Noah, which committed him to caring for all his creatures when humanity continued to drop the ball.[20]

What a Wonderful World! God's Wonder, Delight, and Wise Order in the Poetry of the Bible

God's Word doesn't just give us laws for caring about creation. Scripture sings out in poetic song, declaring the wonders, delight, and wise order we encounter in God's world. Indeed, chief among those who delight in creation is God himself!

Remember the book of Job? When the Lord finally showed up to answer Job's understandable complaining, he didn't give Job a systematic theology lesson. He spewed out chapters and chapters of poetry, many which celebrate the complexity and beauty of the world God created *and delights in.* Here are a few highlights:

Where were you when I laid the earth's foundation? (Job 38:4)

On what were [the earth's] footings set, or who laid its cornerstone—while the morning stars sang together and all the angels shouted for joy? (vv. 6–7)

Have you journeyed to the springs of the sea or walked in the recesses of the deep? (v. 16)

Do you send the lightning bolts on their way? Do they report to you, "Here we are"? (v. 35)

Do you hunt the prey for the lioness and satisfy the hunger of the lions? . . . Who provides food for the raven when its young cry out to God and wander about for lack of food? (vv. 39, 41)

Does the eagle soar at your command and build its nest on high? (Job 39:27)

Look at Behemoth, which I made along with you and which feeds on grass like an ox. What strength it has in its loins, what power in the muscles of its belly! . . . It ranks first among the works of God, yet its Maker can approach it with his sword. (Job 40:15–16, 19)

I will not fail to speak of Leviathan's limbs, its strength and its graceful form. . . . It makes the depths churn like a boiling caldron. (Job 41:12, 31)

God's poetic responses to Job's questions display the Creator's delight in his own works. Yahweh invited Job to consider the glory, diversity, power, and uniqueness of the creatures he made and to embrace an appropriately deep humility before both him and his works.[21] Even Leviathan (crocodile?) and Behemoth (hippo?), the terrifying creatures of the deep that occupied the nightmares and religious myths of the ancient world, are no match for God . . . indeed, he delights in their existence!

Old Testament scholar Ellen Davis suggests that our contemporary world's abuses of creation stem from a failure to *see* creation for what it really is in all its beauty and inestimable goodness.[22] Beginning in Genesis, Yahweh *sees* his creation is good. In the book of Job, Yahweh relentlessly confronts us with *his view of the world*: beautiful, powerful, good. God's poetry holds up all creation before us and invites us to see it as he does.

Even more incredibly, the Lord doesn't just delight in creation . . . he continues to care for it. The eagle soars at his command! The ravens cry out to him for food! And the creation itself responds by testifying to the grandeur of our God: "The heavens declare the glory of God; the skies proclaim the work of his hands" (Ps. 19:1). Every created thing and every creature exists for God's delight *and* to bring him praise.

The Psalms are filled with songs celebrating this.[23] Psalm 104 celebrates Yahweh as the one who "stretches out the heavens like a tent" (v. 2), sets the boundaries for the seas, acts as a gardener actively watering the mountains and satisfying the earth, takes care of the homes of rock badgers and wild goats, causes vineyards to grow up and give wine to gladden the hearts of people, and forms the fearsome creatures of the sea to frolic in the waves. As theologian Walter Harrelson beautifully suggests, the poet celebrates how God looks after creatures and ecosystems that have no immediate or obvious connection to daily human life or economic activity:

> God has interest in badgers and wild goats and storks for their own sakes. He has interest in trees and mountains and rock-cairns that simply serve non-human purposes. . . . Man's work is significant, but so is lion's work. Ships doing commerce on the high seas are doing significant work, but so also is Leviathan, trailing behind the ships, blowing and cavorting.[24]

The only response to Yahweh's creativity and care for all creatures is one of humble wonder and raucous praise: "How many are your works, Lord!" the psalmist sings. "In wisdom you made them all. . . . May the glory of the Lord endure forever" (Ps. 104:24, 31). As humanity joins all creation in praising Yahweh, we find ourselves as part of the creaturely choir, one of those creatures among others, called to give God the worship he deserves.[25] The very last verse of the entire psalter is this: "Let *everything* that has breath praise the LORD!" (Ps. 150:6, emphasis added).

Because Yahweh delights in and is praised by earth and sky, flora and fauna, creation bears witness to his wisdom and the wise ordering of his world. And while this does not mean we can simply read God's design for the world by observing it, it does mean that as God's people we are invited, commanded even, to look to creation in wonder and delight, to care for creation with love and respect, and to learn from creation something of the wisdom of the Creator. Thus, in Proverbs 8, we encounter wisdom not as a concept but as a character, Lady Wisdom, standing at Yahweh's side as he creates the world, dancing and delighting before him as he spins out galaxies and mollusks and redwood forests.[26]

The Prophets: God Will Do a New Thing, but Who Can Perceive It?

Nevertheless, the problem at the heart of creation, the sin hidden in human hearts, remains. Jeremiah writes that Israel's idolatry "polluted the land" (Jer. 3:2 ESV). The result of this idolatry was the laying waste of the land itself "because there [was] no one who care[d]" (Jer. 12:11). There seemed to be little left to do but lament for the earth itself in the face of God's judgment on his corrupted, would-be stewards.

And yet. In the face of rebellion, the Creator continued in his committed care for his creation *and* his chosen stewards of it. The prophet Isaiah is justly famous for prophesying that Yahweh would send one from David's line to do what Israel and all humanity had failed to do (see Isa. 11). Isaiah was equally insistent that Yahweh's saving work would encompass the renewal of all creation. When Yahweh acts, people will be saved *and* "the wolf shall dwell with the lamb . . . and a little child shall lead them" (v. 6 ESV). Infants shall play with serpents rather than being led into rebellion by them (see v. 8). The mountains and hills will join God's people in joyous songs of praise while all the trees of the field applaud (see Isa. 55:12). Where human rebellion had planted thorns and briars in the midst of God's garden, Yahweh's salvation will establish a verdant forest in a curse-free new creation (see v. 13). The earth and its inhabitants will live in the joyous peace of the Lord forever (see Isa. 65:17–66:24).

The entire Old Testament, then, bears witness to God's creation of a good world that displays his wisdom and inspires joyful wonder and delight in God himself and his people. More incredible still, the Old Testament constantly reminds us of Yahweh's insistence that humanity fulfill their calling as members of his royal family who co-rule over creation with the same care, gentleness, and delight that he does.

The Old Testament, though, leaves us still waiting and wondering: Who will come and defeat the Serpent? Who will come and do what Noah could not, transforming and restoring *the stewards* to their jobs as caretakers? In the face of humanity's failures, including the failures of our best and brightest heroes, such as David, Moses, and Abraham, what can be done? Will anyone come from among Abraham's descendants who can bring forth the lacking fruit of righteousness and justice?

God's promises, it turns out, are so great only God can fulfill them. This is what the Gospels tell us in various ways about King Jesus, the Son of God, who came to redeem people and rescue his creation.

The Redeemer *Is* the Creator

The New Testament describes King Jesus's birth as an *incarnation*.[27] Miraculously, the Creator God entered creation as one of his creatures! The New Testament proclaims that this Jesus is both the One through whom all things were made[28] and God-made-flesh[29] on a mission to reconcile heaven and earth.[30] Jesus deserves our worship as both Creator and Redeemer.[31]

The New Testament goes out of its way to show us that where every other human failed in their calling to reflect God's image, Jesus showed up as the perfect image of God (see 2 Cor. 4:4; Col. 1:14; Heb. 1:3). Like Noah, Jesus passed through the waters at his baptism. Like the people of Israel, he was tested in the wilderness at the beginning of his ministry.[32] And like Adam, he faced temptation in a garden (see Matt. 26:36–46; Mark 14:32–42). But while Adam was led astray by one of the very creatures he was entrusted to rule over; Noah ended up drunk, naked, and ashamed; and Israel spent forty years failing to follow Yahweh, Jesus passed the test with flying colors. We may not see humanity coruling with God over creation yet, *but we do see Jesus,* born a human like us, "now crowned with glory and honor because he suffered death, so that by the grace of God he might taste death for everyone" and bring many humans into his royal family (Heb. 2:7–10). That has been the Creator's intention all along.

The Return of the King and the Resurrection of Creation

What about the future? Just before returning to the Father, Jesus announced his authority over all of heaven and earth as the basis for his sending out the disciples (see Matt. 28:18–20). "The risen Jesus thus claims the same ownership and sovereignty over all creation as the Old Testament affirms for Yahweh."[33] The earth remains the Lord's.

This very fact should prevent us from understanding the New Testament as uninterested in care for creation. Unless we want to assert that God scrapped his Old Testament priority list in the New Testament, we've got to assume he cares as much about creation as he ever has. As we discussed in the introduction, the good news of God's kingdom includes the life-giving message that God has not given up on humanity as his royal family. He is not just forgiving us so we can go about our business. He's restoring us to our vocation as co-rulers with him. This includes God's desire for us, the people of his church, to take up our vocation as those who lovingly care for and steward the good world of mountains, streams, hummingbirds, horses, and all the rest.

Indeed, while Jesus is *already* renewing us as his faithful caretakers in the present, we also look forward to a new work that has *not yet* arrived because Jesus hasn't returned to complete the kingdom work he began here in his earthly life and ministry. This "already *and* not yet" dynamic of the kingdom in the New Testament applies both to Jesus's human followers and to the created world itself.[34] Christians look forward to the resurrection of the body. While our resurrected bodies will be free from sickness and death, they will still be recognizably ours. We know that this is our final destiny because Jesus's own body was restored and re-created rather than rejected.

The created world groans for this very same thing. Creation, which has been subjected to frustration through sin and death, groans to be liberated from its bondage to decay "and brought into the freedom and glory of the children of God" (Rom. 8:21). The earth and sky and animals and waters (see Gen. 1), along with all their living creatures, long for the new creation in their own way, just as we long for resurrection bodies in our own way. Astoundingly, the rest of creation's liberation is bound up with the liberation of God's image bearers: the good news that Jesus is rescuing sinners and restoring them to their vocation as co-rulers of God's world is also good news for the rest of creation as well.

When the fullness of this new creation comes with the return of King Jesus, it will mean the restoration of the entire cosmos in glory. That is why when John saw his vision of the new heavens and new earth, he didn't see ghostly souls or even resurrected bodies being beamed up to heaven; he saw the New Jerusalem coming *down from heaven*. Now, God will make his dwelling among resurrected people, ruling and reigning forever in a resurrected world. We do not care for creation simply because we look back to Eden; we care for creation because we look forward to the resurrection of the cosmos, the liberation of the created world, which is bound up with our own new life in Christ.[35] As Hannah says of Port William, a fictional agrarian Kentucky town in Wendell Berry's novel *Hannah Coulter*, "Someday there will be a new heaven and a new earth and a new Port William coming down from heaven, adorned as a bride for her husband, and whoever has known her before will know her then."[36]

The Creation Care Key in Scripture: Summary

Contrary to what many might expect, Scripture has a great deal to say about care for the natural world. Scripture teaches that God created everything, that God loves everything he created, and that he himself simultaneously delights in and sustains every atom in the universe. Creation itself looks to Yahweh for protection and care and worships him simply by being itself; the heavens *declare the glory of Yahweh*.

Incredibly, the Lord entrusts his creation to humanity, made in his image and called to co-rule over his world with him. In addition to developing creation and unpacking its potential, we see in Scripture that we are to care for the created world, particularly in the laws of the Old Testament, laws that direct God's people to respect the intrinsic goodness of the land and other creatures in the course of their economic lives.

Humans have always fallen short of our God-ordained job description, not least by our abuse of God's world. But in the place of faithless humans, the Creator God who loves the world sent his own Son, Jesus Christ our Lord, the Faithful One, to renew, restore, and resurrect his human image bearers *and* the created word that he now rules. Worshiping this Creator King requires us to evaluate our economic lives in light of God's love for the whole creation.

THE CREATION CARE KEY TODAY
STORIES AND PRACTICES OF STEWARDSHIP

How should we *practice* the King's economy in ways that honor (1) the goodness of the original creation and (2) the resurrection destination of creation when Jesus returns?

Our culture has trained us regarding not only what to do with money but also how to view the rest of creation as a set of commodities to be used for narrow economic goals. But economic practices that reduce the world to a set of commodities to be used and discarded are in conflict with God's delight in the goodness of creation for its own sake.

Once again, God's solution is not to get rid of humanity. Rather God intends to restore us as ambassadors of his loving rule. Indeed, some ecologists, apart from any commitment to the Christian faith, have recently suggested that the brokenness of the created world at the hands of humans requires more active, intentional, and creative engagement with creation for the sake of creation.[1]

This confirms the scriptural story of humanity as broken-but-redeemable stewards of God's good world. Because Jesus, in his death and resurrection, has already won the great victory over sin and death, the King's people now implement this victory in the power of the Spirit. As people of the age to come, it is our responsibility to cultivate practices in the present that anticipate the promised future hope for the land and other creatures.

Creation Care and the Cultural Mandate: Two Sides of Our Vocation[2]

Before we look at stories and practices that reflect a commitment to the earth as God's property placed under our management, God's good gift for us to cultivate for his glory, we have two big-picture thoughts about vocation.

First, as we noted in the introduction, human stewardship includes both preserving and protecting the created world *and* pursuing economic and cultural development through creatively cultivating that world. Understood within God's good creation order, then, creation care is not in irreconcilable conflict with pursuing economic and cultural development (what theologians sometimes call the "cultural mandate").[3] Wise stewards will pursue development without foolishly diminishing creation for short-term gain.

Every human is responsible to steward creation well in both of these senses. However, there are times when, in a fallen world, we feel tension between our call to care for creation and our call to generate culture and economic sustenance *from* the rest of creation. We don't know how to resolve all these tensions, but we do know that both elements of our vocation are absolutely biblical.

Because the creation care aspect has often been sidelined, in this chapter, we're focusing specifically on the "preserving and protecting" element of our vocation (see Gen. 2:15). This calling is universal. So no matter what work you do, you are responsible to think through how your industry, entrepreneurial efforts, and snack rooms impact the rest of God's good creation.

Second, some people will have specific vocations focused on healing the creation and also protecting and securing its flourishing. Hence, in addition to people serving King Jesus in engineering, banking, and manufacturing, we need people with vocations in renewable energy, energy entrepreneurship, marine biology, forest ecology, soil ecology, and much more. We must learn to practice allegiance to our King both in particular vocations and in normal, everyday work and rest, eating and drinking, for he sits in authority over every power in heaven and on earth.

Creation Care: It's Been with Us from the Beginning

As we dig in to stories of God's people caring for creation, we want to counter right out of the gate a suspicion you may have: that all this creation business is some recent liberal development. In fact, the truth is that care for the created world goes all the way back to not only the Garden but also the early days of the church. In the fourth century, Athanasius wrote that the "renewal of creation has been wrought by the self-same Word who made it in the beginning."[4] Athanasius and the early church understood that the good news Jesus brought was good news for humans *and* the rest of creation.

Or consider the story of the SPCA—the Society for the Prevention of Cruelty to Animals. Animal welfare began in the United States and Great Britain as a result of committed Christians who cared for people and animals. In nineteenth-century England, a group of Christians fought simultaneously for the abolition of the slave trade, the implementation of child labor laws, and for the prevention of cruelty to animals. They were constantly told this last cause was hopeless. "You'll never change this," many argued, "but you will lose your own credibility."

Nevertheless, twenty-two men who were willing to suffer to see God's world reflect God's ways met in June of 1824 to organize on behalf of animal welfare.[5] At one point they had a nearly £300 debt they could not repay. British authorities imprisoned their founder, Anglican priest Reverend Arthur Broome—"a most unfortunate position for a clergyman"—since he was their treasurer.[6]

This group had a difficult start. But they persevered, and eventually their cause made its way before the Duchess of Kent. In 1835, she lent her name and title to their cause as one of their "Lady Patronesses."[7] Then two years later this duchess became Queen Victoria, and "her encouragement of the Society's activities was immediate and generous."[8] Ever since, this society has been referred to in England as the *Royal* Society for the

Prevention of Cruelty to Animals. In the United States, a new movement among Christians across our country is taking up a similar call to care for creation.

The Answer Was a Farm: EdenThistle

Before they returned to Lookout Mountain to found EdenThistle,[9] Marshall and Katherine Teague lived in Bend, Oregon, working with horses. As Marshall learned to work "with the design of the horse," he began to ask questions about how our culture might be working with—or against—the grain of God's good design. Meanwhile, Katherine began pondering food sourcing and how God expects his people to treat our fellow creatures. As committed Christians, the Teagues felt called to understand the *overlap* between our theology of creation and our practice of living off the land and other creatures.

The answer to Marshall and Katherine's questions, in the end, was a farm. Basing their work in part on Joel Salatin's Polyface Farms, Marshall and Katherine have invested sweat, blisters, their savings, and countless hours to make EdenThistle a farm that provides food for people and flourishing for creation by working with the grain of God's universe. They do more than simply produce high-quality meat; they are simultaneously cultivating land with growing potential for long-term, sustainable production. They call their business a "land stewardship company" to capture this comprehensive vision.

"What we're really farming, or stewarding rather, is more than just the pigs, chickens, quail, and other animals you see here," Marshall explains. "We're stewarding the grass under their feet and the soil out of which that grass grows. We're stewarding the water captured by the soil that grows our plants and waters our animals, the bugs living in our fields, and the trees shading our forests. We're stewarding the hawk that wants to prey on my hens and the wild hare that grazes on our grass when we're not around. We're stewarding the relationship between all these creatures and places on our farm. And we need to steward well the relationship that can exist between the larger human community and the living, teeming creatures here on our farm. Farming is a daunting task. It's well beyond us."[10]

All the animals the Teagues raise depend on grass and foraging for a substantial part of their diet. Rather than separating all these animals from one another like many large-scale farms do, the Teagues use technology and intensive animal husbandry practices to keep these animals in the sorts of relationships they would have in the wild. So, for instance, by using mobile electric fencing, the Teagues are able to manage an intensive grazing cycle that honors all the creatures involved *and* creates high yields. Marshall explains the process like this:

> First, we bring in the larger animals, like cows and horses, to a particular part of one of our pastures. As they graze there, they massage and aerate the soil of our fields. The mobile fencing allows us to move where they're grazing regularly, and such temporary grazing teases out new growth from our grass. Meanwhile, these cows or horses also provide nitrogen-rich fertilizer for the soil as they create manure.
>
> After a few days, we move the large grazers on to new fields so that they don't overgraze or overfertilize. Then we can bring our chickens and quail behind these larger animals. Before the larger animals grazed, the grass would have been too high for our birds, but because the grass has been trimmed down a good bit, the birds can now graze for grass, grit, bugs, and more. As they do, their scratching around actually accelerates the decomposition process of the manure so that its nitrogen is actually more rapidly assimilated by the soil. This makes the soil more readily available to grow new, future grass.
>
> Once the birds graze an area for a while, they're also moved on to fresh, clean pastures while the grazed area is left to be rinsed by the rains, dried and cleaned by the UV radiation from the sun, and grown into more harvestable grass for our animals.
>
> Meanwhile, our pigs move through our farm's woodlands, grazing on grubs, acorns, roots, and vegetation. Their rough digging injects oxygen into the ground and mulches the leaf beds into the soil. In some areas in our woods, we can actually grow wheat, radishes, and other crops during the winter. The pigs prepare the soil, move on while we scatter seed, and then come back and graze what we've planted.

This symbiotic dance of domestic animals attempts to go with the grain of God's creation, but it also embodies the wise stewardship of God's image-bearing farmers (in this case, Marshall and Katherine). Their selective, creative use of technology enables them to pursue the flourishing of land and animals on their way to creating delicious meat and eggs for their customers.

Some may see all this as a sort of unnecessary, Amishesque attempt to get back to an imagined golden, agrarian age. But compare the Teagues' practice to that of some of the other mainstream practices of pig farming described by Old Testament scholar Sandra Richter. Richter writes:

> Regarding America's most lucrative agricultural product, pigs, confinement has been distilled into an exact science: 20 230-lb. animals per 7.5-foot-square pen, housed on metal-grated flooring, in climate controlled conditions, never actually exposed to the light of day. These animals are sustained in such crowded and filthy conditions that movement is difficult, natural behaviors impossible, and antibiotics are essential to control infection. Sows, typically a 500-lb. animal, are separately housed. They live out their lives in 7-foot x 22-inch metal gestation crates from which they are never released, even in the process of giving birth. They are artificially inseminated to deliver an average of eight litters, litters inflated beyond their natural carrying capacity by fertility drugs. A staple of their diet is the rendered remains of their deceased pen-mates. Surely if God is offended by boiling a kid in its mother's milk, we should be concerned that dead sows are routinely ground up and fed to their offspring (Deut. 14:21). But as the "new agriculture" reports, all of these innovations make these production units (that is, animate creatures) easier to manage, maintain, medicate and slaughter.[11]

We find it difficult to believe that such practices, however "economically viable," fit God's heart for the land and its creatures. Nor is pig farming the only problem. More than 90 percent of egg-laying hens in the United States are kept in "battery cages," which "provide as little as 0.6 square feet of space per hen. That is smaller than a regular sized sheet of paper," and because of such cramped quarters, many operators remove the chickens' beaks by burning or cutting in order to keep them from pecking each other to death.[12]

A large body of scientific evidence suggests that excess fertilizer from crop farming and animal waste from industrial farms is responsible for creating a "dead zone"—an area of the ocean with such low oxygen concentration that nearly all aquatic life either dies or moves away—the size of Connecticut in the Gulf of Mexico.[13] This has obvious implications for the fishing industry, on which many livelihoods depend. Poor stewardship of creation often results in harming humans.

Rusty Pritchard, a natural resource economist who works with Tearfund, reminded me of another example of how creation care and human care go together. When the city of Atlanta, Georgia, made a massive effort to get cars off the road during the Olympic Games, ER visits for asthma attacks temporarily went down by almost half, only to return to their previous levels as soon as the Olympics ended and traffic returned to normal.[14] Such a story demonstrates how our unwillingness to consider creation care as an essential part of our economic lives results in devastation for the land, animals, *and* humans.

Such contrasts clarify just how important the Teagues' work is. While EdenThistle will certainly not solve every environmental or agricultural problem, it represents a serious, sustained, and successful attempt to engage creation economically in ways that honor God's world.

Because of their intensely theological vision for their work, the Teagues also educate visitors, students, interns, and customers regarding healthy land stewardship. They are a for-profit business with an online marketing presence and multiple sales channels. But their bottom line is not reducible to profit maximizing. EdenThistle is rooted in a theological imperative that produces food without the ecological amnesia that results from our tendency to try to keep the impact of our work on creation out of our economic calculus. EdenThistle runs on a refusal to forget that stewardship is central to God's call on the whole of our lives.

"The First Piece of the Puzzle"[15]

"Bonton is a South Dallas community where 85% of men have been to prison, poverty is rampant, and jobs are scarce."[16] The USDA also classifies this community as a "food desert."[17] Since 63 percent of residents in the community lack their own transportation and the nearest grocery store is three miles away, taking a bus to get fresh food requires a three-hour round trip. Low access to healthy, whole foods is just one more challenge for this neighborhood, and one that is far too common for communities of concentrated poverty.

What are the hidden costs of little or no access to such goods? The fact that Bonton residents have lacked access to affordable, healthy foods for decades contributes to another terrible set of realities.

- On average, men from Bonton live eleven years less than men in Dallas County as a whole.
- The heart disease, diabetes, stroke, and cancer rates in Bonton are double what they are in the rest of the county.
- Childhood obesity rates are much higher in Bonton than in other Dallas communities.

A near-constant diet of packaged junk food and soda, popular eats readily available in the community at overpriced corner stores, has contributed to these massive health problems. In the face of this set of challenges, Daron Babcock and Patrick Wright are doing something about this food issue that seeks to honor the people, land, and animals that come together at Bonton Farms.

Just a few years ago, Patrick was depressed, jobless, and struggling with a drug addiction. Meanwhile, Daron was thriving financially with his sons in Frisco, Texas. When Daron relocated to Bonton as an "urban missionary," he quickly saw how community disintegration was related to healthy food and good work.

Today these two men are indispensable partners at Bonton Farms, the public face of Bonton Farm-Works, an urban farm project launched through H.I.S. BridgeBuilders.[18] The relational partnership between one who was materially resourced and one who was materially challenged strikes us as hopeful on many levels. Bonton Farms addresses issues of food scarcity, job scarcity, education, and land care in an integrated way on a daily basis.

On their website, Bonton Farms narrates their larger purpose as "the bigger story" of "a small urban farm boldly *growing hope* through vegetables, fruits, eggs and honey and a community, plagued by poverty, transformed in the process."[19] In keeping with their holistic approach to emplaced, relational community development, they remain determined to grow the best tasting, healthiest and freshest food in Dallas, taking great care to adhere to organic standards. [They] divert organic waste from many channels to create compost that continually replenishes and brings biodiversity to [the] soil. When plants need additional food, [they] use only OMRI (Organic Materials Review Institute) certified fertilizers.[20]

At Bonton Farms the gospel of Jesus Christ is reintegrating people and place, work and food, and land and animals in a rich, relational partnership. Since God is reconciling people to himself through the gospel, Jesus is reconciling every type of broken relationship through his people serving together in renewed hope.[21]

"We're Gonna Have a Garden . . ."

Similar signs of hope are springing up in my (Michael's) backyard. Marlon Foster, the South Memphis pastor and nonprofit leader we met in chapter 4, started a community garden because one of the matriarchs of the neighborhood, a vegan his mother's age, straight up told him: "We're gonna have a garden. These kids need to know where their food comes from." Today that garden has become Green Leaf Learning Farm, a flagship ministry of Knowledge Quest that ties education, community development, and improved health and nutrition together. But Marlon believes the garden has stuck because of the way it has brought together the community and its history in a redemptive act of place making.

"Farming is bound up in a lot of pain and ugliness for African Americans," Marlon says. "The legacy of our ancient connection to land and agriculture was lost in some ways because of that ugliness. If you don't honor and acknowledge that, then you miss some things. The reason that grandmother may not want her grandchild out there with that garden hoe is that she remembers what that hoe meant for her family."

So Green Leaf has sought to reclaim agriculture from this oppressive past for the sake of the future. Indeed, as my dear friend and former Knowledge Quest staff member Christian Man (yes, that really is his name!) chronicled in his research on Green Leaf, the farm has enabled older residents who grew up in the rural South under Jim Crow to reclaim the beauty and dignity of growing food for their community. Walter Gates, an expert gardener who grew up on 120 acres and lives nearby, oversaw the work at Green Leaf for several years. When asked about his experiences, Walter said, "It's no longer survival. It's love." When asked if he sang while working the fields in his childhood, Walter replied, "No, but I do now."

Walter's vision for Green Leaf is that it leads to a garden in every yard, while Pastor Stephenson, another community participant with roots in the country, says, "We have a garden, and we want to bless anyone we can. We want the city to know that if you need a helping hand, you can come by. Serving the Lord is good. We couldn't do it without him."

It's these sorts of stories, this sort of ownership from the neighbors around Green Leaf, that Marlon sees as essential to the farm's success. While many community gardens have a sort of "if you build it, the community will come" mind-set, for Marlon and his team, the Green Leaf farm simply—pardon the pun—grew up from the soil of the neighborhood itself, through the love and care of the stewards who've long lived there.

Today Green Leaf covers three acres, including an orchard with apples, pears, persimmons, figs, pomegranates, blackberries, and blueberries in addition to seemingly endless veggies grown in raised beds and hoop houses. Last year, this small plot produced five thousand pounds of fresh veggies in the heart of an isolated neighborhood, while simultaneously giving hundreds of urban young people the chance to engage science and gardening through an applied, hands-on approach. Foster, Knowledge Quest, and the people of South Memphis bear witness to the beauty of God's creation and the glory and dignity that belong to us as human stewards of it.

The Memphis Center for Food and Faith, Noah Campbell, and Memphis Tilth

What about those of us who aren't called to quit our jobs and start farms? How can we participate in creation care in our economic lives? Part of the answer comes by way of an act that most of us perform several times every single day of our lives: eating.

"Eating is an agricultural act," writes Wendell Berry.[22] And for Noah Campbell, an ordained minister and founder of the Memphis Center for

Food and Faith, eating in ways that contribute to the flourishing of creation is one part of what it means to grow up into the fullness of Christ. "How we steward creation," Noah says, "is directly tied to love of God, and often, either directly or indirectly, related to loving our neighbor."

This loving stewardship impacts how we eat. "Food is the currency of creation," Noah says, "the thread that connects economics, ecology, and community." So in 2012, the Memphis Center for Food and Faith (MCFF) launched with the mission of promoting healthy land and community by helping faith communities join in creation-honoring ways of engaging directly in the "production, procurement, aggregation, distribution, and preparation of locally grown and raised food."[23]

In addition to leading clergy workshops and church studies on creation care and food, MCFF launched Bring It Food Hub (brought from idea to incarnation by Christian Man, who got his urban agriculture start working for Green Leaf Learning Farm). Bring It offers a market-based solution to creating healthy food economies by purchasing fruits, vegetables, grains, and humanely farmed proteins from urban and rural farms in the area and then selling them directly to families in the form of subscriptions for a box of good food delivered weekly. When consumers buy subscriptions for these boxes, they help farmers access a more predictable and reliable market for their products. Bring It also has an expanding wholesale operation that includes selling to local Memphis institutions. Overall, during their 2016 season, they served 478 total customers, distributing roughly four thousand pounds of produce each week. These sales allowed Bring It to buy more than $150,000 worth of produce from more than thirty local farmers.[24]

At the same time, Bring It has intentionally targeted churches, nonprofits, and other faith-based organizations in marketing their products. Noah hopes such efforts help the church move beyond the rhetoric of caring for creation and into faithful action. Bring It provides a tangible way for God's people to support economic activity that, like the Sabbath agriculture of the Old Testament, blesses rather than curses the land and its creatures.

MCFF hasn't stopped there. They recently launched Memphis Tilth, an emergent organization focused on food issues in Memphis. Through this partnership, MCFF has helped launch and lead urban farms and community gardens, including the St. Paul garden at Advance Memphis. Through this collaboration, some community garden produce can be sold through Bring It. At the Advance Memphis site, participants in the job-training program can gain the ServSafe food handling certification that can help them land a job in the food industry, while also learning about God's design for creation and humanity's role as stewards of it. The garden will soon have an on-site fruit and vegetable stand selling produce. Memphis Tilth's community kitchen, also located at Advance Memphis, gives my (Michael's) low-income neighbors access to culinary education, shared meal preparation, and value-added production.

Several years ago Noah, Steve Nash (executive director of Advance Memphis), and I kicked around the idea of throwing a party that felt like an Old Testament feast in the heart of South Memphis. A feast that would embody the new economy and community God wants for his world. A feast like the ones we describe in chapters 3 and 4. Several months ago, an Advance Memphis job-training cohort threw a feast with food they had helped grow, harvest, and prepare. In these and so many other ways, Advance Memphis, MCFF, Memphis Tilth, and others are creating expressions of the King's economy. That's good news for the land, the creatures that live on it, the workers who labor in it, and the community at large.

Practicing Creation Care

So how do we begin to practice the King's economy in ways that cause creation to flourish rather than treating creation as a commodity to be used however we see fit? Throughout the rest of the chapter we offer some suggestions for how you can begin practicing creation care in your economic life in your home, workplace, and church.

Before we get there, we want to clearly state that this is new territory for many of us and oftentimes we may disagree about the precise way to practice our agreed-upon need to care for creation in our economic lives. We believe the practices we suggest reflect meaningful, appropriate steps for families, churches, and businesses to consider. Because there is room for debate, though, some of these practices may strike you as more or less convincing. That's okay. Once again, a central argument in this book is that we can't see or know how to make it through complex problems until we've begun *practicing* economic discipleship in our lives. Pick something that makes sense and get to work.

Practicing Creation Care at Work

Consider: Do you have influence at work? How could your workplace and coworkers bend your business toward respecting God's good creation and contributing to its flourishing?

Some ideas for practicing creation care at your workplace include the following:

- *Foster better food practices at work.* When you order food in or go out to lunch, choose restaurants that prepare food raised in ways that treat animals with dignity and the soil with care. Have your workplace be a community-supported agriculture (CSA) pickup site. (CSAs provide weekly boxes of fresh food to folks who sign up and pay for these subscriptions ahead of time. These programs help families get fresh food, and farmers fix a major cash flow challenge by getting cash in hand toward the beginning of the growing season. They also typically work exclusively with farmers who embrace a very high standard in terms of care for animals and the earth.) Consider subsidizing the cost for some or all employees.

- *Change your waste-management policies.* What goes to the landfill? For instance, every year the United States sends 254 million tons of trash to landfills that are rapidly filling up.[25] In fact, the average American worker contributes five hundred disposable cups per year to those dumps, "cups that will still be sitting in the landfill five centuries from now."[26] What would it look like to use paper, Styrofoam, and plastic less?

  What other waste do you create in the course of your business? What waste-management alternatives might create less harm to the created world and human communities? Consider creating a paid internship or apprentice program for students with training in sustainability and ecological management or sustainable development (see Resources for Further Study at the back of this book for more information). You might be surprised by what happens when God's "bottom line" fits where it belongs. Focus their internship on making things "right" both ecologically *and* fiscally.

- *Let your entrepreneurial skills flow.* You have many opportunities to partner with architects, engineers, scientists, and farmers to solve various problems that could make spaces, structures, and systems more honoring to creation and more profitable. When I asked Marshall Teague how God's people could help places like EdenThistle, he saw an enormous need and opportunity for businesses and entrepreneurial types of all sorts to apply their acumen to the questions of how to feed our neighborhoods and world well while caring for God's creation in the process.

- *Start a social enterprise with the goal of ecological flourishing.* In your community, who will lead the charge to find new energy, new design, new partnerships to champion care for creation in our economic lives? Consider joining an ever-growing army of social entrepreneurs who are seeking to solve ecological issues.

Practicing Creation Care at Church

Consider: How much influence do you have in the body of King Jesus? How could the believers with whom you gather grow in regard to respecting God's good creation?

- *Preach, teach, share.* If you preach or teach or lead Bible studies or participate in a small group at your church, ask yourself, "How well do the people God has invited me to influence know God's perspective about the creation itself?" If you have one of these roles, make sure you teach about our vocations as caretakers of creation.

- *Practice better eating together.* Nearly every church has meals together. Increase the amount of healthy, fresh food that's prepared, served, and shared. Cut back on the amount of paper, plastic, and Styrofoam you use at those events. Every day the United States sends the equivalent of 63,000 garbage trucks of waste to the landfill.[27]

What if church meals became places where we learned to reduce this harmful environmental waste?

When you cater food, consider paying a bit more to order from businesses that grow food well and treat animals and the land with dignity and respect. In particular, we believe we can say with confidence that in the new heavens and new earth, chickens won't be crammed into tiny cages for the whole of their short lives and pigs won't sit in their own filth waiting to be fed the ground up remains of their cagemates. While there is room for debate and disagreement about what constitutes just practices of animal husbandry and crop farming, churches must educate and lead the way in supporting farmers who are reaching out toward the new creation reality in their practices today. In our opinion, certified pasture-raised chickens and eggs, foraged pork, and pasture-raised beef represent examples of products that ensure the chickens, pigs, and cows we eat were treated ethically (all these certifications indicate that the animals were raised in pastures rather than cages). While these decisions will cost more money (or require us to eat less), consider this part of your work of participating in Christ's renewal of his economy and his world. Furthermore, a lot of debate surrounds the practices (and certification process) behind these various labels; if we're going to take this aspect of our discipleship seriously, we'll have to be willing to do some further research on what is available where we shop (see the Resources for Further Study section in the back of the book).

This all could happen even better in small groups, community groups, and other home-based ministries of the church. As Katherine and Marshall Teague reminded us, it takes awhile to learn how to integrate many of these better eating practices into our lives. So do it together! Have small group feasts where you splurge on humanely raised meat or learn how to make delicious meals out of fresh veggies. Maybe even invite the farmer to come and share.

- *Practice better food shopping together.* Establish your church as a CSA drop-off site, and buy or subsidize boxes for lower-income members. Meet farmers working to care for creation and help them connect with congregants as potential customers. Advertise or attend farmers markets together. These direct connections to local producers are often the best way to ensure that the animals we eat were treated with the highest ethical standards.

- *Practice raising food together and put your space to use.* Could your church have a congregational community garden (or space for families to manage a raised bed)? Plant native trees on the church's property? Plant seedlings for distribution for the members' gardens or organize seedling swaps? Organize a workshop on how to grow tomatoes? Find ways to encourage families to participate in gardening together.

- *Organize students (of all ages) to learn and take care of the natural resources in your region.* Our culture is shaping our children into empty consumers who need to be "filled" to experience "success." But our discipleship plans should help them see Jesus's kingship over all he has made and sustains. Get the students in the woods, on a farm, learning about rivers, streams, and forests. Introduce them to people who earn their livelihood by working directly with land and animals. Done well, this is a multigenerational investment.[28]

- *Discover the "food deserts" in your region and organize others to help you and your fellow members take action.* Remember the example of Bonton Farms? Are similar communities near you? Do you live in one? If the people in your city with the least amount of money have no access to healthy food, you can pray and meet with others to begin dreaming about how to help—without hurting.[29]

Practicing Creation Care at Home

Finally, our homes are usually the places where we can exercise the most influence. And in becoming better stewards of creation, for most of us, our homes are the front lines we should not skip.

Vote with your money for the world that is to come. Our demands increase supply. So if we buy more from producers that treat animals with dignity and refuse environmentally harmful practices, we bend our economic lives toward creation care. You can do this by doing the following:

- *Commit to a local CSA.*
- *Buy meat (and other animal products) from farmers that treat animals with dignity.* Will the meat we eat arrive at our table via models that ignore God's delight in his beloved creatures or via farms and farmers that honor the design of animals? See the discussion above.
- *Shop at farmers markets.* Oftentimes, farmers on the cutting edge of trying to integrate creation care with sound economics are on smaller-scale farms that sell primarily to local markets. As a result, shopping at farmers markets can make it easier to find food that's been raised with care *and* support businesses that may struggle to sell their crops amidst cheaper alternatives that do not exhibit the same care of land and animals. Meet the farmers and ask them about their farms to better understand the complexity of the issues and how to participate.
- *See spending more on food products created with care as an act of Christian discipleship, and be willing to change eating habits as a result.* The Teague family reminded us that living with the grain of the universe almost certainly means eating less meat. And by cutting back, we can afford to spend more on meat that was ethically raised. Katherine Teague keeps a wonderful blog of recipes and other ideas on the EdenThistle website. Her writings include helpful tips about purchasing, preparing, preserving, and cooking.
- *Compost and garden at home.* Our family greatly reduced our waste when our son convinced us that this practice fit the view of the world we had taught him. Now, large portions of our waste go back into the urban soil we cultivate to grow fresh fruits and vegetables. Small portions of land produce way more than one family can consume in a given season. The opportunity to share presents itself readily.

And while gardening won't solve the world food crisis, it is an excellent formative practice, a spiritual economic discipline that's good for our health. When we garden, we grow in appreciation for those who raise the food we eat (because gardening is harder than it looks). We grow in our understanding of the rhythms of creation and the seasons. We grow in wonder at the world God has made, just as Job did when he encountered the wildness of God's world. And when

I (Michael) grow fresh veggies, I find myself infinitely more likely to eat them. For all these reasons, we believe gardening is a powerful discipline to shape us for creation care.

Start Practicing

Before moving on, take a moment and contemplate where to begin practicing creation care in your own life. Where are your easiest first steps? Consider: Who in your community is already passionate about or engaged in creation care? What do you know about the local food economy? What do you need to know about your neighborhood and city to grow in practicing creation care? Before finishing this chapter, identify how you, individually or with a group, can practice creation care within the next month.

I will practice creation care within the next month by . . .

_____

_____

_____

_____

The Creation Care Key: Conclusion

Since God created us to serve and take care of his good creation (see Gen. 2:15), his work to redeem us restores us to our basic job. We were created to glorify God as embodied creatures in his good creation order. God's rescuing grace restores us to this calling. As disciples of King Jesus, we must anchor our economic activity in commitments to honor the land and other living creatures as gifts to be cared for and stewarded. Such careful stewardship will require us to recognize creation's fundamental role in glorifying God both now and in the new heavens and new earth, and embrace economic practices that avoid harming and pursue the flourishing of creation.

"THE LORD HAS GIVEN YOU THE SABBATH"

THE REST KEY IN SCRIPTURE

> See! The LORD has given you the Sabbath.
>
> Moses to rescued Israel,
> Exodus 16:29 ESV

> The Sabbath reminds God's image that they are his regents to serve him. . . .
> A person who feels inclined to work seven days a week should examine what
> god he or she worships.
>
> Bruce Waltke

> If rest is learned through habit and repetition, so is restlessness. These habits
> of rest or restlessness form us over time. . . . Sleep exposes reality. We are
> frail and weak.
>
> Tish Harrison Warren

> The Sabbath teaches all beings whom to praise.
>
> Abraham Joshua Heschel

> Sabbathless toil is a violation of God's intention for our lives and our whole
> economy. . . . Any serious commitment to Sabbath involves doing our best

237

to ensure that the people who serve us—especially those who serve out of sight, not just the waitress but the dishwasher, not just the store cashier but the nightshift cleaning crew—are provided wages and benefits that allow for hourly, weekly, and yearly rhythms of rest.

Andy Crouch

Sabbath is a school for our desires.

Walter Brueggemann

Running on Fumes . . .

Just for a moment, try a little experiment. Grab a pen and write down in the boxes below every metaphor or expression you can think of for these two states of being: (1) *exhausted* (example: "I'm beat") and (2) *super busy* (example: "I'm swamped"). Go ahead. Take a couple of minutes. Make two lists using the space provided below, using one for exhausted and one for super busy.

Exhausted	Super Busy

Okay. How many expressions did you think of? What were they?

Here are a few (thirty-two to be exact) common metaphors and expressions for describing exhaustion:

"I'm beat." "I'm burned out." "I'm wiped out." "I'm spent." "I'm shot." "I'm sapped."

"I'm fried." "I'm cooked." "I'm baked."

"I'm drained." "I'm pooped." "I'm frazzled." "I'm coming apart at the seams."

"I'm wearing thin." "I'm worn out . . . strung out . . . wrung out."

"I'm at the end of my rope." "I'm hanging on by a thread."

"I'm running on empty." "I'm running on fumes." "I'm out of gas."

"I'm dragging." "I'm run-down." "I'm zonked."

"I'm sinking fast." "I'm about to crash." "I'm ready to drop."

"This job/project/relationship is eating me alive."

"I'm dog-tired." "I'm bone-tired." "I'm dead-tired."

Here are a few (only eighteen this time, because I was too busy to think of . . . wait . . . never mind) common expressions for being overly busy:

"I'm running myself ragged." "I'm running around like a chicken with my head cut off." "I'm chasing my tail."[1]

"I'm under a pile." "I'm under an avalanche." "I'm snowed under."

"I'm stretched too thin." "I'm stretched to the corners."

"I'm weighed down." "I'm overloaded." "I'm overtaxed."

"I'm swamped." "I'm drowning."

"I've got too much on my plate." "I'm spinning too many plates."

"I've got too many plates in the air."

"I'm working myself to the bone." "He's gonna work himself to death."

Need a nap? Yeah, us too! Now, how many metaphors or expressions can you quickly think of for "well rested and refreshed"? Fill these in using the space below. Take your time.

Well Rested and Refreshed

Get the point?

Expressions for our exhaustion and busyness fly off the tongue readily. But it is much harder to think of one for anything approaching calm and rested. Metaphors are like linguistic lenses through which we view the world. Moreover, they assume, reflect, and reinforce aspects of our culture that we take for granted. This is why they are so hard to translate from one culture to another.

No wonder, then, that we find it so much easier to conjure up expressions of exhaustion than of rest! We in the West are super busy, super tired, and increasingly aware that, to use yet another metaphor, we're just spinning our wheels. We know it deep in our dead-tired bones. Who will rescue us from this frantic freneticism of death?

Throughout the book, we've explored a series of spiritual disciplines for our economic lives, a toolbox of practices to shape our hearts toward God's economy. Many of these practices call us to labor in new and exciting ways toward a renewed vision of God's world and our work in it.

The bad news is that most of us have spent the better part of our lives engaging in practices that *deform* us. In fact, as workaholism, endless activity, and constant technological connectivity increasingly emerge as ways of life for us, any new effort has the danger of becoming a deforming practice. Where will we get the wisdom to practice the King's economy well? This final key is about a God-given practice called Sabbath that, in many ways, ties all the rest together. This practice demands that we not only *do* something but also *receive* something as a blessed and holy gift from God.

Creation: Climactic Rest

Once again, we return to the beginning. While we've emphasized the importance of humans as God's image bearers and creation as God's beloved garden, neither are the lead actors in the drama of Scripture. No, Yahweh is the star of the show from the moment the curtain rises in Genesis 1:1. Intriguingly, his *resting* marks the climax of the first scene in the opening act of the play.

In the ancient world, kings rested after they conquered their enemies and established their dominions. So the Creator's rest reminds us of God's rule over every dominion. God's work was done. God's good order was in place.[2]

Genesis 2:1–3 further unpacks the character of this Creator God who rested at the end of his workweek:

> So the heaven and the earth and all their host were finished. On the seventh day God finished his work which he had done, and he rested on the seventh day from all his work which he had done. God blessed the seventh day and set it apart as holy, for on it God rested from all his work which he had done when he created.[3]

Remember, this is Yahweh, who makes people in his image and calls us to imitate him. So just notice for a moment the pattern of God's work as it's presented in this passage:

God finished his work (he stopped).

God rested from his work (he enjoyed the results).

God sanctified time (he set it apart as holy).

That's the way God works . . . and rests. God didn't come to the office to "check on creation in anxiety to be sure it was all working."[4] What does that mean for the rest of us? To find out, let's fast-forward to the next book of the Bible: Exodus.

Exodus: Rescued from Bondage to Rest

Now, imagine for a moment the first audiences to hear that creation story as Scripture. They were the descendants of Abraham, Isaac, and Jacob who followed Joseph into Egypt (see Exod. 1). While Abraham's family did okay in this foreign land while Joseph lived, as we've seen in earlier chapters, under Pharaoh's reign, they became taken-for-granted, marginalized, subdominant slaves. In covenant faithfulness, Yahweh came to rescue them. He bore them up on eagles' wings and brought them *out* of bondage and *to* himself (see Exod. 19:4).

This story is all about different kings and different kingdoms. You see, Exodus recounts the Israelites groaning under the hard service of Pharaoh and his government (see Exod. 1:14; 6:5). But this same language is used in Exodus 7:16 to describe Yahweh telling Pharaoh to "let my people go, that they may *serve* me in the wilderness" (ESV, emphasis added). The Israelites' problem, then, wasn't simply that they were slaves needing to be set free but, rather, that they were "slaves to the wrong master and [needed] to be reclaimed and restored to their proper Lord."[5] Exodus tells the story of Yahweh rescuing the Israelites from the darkness of Pharaoh's kingdom and transferring them into his own kingdom.

So let's compare kingdoms. Exodus chapters 1 and 5 give us important details about how the pharaohs reigned.

- Rooted in fear they practiced: top-down control, violent brutality, and heartless cruelty (see Exod. 1).
- Rooted in cynical pride they practiced: unreasonable demands, deceptive propaganda, and demeaning speech (see Exod. 5).

So Israel languished in misery and bitterness under heavy burdens, mass genocide, and deceptive regimes. Old Testament scholar Ellen Davis describes Egyptian cave paintings depicting starving gleaners begging for or even viciously fighting over a few scraps—right next to the Egyptian workforce raking in an abundant harvest. Such was economic life under the pharaoh.[6] Now, put yourself in the Israelites' sandals as they stood on the freedom side of the Red Sea and began to get to know their new King. Earlier in this book we described the Israelites in the desert as entering God's Wilderness School of Economics. But if manna made up God's Econ 101, it also introduced the topic of God's 300-level Advanced Econ class: Sabbath.[7] The Sabbath as embodied already in the manna economy was central for *reforming* Israel's economic imagination, perhaps even the primary classroom for *reshaping* Israel's economic desires. Sabbath isn't simply "the pause that refreshes. It is the pause that transforms."[8]

Can you imagine hearing Yahweh, your new Almighty Overlord who just snatched you out of slavery in Egypt so you could serve him, say, "Tomorrow is to be a day of rest, a holy Sabbath to the Lord. I'll give you twice as much as you need on the sixth day so everybody can take a day off on the seventh" (see Exod. 16:22–23)? How many days off do you think those oppressed Israelites got when they were stuck on Pharaoh's assembly lines? Imagine the relentless groaning of broken men and child laborers in Egypt, the noisy crack of the slave masters' whips giving way to the previously unknown silence of a day off, an afternoon manna picnic, perhaps even a midmorning nap. Picture the people adjusting to this aspect of the new economy under the true King:

Youngest child: "Mom, what should we do today?"

Mom (sleeping in later than usual): "Let's just soak in all that's happened."

Firstborn: "Dad, shouldn't we go gather manna first?"

Dad: "No need, child. Yahweh's taken care of that . . . just like he said he would."

How wonderful this message must have been in the ears of the recently rescued slaves: "No work. A break from labor. The world won't end if we take our hands off the levers. Creation won't crumble if we don't clock in." Sabbath rest is heard as something that would have been impossible in Pharaoh's Egyptian economy:

"We have dignity."

"We are more than our brick quota."

"We are more than brick producers."

Of course, these people had lived in bondage for generations, so some of them went out on the Sabbath expecting to find manna anyway (see Exod. 16:27). A lifetime in the "economy of scarcity" was hard to shake.[9] Having had to grasp for scraps from Pharaoh's table, the Israelites found it difficult to accept the unmanageable, uncontrollable gift of God's table in the wilderness.

So when some of them rejected God's Sabbath day off and headed on into the office, Moses rebuked them with a question . . .

> How long will you refuse to keep my commands and my instructions? (Exod. 16: 28)

. . . *and* a word of grace.

> See! The LORD has given you the Sabbath; therefore on the sixth day he gives you bread for two days. (v. 29 ESV)

Freedom and reliable provision would take some getting used to. Yahweh hadn't really explained the Sabbath yet, manna was a miracle, and in any case, "One might expect some sympathy for wilderness travelers (and former slaves) who try to exercise some moderate control over the food supply."[10] But Moses and Yahweh insisted on this early Sabbath practice in relation to manna because they knew that it was essential to draw an "absolute contrast" between Egypt's economy and Yahweh's economy.[11] Yahweh used Sabbath rest and dependence to shape his people's hearts to trust him enough to embrace his economy.

> Yahweh used Sabbath rest and dependence to shape his people's hearts to trust him enough to embrace his economy.

Mount Sinai: Regulating Rest

When Yahweh brought the Israelites to Mount Sinai, he reminded them of their ultimate mission and identity: "You will be for me," Yahweh declared, "a kingdom of priests and a holy nation" (Exod. 19:6). Through embodying the justice and righteousness of God, the Israelites were to not only create the kind of neighborhood where we all want to live but also show the world what it means to live as image bearers of Yahweh. Central to all this were the ten guidelines (which we know as the Ten Commandments) for the good neighborhood. The commandments provide one of the clearest descriptions of Yahweh's kingdom. His neighborhood shall be a place:

Of honor and long life (see Exod. 20:12)

Free of violence (see v. 13)

Where no one shacks up with your spouse (see v. 14)

Where no one takes your stuff (see v. 15)

Where you can trust your neighbors (see v. 16)

Where people *want* what's best for one another (see v. 17)

This paraphrase of the second half of the Ten Commandments describes an actual community. People will share life together, and it will be good. How will that work?

The first half of the commandments, which call the Israelites to worship Yahweh alone, is the key. God will dwell in their midst, and if they'll listen to his voice and practice what he prescribes, life will go well. So this means the following:

No other gods (see v. 3)

Not even idols or images (see vv. 4–6)

Don't misuse the name of the one true God who rescued you—Yahweh (see v. 7)

So far, so good. Notice, though, what stands in the middle. The longest commandment, which pulls the two parts together, is the fourth—the Sabbath commandment.

Remember the Sabbath day, to keep it holy. Six days you shall labor, and do all your work, but the seventh day is a Sabbath to the LORD your God. On it you shall not do any work, you, or your son, or your daughter, your male servant, or your female servant, or your livestock, or the sojourner who is within your gates. For in six days the LORD made heaven and earth, the sea, and all that is in them, and rested on the seventh day. Therefore the LORD blessed the Sabbath day and made it holy. (Exod. 20:8–11 ESV)

The version in Deuteronomy 5:14–15 begins the same but provides a different justification for the Sabbath:

Remember that you were slaves in Egypt and that the LORD your God brought you out of there with a mighty hand and an outstretched arm. Therefore the LORD your God has commanded you to observe the Sabbath day. (Deut. 5:15)

This fourth commandment ties the two parts of the Big Ten together. The first part of the law is our duty to God. The second part is our duty to other people. This fits Jesus's own testimony that the two greatest commandments are to love God and love neighbor (see Matt. 22:37–40). But right there in the middle of these two sections is the Sabbath, standing somehow as the glue that holds love of God and neighbor together. Indeed, as we shall see, the Sabbath is a day set apart for outrageous love of God and others.

> Sabbath rest reminded the Israelites that they'd been rescued from the relentless labor of Pharaoh's economy and welcomed into a pattern of work and rest that reflects Yahweh's own habits and the very structures of his created world.

Furthermore, the Sabbath command connects Israel's redemption to God's purposes as Creator (in Exodus) and Redeemer (in Deuteronomy).[12] Sabbath rest reminded the Israelites that they'd been rescued from the relentless labor of Pharaoh's economy and welcomed into a pattern of work and rest that reflects Yahweh's own habits and the very structures of his created world.

In the Ten Commandments, then, is a central *command* from Yahweh about how to imitate his workplace policy on labor and rest.

Remember it.

Keep it holy.

Do no work.

Sabbath practice was part of God's process for shaping his people into his just and righteous kingdom and priests. Let's unpack how this worked, particularly in relation to the Sabbath as a way to love neighbors.

Sabbath: Giving and Receiving Rest

First, let's consider the original *recipients* of this gracious Sabbath gift. In several reiterations of the Sabbath command, Yahweh made it clear that the Sabbath was for:

> You, your children, your servants, your animals, and immigrants in the community . . . (Exod. 20:10, paraphrase)

> . . . so that all of these groups, including the most marginalized, "may rest, as you do" (Deut. 5:14) and so "be refreshed" . . . (Exod. 23:12)

> . . . because Yahweh rescued you from harsh slavery to Pharaoh and brought you out with a mighty arm (Deut 5:15, paraphrase).

Sabbath was, in other words, a law with a life-giving purpose: to give a regular opportunity for rest to even the most marginalized members of the neighborhood.

This was truly remarkable. God's purpose for "you shall do no work" was explicit: *rest and refreshment* for servants, hired workers, immigrants, and even animals. Apparently interpreting a law like this as God's gifts of rest and refreshment *for themselves* came fairly naturally to the Israelites. Applying a law like this to animals, servants, and strangers was less natural. But Scripture makes Yahweh's intentions explicit. Sabbath was a life-giving gift for his kingdom of priests and anyone, including the animals, connected to them. Because endless work runs counter to God's good created order, when Yahweh was in charge, nobody was enslaved to their jobs. Everybody got a break. As G. K. Chesterton so memorably put it, once people got around to making a holy day for God, they found they'd gotten a holiday for people.[13]

Take a moment and consider the economics of this command. First, realize that even relatively wealthy Israelites by ancient standards would have been dangerously close to impoverishment according to our standards today. Keep in mind that the family farm was everything economically and that agriculture required constant attention (and during some seasons, a rush of activity to ensure that everything got planted or harvested before the weather ruined all their hard work). Now imagine Yahweh legislating that the head of the farm—and everyone involved in the family business—had to stop working completely one day out of every seven.

Practicing Sabbath, in other words, required the Israelites to trust Yahweh completely. The Sabbath clearly says "thus far and no further" to the work lives of God's people. You can almost hear Israel's Economic Policy Council saying to Moses, "This Sabbath rest is just job-killing regulation! It'll limit productivity!" And so—in part because of how radical this gift-law was—Yahweh made sure the Israelites didn't try to hedge their Sabbath bets. They couldn't "trust" Yahweh by taking a break themselves while quietly sending their servants and foreign hired workers out into the fields with their ox and donkey. They couldn't give religious-language lip service to their trust in God while making sure their bank accounts remained bent on building as much wealth as possible. The Sabbath, with its limitations and boundaries, was a *requirement* for everyone and a *gift* to everyone. Everyone could rest because God had committed to provide.

Moreover, the phrase "rest *as well as you*" (Deut. 5:14 ESV) identifies the Sabbath as "the great day of equality when all are at rest."[14] To take a quick look at where we're going, in the words of one Old Testament scholar:

> Not all are equal in production. Some perform much more effectively than others. Not all are equal in consumption. Some have greater access to consumer goods. In a society defined by production and consumption, there are huge gradations of performance, and, therefore, of worth and significance. In such a social system everyone is coerced to perform better—produce more, consume more—be a good shopper! Such valuing, of course, creates "haves" and "have nots," significant and insignificant, rich and poor, people with access and people denied access. But Sabbath breaks that gradation . . . Because this one day breaks the pattern . . . all are like you, equal—equal worth, equal value, equal access, equal rest.[15]

Because all are equal in God's sight, all ought to experience work as the Lord designed it. As Mark Glanville points out, the way Deuteronomy uses service/slave language in the Sabbath commandment draws a close connection between the Sabbath and the exodus from slavery. This connection "suggests that work is exploitative if there is no provision for rest . . . bad work requires deliverance while good work requires rest."[16]

From Sabbath Days to Sabbatical Systems

There's more, though. As God's Word unfolds, we find the Sabbath day opened up an entire way of marking time that included Sabbath *years* and *cycles of years*. And Yahweh prepared his people for hearing about this expanded Sabbath by creating empathy among them for the marginalized in their midst.

Perhaps we have paid too little attention to the "empathy orientation" that grounds the Sabbath practice. The first people to receive Scripture as Scripture were rescued slaves. Not mystics seeking God. Not theologians seeking (or preserving) the transcendental truths of the universe. Not kings conquering enemies. Not seers or diviners or magicians. They were slaves. And Yahweh wanted their experience of slavery, sorrow, and rescue to shape how they worshiped and followed him. Listen to Yahweh's words about this history and its expected impact on the Israelites' hearts and minds:

> You shall not oppress a sojourner. You know the heart of a sojourner, for you were sojourners in the land of Egypt. (Exod. 23:9 ESV)[17]

This reminder, meant to engender empathy for others experiencing any form of sorrow or oppression, leads immediately into the law regarding the sabbatical year.

> For six years you shall sow your land and gather in its yield, but the seventh year you shall let it rest and lie fallow, that the poor of your people may eat; and what they leave the beasts of the field may eat. You shall do likewise with your vineyard, and with your olive orchard. (vv. 10–11 ESV)

The description of the Sabbath years in Leviticus 25:1–7 and Deuteronomy 15 add the land, wild and domestic animals, slaves, hired servants, and indebted neighbors to the list of those blessed by this Sabbath rest. Such a year of rest allowed the land to produce food for the marginalized. Furthermore, as Deuteronomy 15 makes clear, the Israelites were also required to give a "rest" to those who owed them money. Thus, forgiving debts was added to the list of those practices appropriate to people whose lives are marked by Sabbath (see the chart).

Passage	Beneficiaries	Benefit
Exodus 23:10–11	the land, the poor, animals	rest/refreshment
Leviticus 25:1–7	the land, you, family, slaves, hired servants, immigrants, domestic animals, wild animals	rest/sustenance
Deuteronomy 15	poor indebted neighbors	debt cancellation

Several aspects stand out as we engage this Sabbath year. First, notice that it means 365 days of straight Sabbath. Wrap your mind around that: the weekly Sabbath was preparation for a yearlong Sabbath every seventh year! Can you even imagine? A whole twelve months of rest and restoration, an interruption in the relentless rush of economic life? Surely this law was a gift of divine grace.

Second, notice that the principle of resting from relentless work spilled over into new territory. In the Sabbath year, God called his people to both rest and give rest in the face of other economic practices that enslave. The sabbatical year required that loans were forgiven (see Deut. 15:1–11). In the ancient world, debt was often used to get the labor or the land of the one who had borrowed. Releasing these debts every seven years jammed a spoke in the credit and debt wheel that so often rushed relentlessly on toward dispossession and enslavement.

The Sabbath year spelled out the implications of embracing an economy of abundance and trust rather than of grasping and scarcity. The sabbatical year ensured that Israelites could neither enslave themselves *nor others* in the endless pursuit of more. Indeed, Sabbath rest from work and debt "reenacted" the exodus from bondage.[18] Sabbath days and Sabbath years represented a refusal to run the rat race for oneself and the rejection of coveting in relationship to one's neighbors.[19] Once Israel recognized they were not in control, once they took their hands off the wheel, they found themselves free to rest and to give rest to others.

Third, this Sabbath Year wasn't just some liberal social program. The Sabbath year was kept to Yahweh (see Lev. 25:2, 4), just like the regular weekly Sabbath. This was deeply religious, an act of worship, a yearlong celebration dedicated to honoring and giving glory to the divine King.

Finally, though, let's answer the question many of us start asking the moment we encounter this bizarre bit of Old Testament legislation: How did these people eat if they couldn't prepare crops (sow fields or prune vines) or harvest crops (reap or gather any produce)? The answer is simple—they had the "Sabbath produce of the land to eat" (Lev. 25:6 NET). In the absence of organized planting and harvesting (see Lev. 25:5–6),[20] the land provided for all simply through the gratuitous abundance of God's good creation order in action. In other words, the Sabbath year made everybody get out and glean together.

Remember the manna economy? This is what it looked like in the land. For an entire year, the wealthiest landowners in the village, the poorest beggar on the street, and the most recently arrived refugee all got out and reminded themselves through a year of abnormal economic activity that all ate only because of God's grace. The Israelites had already experienced this with the manna, but the farms and fields of the promised land could tempt them to believe that they deserved the economic rewards of their labor, that their own hard work had won abundance for them (see Deut. 8:11–18). So Yahweh gave them a year to remember that everybody, from the top of the social hierarchy all the way down, is merely a gleaner in the fields of the Ultimate Landowner, Yahweh himself. Even the Israelites were simply "foreigners and strangers" in God's land (Lev. 25:23).

Just imagine it: every family business shuts its doors for regular work for a year. For twelve long months, the business owner and his family take a break from hiring, lending, paying wages. Together with a Middle Eastern janitor and an undocumented high school dropout who works the register, the family gathers in the goods that God himself makes spring up out of the ground.

Rich and poor gleaning together—receiving life as a sheer, unearned gift.

Native and foreigner gleaning together—no divisions among them.

Humans and animals benefitting from the land, even as the land itself enjoyed a Sabbath rest to Yahweh.

This practice, this way of scheduling economic and social time, engrained humility, gratitude, and wonder in rich and poor, local and foreigner alike. Indeed, such a practice undergirded an entire economic way of life aimed, as we saw in chapter 4, at the potlucking community. The Israelites released debts because the borrower was a *brother* (see Deut. 15:7). They limited debt and took an economic break so that members of the extended family could remain members of the community living in God's land (see Lev. 25:36).

Yet such family self-care welcomed even immigrants into the Sabbath way of life, into a generous kingdom, a family of justice and mercy, marked by economic and ethnic diversity. Here all kinds of people were unified, receiving life as it was intended, as a rich gift to be enjoyed and shared justly. This picture of our ancestors is an image of the world as it should be.

Oh, and by the way, the Sabbath system got even better. The culmination of Yahweh's system of Sabbaths was the Year of Jubilee (see Lev. 25:8–55) that we discussed earlier. In the Equity Key, we focused on the Jubilee's insistence that nobody get permanently disenfranchised from a piece of the economic pie, that nobody get permanently pushed off their plot of the promised land. But for our purposes here, note that this fiftieth year also would have been the second year in a row that no one was allowed to work.[21]

Old Testament scholar Chris Wright has argued that the institution of the Jubilee was designed "to have a built-in future dimension."[22] In other words, Yahweh demanded that Israel's economic arrangements always look ahead toward this giant Jubilee party. It limited long-term negative arrangements and encouraged just transactions in relationship. With its focus on release from bondage and restoration to ancestral lands, the Jubilee wove hope into Israel's macro-rhythms of time, even as the weekly Sabbath wove trust and submission into their micro-rhythms of time.[23] And it brought together each Israelite's dependence on the grace of the Lord and their love of neighbor, because the Jubilee was proclaimed on the Day of Atonement. "To know yourself forgiven by God was to issue immediately in practical remission of the debt and bondage of others."[24]

As a whole, then, the sabbatical systems helped the Israelites remember, celebrate, and live out their redemption from bondage in Egypt by their redeeming, creating King. The Sabbath system set up "God's Temple in time,"[25] creating a *place* within the rhythms of economic and social life to meet God, delight in his gifts, and welcome neighbors in love.

> The institution of the Jubilee was designed "to have a built-in future dimension." . . . Israel's economic arrangements always look ahead toward this giant Jubilee party.

Of course, such a radical way of economic life was difficult to embrace. After their redemption from Egyptian bondage, the Israelites would need rescue from another form of bondage, one they chose for themselves by worshiping idols, oppressing their neighbors, and ignoring the Sabbath. They would need a new exodus.

New Exodus: Rescue from Idolatry to Serve the Living and True God

Again and again the prophets announced coming judgment on Israel and Judah due to their worship of lifeless idols. As we saw in chapter 1, again and again God's people went after gods who promised to deliver the socioeconomic goods. Worshiping these false gods also freed up the Israelites to oppress their neighbors, not least by rejecting the Sabbath calendar.

So when the farmer-turned-prophet Amos showed up on the scene, he had some strong words for God's people. Imagine for a moment that a prophet bursts into your church this Sunday, points his finger at everyone, and declares: "God hates your choir! Your preaching! Your pipe organ (or bass guitar or mandolin or cello)! He hates what you put in the plate! He hates your stupid Sunday schools! He refuses to hear your meaningless prayers or show up when you take the Lord's Supper! Do you know why? Because your celebration of this day doesn't translate into acts of justice, love, and mercy for your poor neighbors, the refugee family living down the street, the fatherless and underemployed from the other side of the tracks." It would make for an interesting Sunday, you can say that much.

That's essentially what Amos said when he found wealthy members of God's people spending the entire Sabbath day longing for it to wrap up so they could get back to cooking the books in their trade and selling the poor into debt slavery for the price of a pair of sandals (see Amos 8:5–6). "All the while they keep Sabbath, they are in fact, in their imaginations, buying and selling and trading and bargaining. The appearance is one of *rest*, but . . . the social reality is one of restlessness, for the pattern of acquisitiveness is not interrupted."[26] Because of this trampling of the poor (see v. 4) Yahweh hated their religious feasts . . . and promised to turn them into funerals instead of festivals. Yahweh was serious about his Sabbaths. Apparently the Israelites couldn't worship Yahweh without their full commitment to receive rest and to give rest to others.

In another famous passage, Isaiah rebukes Israel for their empty religious practices that are disconnected from their obligations to the poor. Their "fasting" was for selfish gain (see Isaiah 58:3). Therefore their "devotion" was bound up with oppression of their workers, competitive quarreling, and physical violence (v. 4). Yahweh simply refused to hear it. He detested such religiosity. What he longed for from his people included

- rescuing the oppressed and bringing down oppressive systems (see v. 6),
- treating the hungry poor like family (see vv. 7, 9–10), and ultimately
- seeking him for support and protection (see vv. 8–12).[27]

Notice, however, that the Bible moves directly from this famous passage on the fasting God required to the Sabbath he demanded (see vv. 13–14). God wasn't changing subjects here. Proper Sabbath observance went hand in hand with proper fasting—honor God by serving his image bearers in their distress. If one was not to turn away when a neighbor's ox or sheep or donkey went astray or fell down (see Deut. 22:1–4), surely one was not to ignore situations or systems that cripple a neighbor.

To "call the Sabbath a delight" (Isa. 58:13 ESV) was both to take "delight in the LORD" himself (v. 14) *and* to act in liberating love toward one's neighbor. As we will see, the more we know the generous God of liberating grace, the more we will want to see others released from any form of dehumanizing bondage: systemic, economic, political, personal, spiritual, emotional, or psychological. If our lives are shaped by living in God's liberating Sabbath time, we will find ourselves committed to offering that same liberating life of debt forgiveness, justice, and rest to others.

Jesus: Lord of the Sabbath—King of Jubilee

What about the New Testament? We would do well to begin where Jesus began with his Year of Jubilee announcement in his first sermon at Nazareth (see Luke 4:16–21). At the start of his ministry, Jesus "got behind the pulpit" on the Sabbath to announce the imminent arrival of the sabbatical year.

This sermon is critical and summarizes the initial launch of Jesus's kingdom activities. Jesus declared his purpose was to "preach the good news of the kingdom of God" (v. 43 ESV).[28] Luke 5 then recounts how Jesus proclaimed and enacted that kingdom (cleansing a leper and healing a disabled person).

These gracious words and merciful deeds led to a conflict with some Pharisees (on the Sabbath), who thought Jesus's disciples were Sabbath breakers because they gleaned grain on the Sabbath. In the ensuing conflict, Jesus declared himself to be the one who holds authority over holy Sabbath time: "The Son of Man is Lord of the Sabbath" (Luke 6:5). In Mark's version, we get the fuller explanation for Jesus's apparently easygoing approach to his disciples' Sabbath behavior: "The Sabbath was made for man, not man for the Sabbath" (Mark 2:27).

Jesus claimed the authority to define and describe the Sabbath. He is Lord of it. And he used that lordship to remind his Pharisee adversaries of the point of the whole institution: the Sabbath is a gift for God's people. There's an interpretation we can live with! It's a day made for us—for our benefit. The Pharisees' boundary-making, external purity-driven approach missed the point entirely.

Since the Sabbath is made for *humanity*, Jesus was quick to point out that "keeping Sabbath" can't serve as a shield to protect us from loving our neighbors. Because we have the whole day to rest and celebrate, if someone needs care and attention, we have resources, including time, to share. If someone owes us money, we live in an economy with rhythms that include a release from debt that mirrors our own forgiveness from God (see Matt. 6:11–12).

For many of us, perhaps, the idea of the Sabbath has been reduced simply to stopping. God knows we have enough trouble with just that part. Yet, as we have seen, the Sabbath also clears out space for love, worship, and welcoming service. It pauses our relentless economic quest for ourselves so that we might embrace economic service and sharing with others as part of our worship of God. Jesus, if anything, turned up the volume on this Sabbath-for-the-marginalized aspect.

This is the obvious point of Jesus's statement on the Sabbath. His characteristic Sabbath actions make his words even clearer. If we want to understand what the Lord of the Sabbath would say to us about this good gift to humanity, all we need to do is watch what he did.

Throughout the Gospels Jesus fulfilled the Jubilee by enacting the liberating righteousness and mercy described in that early Nazareth sermon's quotation of Isaiah (see Luke 4:16–21). He healed a man with an unclean spirit (see Mark 1:21–28), Simon Peter's ill mother-in-law (see vv. 29–31), those who were sick or oppressed by demons and many others who were ill with various diseases (vv. 32–34), a man with a withered hand (see Mark 3:1–6; Luke 6:6–11), and one who had been disabled for thirty-eight years (see John 5:1–17), as well as a man born blind (see John 9)—all on the Sabbath and all in the face of condemnation from the religious elite. For Jesus, the Sabbath was just the right day for setting others free from all that oppressed them. For Jesus, the question was simple: Is the Sabbath for doing good or doing evil? For saving life or taking it? (See Mark 3:4.)

King Jesus Is Risen from the Dead—the Firstfruits of the New Creation

Jesus's greatest miracle of all—his death and resurrection—deepens and transforms our perspective on Sabbath time.

> After this, Jesus, knowing that all was now finished, said (to fulfill the Scripture), "I thirst." A jar full of sour wine stood there, so they put a sponge full of the sour wine on a hyssop branch and held it to his mouth. When Jesus

had received the sour wine, he said, "It is finished," and he bowed his head and gave up his spirit. (John 19:28–30 ESV)

According to John, Jesus's death happened at the end of the sixth day. Just as Yahweh finished his work on the sixth day of creation (see Gen. 2:1–3), Jesus brought his work to completion on the sixth day. He finished his greatest act of setting prisoners free just before the Sabbath, and on that last Sabbath, he rested the rest of death itself. In this way, Jesus fulfilled the law in its entirety. He finished his work on the sixth day. He rested on the last Sabbath of the old order of things.

Of course, the story doesn't end there. Early on the first day of a new week, Jesus rose from the dead. Standing in a garden and mistaken for a gardener, this second Adam began the work of re-creating and reconciling all things (see John 20:15).[29]

Throughout the entire old covenant, God's people worked six days and rested on the seventh day. But once the Lord of the Sabbath came, announcing good news, enacting salvation, dying on the sixth day, resting on that final Sabbath, and rising on the first day of a new week of New Creation, God's new covenant people began to gather in celebration "on the first day of the week" (Acts 20:7; see also 1 Cor. 16:2). Pretty quickly, they started calling this new day "the Lord's Day" (Rev. 1:10). This shift in the calendar shapes our hearts to experience a greater rest than could ever have been made available to God's people prior to the resurrection of our King.

As a pastor, this is one of the things I most want to sink deeply into the hearts and minds of God's people. I want them to experience deep soul rest due to the finished work of King Jesus. In the old covenant, we worked *toward* rest, as the culmination of six days of labor. Now that King Jesus has finished the work he was sent to accomplish, we work *from* rest. We begin each week in rest and in celebration of his victory over sin and guilt and shame and death and violence and every evil power. Jesus has completed his work!

When we begin each week in rest and celebration, we are confessing that his work on our behalf is perfect. Nothing is left for me to do to be reconciled to God. When we begin each week in rest and celebration, we are hailing his victory, his rightful rule over all things, even before everyone acknowledges the same (see Phil. 2:9–11). Every week begins in hope. Jesus Christ is risen from the dead. When we begin each week in rest and celebration, before we resume normal activities as his servants, we delight in his finished work with God's gathered people and collectively receive the riches of his presence in the Spirit according to his promise (see Matt. 18:15–20; 28:20; Heb. 7–12). We do not labor, even labor for the Lord, toward rest. We labor, even labor for the Lord, from rest.

Leaning toward the Glorious Future

Of course, some passages in Paul's writing make it seem as if, by the time we get past Jesus, the Sabbath gets swept away completely (see Rom. 14:5–6; Gal. 4:8–10; and Col. 2:16–17). But we need to recognize that the issue at hand in these letters is not whether a day of rest is a good gift to be received from the Creator. These passages are primarily concerned with Jewish and Gentile believers accepting one another in Christ. For instance, in the case of Galatians 4:10, Paul was trying to make sure Gentile believers didn't get bossed around by Jewish believers zealous to turn them into *Jews*-in-Christ (emphasis on Jews).

Following Christ's death and resurrection, many of the commands given to the Israelites as God's chosen people were no longer binding, such as the prohibitions on eating certain types of food (see Acts 10:1–33). However, the Sabbath reflects God's own example prior to his giving specific laws to Israel; the Sabbath pattern of work and rest reflects the design of his world. Furthermore, Sabbath is one of the Big Ten, and we all know that Christ's fulfillment of the law doesn't free us up to lie, murder, and steal. Unfortunately, most of us act as though there are nine commandments rather than ten.

The three passages mentioned above (Rom. 14:5–6; Gal. 4:10; and Col. 2:16–17) should free every believer from overprescribing how to practice Sabbath rest for themselves and especially caution every believer from overprescribing how to practice Sabbath rest for others. In particular, various professions or seasons (during a medical residency or while working in a disaster relief situation, for instance) certainly complicate the practice of Sabbath in a fixed way. However, Scripture's consistent witness to structuring the rhythms of our lives around cycles of working and resting/giving rest means that we ought seriously to consider how to practice Sabbath rhythms in our lives.

The Rest Key in Scripture: Summary

Summarizing this biblical flyover of Sabbath in primarily economic terms, we can make the following six summary points.

1. *Practicing Sabbath means stopping.* When we reflect God's glory as the Sabbath-making Creator, we get to do something wonderful: we get to stop. This stopping is a confession of our limits, an attunement to our own design as dependent creatures. Moreover, Sabbath is an "act of resistance" that "declares in bodily ways that we will not participate in the anxiety system that pervades our social environment."[30] We can come out of our culture's never-stopping time and enter the time of rest, worship, and neighborliness that Yahweh sets apart as holy and offers us.

   > Moreover, Sabbath is an "act of resistance" that "declares in bodily ways that we will not participate in the anxiety system that pervades our social environment."

2. *Practicing Sabbath means worshiping Yahweh rather than our idols.* Practicing Sabbath creates a "temple in time," making worship of God a regular part of our life rhythms. But this doesn't happen if we choose independence, self-sufficiency, and autonomy instead of Sabbath. Since we are worshipers, if we dodge the God of the Sabbath, we bow down to some other portion of God's creation and make it our blind, deaf, and powerless master. The idols we create for ourselves require our endless, relentless service. They demand more and more bricks without supplying straw. They seek to convince us that we exist for them. If you can't stop or don't know how to rest, look for the demanding deities barking out orders. There's no rest for the weary with these lords.

   When we practice Sabbath in worship of Yahweh, we begin to live lives free of anxiety because "the creator is anxiety-free and publicly exhibits that freedom from anxiety" by practicing Sabbath himself.

"God is not a workaholic. God is not Pharaoh. God does not keep jacking up production schedules. To the contrary, God rests, confident, serene, at peace."[31] When we worship *this God*, we become freed up to join him in this anxiety-free way of being in the world. If we cannot rest, if we cannot stop, it isn't Yahweh we're worshiping. It's probably Pharaoh.

3. *Practicing Sabbath means relinquishing control.* A major benefit of stopping relates to one of our favorite self-deceptions: that we are in control. Our illusions of control have us drowning in anxiety. When we stop by faith, we are acknowledging God—his power, his wisdom, his love. Stopping in unbelief is a hopeless giving up that leads to addiction and escapism. But Sabbath stopping requires and cultivates trust in the One whose job description does include running the universe. Stopping by faith is a major recalibration against the lies that drive us, especially lies about our need or ability to be in control.

> If we cannot rest, if we cannot stop, it isn't Yahweh we're worshiping. It's probably Pharaoh.

We are creatures with limits. We can't know everything. We can't do everything. We can't control everything. If those words sound like problems, we have forgotten who knows all things, who can do all things, and who controls all things! Since we are made in God's image, we can even stop managing our reputations. Since God made us in his image, our identity is a gift to receive rather than a project to manage or a goal to accomplish. God has already finished this work! We are already "fearfully and wonderfully made" (Ps. 139:14).[32]

4. *Practicing Sabbath means delighting in both God's work and our own.* When God rested, he was delighting in the completion of work well done. On the seventh day God enjoyed the very goodness of his work—and so should we. The apostle Paul calls people who denigrate the joys of creation, things like sex and food, dangerous liars proffering demonic teaching (see 1 Tim. 4:1–5). Paul's antidote to these serious heresies of practice is simple. The creation is God's good gift and meant to be received with thanksgiving (see vv. 4–5).

The Sabbath is useful precisely for this. Like God when his work was finished, we should evaluate our work and enjoy the fruit of our labors through regular patterns of work and rest. Indeed, it is ultimately "God, who richly provides us with everything for our enjoyment" (1 Tim. 6:17).

In the contemporary world, our relationship to work seems to grow ever more troubled. Sabbath is part of God's solution. How can we get perspective on our work if we never put it down to reflect on it? How can we know what drives us if we never take our hands off the wheel?

5. *Practicing Sabbath means embracing (economic) limits.* Sabbath means rejecting profit maximizing as the primary driver behind economic decisions. There's just no way around it. Those Israelite farmers had to trust that giving themselves and their workers a day off, sending folks home when work needed to be done and profits needed to be made, wouldn't ruin the family business. They had to be willing to trust Yahweh that life lived with the grain of his good creation would be better than life lived against it. And finally, flowing out of this last point . . .

6. *Practicing Sabbath means giving rest every bit as much as it means taking it.* Sabbath time meant giving the most marginalized a holiday, meant business owners and immigrants gleaning together side by side during the Sabbath years, meant forgiving debts and returning property to those who had lost it. Sabbath was and is a reenactment of the exodus, a way of shaping our lives that reminds us that because God loved us when we were enslaved to sin and death, we seek liberation for others from whatever stands against them. Sabbath means recognizing that business as usual, like business in Egypt, too often creates winners and losers and produces communities isolated from one another along the railroad tracks of our world. Sabbath economics interrupts all that. The moment our economic lives start to turn into

> Those Israelite farmers had to trust that giving themselves and their workers a day off, sending folks home when work needed to be done and profits needed to be made, wouldn't ruin the family business.

one more system of exploitation, Jesus, Lord of the Sabbath, shows up, reminding us that time is for serving and sharing, that worship includes doing good rather than evil, that our economic lives aren't evaluated by outputs but by the effect our economic actions have on our neighbors.

THE REST KEY TODAY
STORIES AND PRACTICES OF SABBATH

God gives his people the good gift of the Sabbath, a time-structuring practice that welcomes us into rhythms of work and rest. What could be better than practicing and receiving such a gift?

How's That Working for Ya?

When we think about our own lives, however, most of us can identify pretty quickly that practicing Sabbath isn't easy for us. Americans work more hours and longer days, are more likely to work nights and weekends, and take less vacation than any other industrialized nation.[1] As I write this chapter in the spring of 2017, I'm ashamed to say that I'm several years overdue for a three-month sabbatical. Nor am I alone in my apparent unwillingness to take even paid time off. A recent study of US workers showed that

- only 25 percent of employees with paid time off used all their vacation days, and
- 15 percent of employees took none of their vacation days at all.[2]

Since God did not design us for work without rest, unsurprisingly, our workaholism is bad for our health. Indeed, studies link workaholism with everything from increased risk of heart attack or diabetes to "poor sleep quality, weight gain, higher blood pressure, depression and anxiety," and "unhappy marriages and higher divorce rates."[3]

That most of us are never more than four feet away from a massive supercomputer known as a smartphone only contributes to the challenges. One 2012 study suggests that "heavy smartphone use caused more 'work-home interference,'" and "went on to show that this led to more burned-out employees."[4] Another study suggests that smartphones are undermining young people's abilities to read emotions, a key skill in developing the sort of empathy for others that grounds God's call for us to give—as well as receive—rest.[5]

> Our culture has interpreted us as nobodies, cosmic orphans in need of the right labels to "count." Identity is a project we must take on, and many companies are willing to sponsor us—at a cost. "Image" is for sale.

Of course, our smartphones and other social media technology allow us to be constantly on the hunt for new products and always engaged in constructing our own image. This is all part and parcel of our culture's broad approach to economic life. In chapter 1, we saw that contemporary economists describe people as *homo economicus*, as solitary individuals committed first and foremost to our own pursuit of pleasure and avoidance of pain. We also saw that such a worldview leads to false worship.

And this false worship eventually leads to a deeply dysfunctional sense of identity. Our economic idols have sold us the following two lies simultaneously:

- We are the center.
- At our center, we are hungry consumers who cannot be satisfied.

Our culture has interpreted us as nobodies, cosmic orphans in need of the right labels to "count." Identity is a project we must take on, and many companies are willing to sponsor us—at a cost. "Image" is for sale.

And for all of you who let yourself off the hook as you read that last paragraph because you hate shopping, our identities aren't just for sale.

They can be *earned*. You see, when many of us examine why we work so hard, whether in investment banking, evangelism and discipleship, or ministries of mercy and justice, we find that we work so that we matter. This is what Tim Keller calls the "work under the work."[6] We live from promotion to promotion or ministry victory to ministry victory in the hopes that the next one will finally make us count.

Even when we stop for worship, we struggle to really stop. Whether it's creating shopping lists on the back of the bulletin or responding to text messages and app alerts that interrupt our cell phone–based Scripture reading,[7] our anxious activity interrupts even the sacred space of the church. After the service, Sunday afternoon lunch is invaded by soccer practice or its equivalent. "Families . . . think of themselves as helpless before the requirements of such commitment. In context it requires . . . enormous, communal resolve to resist"[8] the infinite demand of contemporary society on us whenever we attempt to stop.

When we buy the lie that we're orphans who must consume or earn our way into significance, we find ourselves purchasing lifestyle at the cost of life itself. Sabbath practices can rescue and reorient us to find life from the God who freely gives it. Stopping means you get to be who you are—a person made in God's image rather than a cog in another's machinery or a competitor or a consumer or a loser (if you lack those products, promotions, or ministry successes our culture says will give you acceptable status). Stopping to live is much more humanizing than living to shop . . . or earn . . . or work. God says, "I made you and the world. Stop one day in seven. You don't run the world." The gods of image creation and maintenance respond by saying, "Look, click, compare, buy, back to work . . . or else!" "The Sabbath reminds us there is more to life than work"[9] and that we are more than our positions, salaries, or lifestyles. But that doesn't mean it's easy for us.

Receiving Sabbath in Our Afraid-to-Stop Age

When we receive rest by stopping our relentless activity in Sabbath practice, we quickly learn that living by God's calendar goes with the grain of his universe. This isn't because taking a day off to worship Yahweh and welcome one another looks radical. Quite the opposite—and so much so that we've worried a bit about whether readers might find the stories in this chapter too unsexy to be compelling. But the truth is, the beauty of the Sabbath lies in its simplicity. So let's consider: What happens when Jesus's people take the Sabbath seriously today?

For starters, resting allows us to experience renewal and refreshment in Jesus. Two of my (Michael's) closest friends, Jonathan Wilson and Collins Harrison, taught me to take a day off through their countercultural commitment not to work or study on Sundays while they were in medical school. Med students are notorious for all-nighters and anxious cramming, for surviving insane workweeks and back-to-back shifts. But while in school, my friends decided they would commit to stopping on Sundays.[10]

"Once I made the decision," recalls Jonathan, "Sunday became my favorite day of the week, and this incredible chance to recharge." The day of rest came as a gift to these doctors-in-training because there's always more work to be done, always more studying to do, not to mention occasional tests on Monday morning.

> "Rest, ironically, is an activity that must be prepared for and then pursued."
>
> —Tim Keller

"I think starting the week off in the posture of rest conveys a degree of trust in the Lord that our time is his and we are offering back to him the firstfruits of that gift," says Collins. For him, the "conscious sacrifice" of that first day helped him lay down his anxiety and insecurity about the week ahead. "It was a way to say to God, 'Your kingdom and rest are priceless to me,'" he says. "And it changed my perspective throughout the week." But such a practice also requires preparation. We're so busy we must actively plan to stop. According to Tim Keller, "Rest, ironically, is an activity that must be prepared for and then pursued."[11]

"So if I had that Monday morning test," says Jonathan, "I just knew I had to get the work done on Saturday." When the Saturday evening sun set, his work was done whether or not he felt it was done. While such countercultural practices occasionally felt like they'd lead to the end of their medical careers, as it turns out, both Jonathan and Collins became doctors after all. It is the myth of our anxious culture that tells us we will not survive if we ever stop.

Collins' and Jonathan's story also reminds us of the complexities of practicing Sabbath today, since as residency doctors, they essentially have no control over their schedules. As a result, they have had a hard time maintaining a day of rest and have found it impossible to keep the same day of rest each week. Because of the freedom we have in Jesus, I think we can be grateful that these men are becoming doctors while also working together as members of the body of Christ to discern how to help all God's children embrace patterns of work and rest.

Inspired by my friends, I can also testify to the joy of taking a real break on Sundays. Often I fall asleep midafternoon, a sure sign that my body has been worn down over the course of the week. Equally often I find joy and delight in God's Word, in a conversation with Rebecca, or in a hike with my beautiful children. Strange to say, practicing Sabbath isn't easy (I can't tell you how often I longed to work on this book on Sunday afternoons), but it is almost always rewarding. I, like so many others, can testify to feeling rejuvenation flow into my heart, mind, and body after a day of rest.

All this, though, requires effort. And such efforts to rest work best when we function together as a community. Author Judith Shulevitz writes:

> Most people mistakenly believe that all you have to do to stop working is not work. The inventors of the Sabbath understood that it was a much more complicated undertaking. You cannot downshift casually and easily. This is why the Puritan and Jewish Sabbaths were so exactly intentional. The rules did not exist to torture the faithful. They were meant to communicate the insight that interrupting the ceaseless round of striving requires a surprisingly strenuous act of will, one that has to be bolstered by habit as well as by social sanction.[12]

Second, though, resting from work releases us to welcome one another. In an age marked more and more by multiplying connections mediated by technology, we are becoming increasingly lonely. We can connect with people across the globe but not across the table. Sabbath offers us time to gather as family[13] without distractions incessantly buzzing or beeping. One practice to support such gatherings is creating a box for people to put their cell phones in during family meals. We might all consider creating "Sabbath boxes" to store our phones for the whole day. Such technology-free family time can wonderfully include others with less social connection.

Sabbath community can become larger but not less than family. One of the ways my family (the Holt family) grew to know and love Michael Rhodes was by spending lots and lots of time with him in our home. Some of that time occurred on Sundays, but most of it fit a crazy strategy that blessed our whole family. Right as our three older kids were in the middle of their teenage years and less and less interested in our opinions, Michael was a college student who wanted to be around my wife and me. And of course he was a cool college guy to our kids. So we got really good time with our kids, who wanted to be with Michael, who wanted to be with us. Opening our home for "extended family time" blessed all of us and still does. Meals on Sundays, in particular, can become ideal times for welcoming others into our homes.

> Meals on Sundays, in particular, can become ideal times for welcoming others into our homes.

And, of course, in the church, "family" includes widows, orphans, single members of the congregation, immigrants, and others. In my (Michael's) family growing up, Thanksgiving was often a day for welcoming international immigrants that were a part of the Sunday school my parents led. Welcoming Chinese PhD students alongside our extended family helped me gain a love for hospitality and an appreciation for other cultures. I will never forget how grateful I was for similar invitations when I was living in Kenya, longing to be on the receiving end of such hospitality.

One way my (Robby) family practices Isaiah 58 is through a long-term relationship with good friends who periodically need shelter. One good friend has lived with us several times, as long as a couple of months at a time, due to a lifelong drug addiction and other serious struggles. I'll never forget about a dozen years ago when my youngest daughter, then four years old, noticed his deep sadness during a family walk. Instinctively, she reached up and grabbed his hand to offer comfort. Big tears rolled down his cheeks as love anchored him once again in relationship. That day I watched love break through a heart hardened by the heaviness of chronic and acute abuse, self-hatred, disappointment, and shame. My four-year-old daughter built my faith and encouraged me to move forward in hope through one simple action.

But none of this would have happened if we had shut our home to our friend and neighbor in need. The grace of God has opened our eyes to our own brokenness so that we can open our home to others broken by their own sin and the sin of others. As it turns out, this friend is by far the most empathetic friend I have ever had. He notices and tunes in to mood swings in me before I do. And if you knew his whole story, you would want him in your home too. So who has benefited the most from entering a way of life shaped by the weekly return to God's Sabbath rest?

Life lived in line with Sabbath time can also reshape the way we arrange our schedules more generally. I (Michael) have lived with my family in our low-income neighborhood in South Memphis for nearly six years now. We love our neighbors and spend a good deal of time with them. But one thing I've learned is this: I miss out on an awful lot of my neighbors' barbecues, cookouts, and family celebrations because so often every minute of my life is scheduled. My neighbors don't send Google Calendar invites.

Furthermore, Rebecca and I have had to try to cultivate the gift of being interruptible. I so often live more in Pharaoh time, with its addiction to creating ever more "bricks," than Yahweh time, with its delight in daily bread and days off. I find myself irritated and annoyed when my neighbors' various needs don't happen in nice, discreet blocks of time I've set apart for "ministry." I want to control time and fit others' lives into my schedule. But that's not how neighborhoods work, and that's not how time works in God's neighborhood. Sabbath time reminds me, and Sabbath practice shapes me, to leave space for my neighbor, to resist the tendency to schedule every second in the name of "stewardship" or "efficiency."

Giving Rest in a Relentless Age

Most of the way we've described the problem and possibility of Sabbath, however, has been from a decidedly middle-class perspective. In other words, we've taken it for granted that we're overworked professionals who could choose to work less. But for many of our neighbors, this is far from reality.

Consider members of the working poor, such as my friend and neighbor Juanita. Her work life is literally unimaginable to me. She works two jobs. At one, she moves heavy packages for a shipping company, often overnight. At the other, she provides care for a physically disabled man. Her shifts and workdays change constantly. Her sleep schedule, if diagrammed, would look like the doodling of a deranged maniac. And when she's awake, she's often helping to raise her grandchildren.

Juanita is not alone. One warehouse that hired a lot of my neighbors paid decent wages but had all employees on swing shifts, so that everyone went back and forth between day and night shifts. I'd see employees walking down the street looking like zombies. This constantly off-balance approach to work must have affected their kids, their relationships with parents or spouses, and their participation in church.

The working poor's non-work hours, meanwhile, are often filled with a never-ending set of crises precipitated by payday lenders, sick family members, or a broken-down car. All this, of course, comes with a social cost. One 2014 article on the working poor chronicles these struggles:

> Jason Derr, 37, who earns $10.75 an hour and supports his wife and baby, wishes he and his wife could socialize with the few friends they have. But the lack of money stops them. "We can't afford to do anything," he said. "I feel like we are unable to participate in humanity, that being alive has a buy-in cost."
>
> Similarly, Simon will spend full weekends at home without social interaction. "There will be weekends when I'll just have to sit home because if there's a priority between food and going out, it's going to be food." Powell added that she hasn't seen her friends in "six months because I can't afford to go out with them, and they all want to go out."[14]

Meanwhile, another group of low-income neighbors faces the opposite problem: chronic unemployment or underemployment. Indeed, even financially stable people who are elderly, retired, or have a disability may find themselves without enough meaningful work to do. Ironically, the result of not having work is not rest. It is depression and weariness. I asked hundreds of job seekers in South Memphis, "What does it feel like when you aren't working?" and the answers were always the same:

depressed, irritable, sleepy, angry, like you can't do anything, worthless, miserable.

The plight of neighbors who are considered the working poor or are facing long-term underemployment reminds us that Sabbath is never simply about receiving rest as a luxury. It's also about giving rest to others —particularly the marginalized. How are Christians practicing giving Sabbath today?

Sabbath Is for Welcoming

When I (Robby) was in seminary, I met one of the strictest Sabbath keepers I have ever known. If the phrase "strict Sabbath keeper" has you picturing one cold and dour dude sitting silently in a corner, please know he was just the opposite. He kept Sabbath on Sunday in light of the resurrection. One of his regular family practices on Sunday afternoons was to visit nursing homes with his children. They went to love and comfort the aged who were the most neglected. He left the relentless flow of time tied to efficiency and productivity and entered the temple in time where we can welcome those whom God loves but who cannot help us achieve our productivity goals. That's Isaiah 58 with shoes laced up and walking!

Giving Rest at Work: Refuge Coffee, Broetje Orchards, and Others

Remember our look into Leviticus 25:1–7, where all kinds of people across ethnic and economic lines gathered daily to enjoy God's goodness together during the Sabbath year as equal recipients of God's good gifts? This passage captures the beautiful vision of our friends Bill and Kitti Murray. (No, not *that* Bill Murray.)

Bill and Kitti were empty nesters in 2008 when their world began to flip right side up. While prepping to teach a course on justice and reading John Perkins, they felt the call to make a move: they would live somewhere "among widows, aliens, and orphans," says Bill.

So they relocated to Clarkston, Georgia, in a neighborhood at the epicenter of this small town's enormous refugee resettlement program. As they watched and listened and prayed, they saw people living their new lives in lonely silos and constantly struggling to find any decent work. So they watched and listened and prayed some more . . . and they threw some great block parties.

But Clarkston had no community hub and no coffee shop. Kitti began to dream of addressing both problems at once. From that dream the Murrays launched Refuge Coffee in the heart of Clarkston, about half a mile from their front door. Startup life is no joke, but their efforts have been worth it as they address three "gaps" they saw as they watched and listened to their neighbors.

Opportunity gap. The jobless rate in Clarkston is double the national average, which can lead to hopelessness.

Hospitality gap. Believe it or not, 85 percent of immigrants to our country have never been inside an American home, which can lead to loneliness.

Awareness gap. Most people in Atlanta don't know the United Nations has resettled up to two thousand refugees here every year for the past three decades, which can lead to alienation between Americans and refugees.[15]

Their vision includes job creation, job training (while their trainees earn a decent wage), and creating a multiethnic meeting space to foster community. Today Refuge Coffee employs six refugees. At one point the company's three baristas were from Syria, the Congo, and Ethiopia, respectively. In reference to the job training program, where the refugees also share their own languages and cultures, the employee from Ethiopia said, "We're like family."[16] This matches Refuge Coffee's vision statement:

We believe in the power of welcome. We dream of a vibrant resettled refuge community in Clarkston, Georgia, where our new neighbors are embraced and given opportunities to thrive through the business of hospitality through coffee.[17]

Bill and Kitti speak with a rare mix of joy and conviction. They are people who have learned how to stop and pray. They are learning the value of stopping to watch and attend to others. They are anchored in the rest that Jesus *is*, so they are sharing feasts and jobs and experience and hope and rest with others. They embody the refuge and hospitality of the God who rescues restless wanderers, strangers, and aliens. Sabbath for Kitti and Bill means giving refugees the opportunity to work and rest, contribute to the community, and care for their own well-being. The God of Sabbath rest has arrested them, and they are glad.

Remember Broetje Orchards from chapter 6? Their passion for loving their employees has extended into practices of giving rest. "A deepening awareness that some families had almost no time together as a unit (fathers working early morning in the fields, and mothers spending swing shifts in the plant) compelled them to build a new state-of-the-art packing facility that could eliminate the need for early evening work."[18] Such decision-making represents this orchard's efforts to bend their economic lives toward giving Sabbath rest to others.

Nor should we ignore the way enormous corporations such as Chick-fil-A and Hobby Lobby, as well as an army of small Jewish and Christian entrepreneurs, choose to close their doors one day a week to give rest to their employees. In each and every case, market logic would seem to require these businesses to maximize profits, productivity, and time by operating seven days a week if they want to remain open. And yet open they remain.

Sabbath Debt

Finally, Christians are finding ways to liberate the marginalized from the Sabbath-less cycle of debt. We shared many stories on wealth building and financial literacy in chapter 8. Recall also the story of the pastor who raised more than $40,000 to help attendees get out of payday loans.

Another interesting model comes from a group that, as best I can tell, isn't explicitly religious but nevertheless has claimed the Sabbath of Sabbaths, the Jubilee, as the name for their movement: Rolling Jubilee. Rolling Jubilee's strategy of debt relief is pretty simple. People give money to the movement, which then buys the right to collect outstanding medical debts from people for pennies on the dollar. In other words, Rolling Jubilee becomes the bill collector. There's a lot of bill collection to go around, since one in seven Americans is pursued by a bill collector at any given moment.[19]

This is where things get interesting. After acquiring the right to collect the debt, Rolling Jubilee writes a letter to the person who owes the money and gives them a simple message: your debt is forgiven. It's hard to imagine a more theologically informed social message. To date, Rolling Jubilee has raised more than $70,000 that has been leveraged to forgive more than $31 *million* dollars of debt. In doing so, they're introducing the never-ending cycle of debt to the interruptive, liberating power of Sabbath time. May we learn from their example!

Practicing Sabbath

So what does it look like to practice giving and receiving rest?

Practicing Sabbath at Church

Consider: How can you help the members of your congregation give and receive Sabbath rest to one another?

- *Practice times of rest that include those who are most likely to miss out on rest: people with disabilities, the elderly, immigrants, and the poor.* It seems to be a fact that most church programs aim at the "normal" members. We forget that the cost of lunch out after the service excludes the working poor, and lack of transportation and assistance prevents the elderly from attending church at all. Practice creating events that give people an opportunity to just be together. Remember that lower-income parents are constantly aware of their inability to afford outings. Help them receive Sabbath rest together as a family through church picnics and gatherings and other social opportunities.

- *Help your congregation practice worshipful rest as the church.* Consider restricting technology-dependent ways of doing church (don't ask people to send emails or texts during the service, consider reading from a physical Bible rather than an iPad, and invite people to turn off their phones during the service). Host retreats that help people get away and ensure those retreats are accessible to those most often left out: the working poor, single parents, etc. Invite people to leave their phones and laptops behind.

- *Liberate people from debt into Sabbath release.* Set aside some mercy-fund money for debt forgiveness, particularly in the face of predatory loans or other unjust situations.

- *Form accountability groups related to Sabbath rest and get in other people's business about their approach to rest.* Brian Fikkert likes to point out that his workaholism is every bit as much a sin as an alcoholic's addiction. The difference is that Brian's sin (which is the same as Michael's and Robby's in this instance) gets him ahead in the world and earns him respect from others, including those in the church. This is unbiblical. We simply must foster habits of accountability. Commit to not accepting more work travel or another extra assignment or a new project without first talking to your spouse or accountability partner. Do a "rest audit" in your community group. Encourage people to say no to stuff. And pastors and other leaders: model taking a rest, even when it feels as though you can't.

Practicing Sabbath at Work

Consider: How can you encourage your workplace toward Sabbath rest and support other workplaces that embrace Sabbath rest? *Create (or encourage others to create) workplace policies that contribute to healthy rhythms of work and rest.* Let's all admit it: many businesses, including those run and managed by Christians, almost seem to require a rejection of Sabbath living (and we're not just talking about whether you're open on Sunday). Do what you can to:

- Give substantial paid time off to all employees (and generous maternity and paternity leave policies). Model and encourage taking that time off.

- *Reduce, as much as possible, the constant uncertainty of people's schedules.* Swing shifts, fifty-hour weeks followed by fifteen-hour weeks, working on the weekends, etc. are often brutal on workers. Find ways to reduce all such Sabbath-threatening work rhythms.

- *Give employees permission (or encourage coworkers) to take time to reflect on their work and their lives.* This can happen through employee gatherings or retreats, as well as through emotional health opportunities. When I (Michael) was at Advance Memphis, they had a policy that paid for all but $20 of any counseling I received. As a result, I was able to get therapy from a brother in Christ. That therapy saved my life. And it happened in part because the leadership of Advance was trying to live toward Sabbath.

- *Every time you look in the mirror say to yourself five times: "Workaholism is a sin, not a virtue. Workaholism is a sin, not a virtue. Workaholism . . ."* Okay, we're being a little tongue in cheek with this last one. But seriously . . .

Practicing Sabbath at Home

- *Take a full day off from anything that remotely counts as "work" (and make it Sunday if at all possible).* Seriously. Regardless of what Monday looks like. Regardless of how much work you have to do. Stop. Make yourself stop. Build stopping into the rhythms of your life. Remember, if you can't stop, if stopping feels impossible, that's an indication that you're worshiping a god *other* than the Lord of the Sabbath, Jesus Christ.

- *Flee from constant distraction.* Put your smartphone in a "technology box" when you walk in the door or while you're at dinner, put the laptops up when you're at home, and simply buy fewer of the latest gizmos. Talk to one another rather than watching TV together. Ask good questions at the dinner table. Most nights we (the Rhodes family) share the happiest and saddest things from our day with our four kids, all six and under. This helps us listen to one another and develop healthy emotional self-awareness and connectivity within our family. Find ways to "cut off" your addiction to work.

- *Identify what drives you to unhealthy work habits.* The next time you feel like you can't stop, write down what feelings lie under those feelings. Then give those underlying feelings—which will often be idolatries—to God to redirect or crucify in your life.

- *Take a retreat.* Find a way, whether it's an hour once a month or a weekend out of town occasionally, to get away from the hustle and bustle, meet with Jesus, and take an honest look at your life. Adele Calhoun's *Spiritual Disciplines Handbook* provides outstanding suggestions for spiritual disciplines, including a guide to spending extended time on retreat with Jesus.
- *Make blessing others part of your rest practice by giving rest.* You can do this in so many ways. Welcome others into your home. Intentionally cook enough for leftovers and then take them to friends or neighbors. Give a gift card to somebody struggling financially. *Be together.* Visit those who are isolated and lonely.

Start Practicing

Before moving on, take a moment and contemplate where to begin practicing Sabbath in your own life. What are your easiest first steps? Consider: Who practices Sabbath well? Are there folks in your same stage of life (either professionally or with family) with whom you could dream about what healthier rhythms of work and rest could look like? Before finishing this chapter, identify how you, individually or with a group, can practice Sabbath within the next month.

I will practice Sabbath rest within the next month by . . .

_____

_____

_____

The Rest Key Conclusion: The God of Rest and Refuge

So then, there remains a Sabbath rest for the people of God, for whoever has entered God's rest has also rested from his works as God did from his. . . . For we do not have a high priest who is unable to sympathize with our weaknesses, but one who in every respect has been tempted as we are, yet without sin. Let us then with confidence draw near to the throne of grace, that we may receive mercy and find grace to help in time of need. (Heb. 4:9–10, 15–16 ESV)

So says the author of Hebrews. The greater rest still lies ahead. But given Jesus's accomplishment, we strive to enter it by faith, knowing that we have a God who has joined us in our humanness so that he might provide the grace and mercy we need.

Some of you reading this chapter are thinking, *Nice idea, but it's not going to happen.* Before you move on, we want to remind you of three things.

First, when we refuse rest in Yahweh, we're choosing to worship something else. Figure out what that is and ask yourself which God you want to serve.

Second, remember that Sabbath, as with all the practices we've recommended, isn't just a good action. It's a *transformative* action. Sabbath is a school for desire. It shapes and transforms us. We too often hope to become healthier people who will then practice Sabbath. But Sabbath is a significant prescription God has given us to become healthier people.

Third, for many of us, including the authors, this entire book has called us far out of our comfort zones and maybe even laid on our backs a big load of guilt. To you and to ourselves, who have struggled with guilt, we say this: all our work, including the work of practicing the King's economy, flows out of our rest in our Savior. We begin in rest. We work from rest. Christ has done the hard labor. And then, miracle of miracles, he welcomes us into his work so that we may rejoice together with him (see John 4:36–38).

Therefore, we welcome you, not just into the practice of Sabbath keeping, but into an entire way of economic life marked by the practices explored in this book. Such a life, we suggest, requires our active efforts to exercise our hearts, minds, and habits for life in God's economy rather than our culture's. But such a life, such an economic adventure, is also nothing more than the sheer, life-altering, generous gift of Jesus.

May we receive it.

CONCLUSION

Worship, Community, Work, Equity, Creation Care, and Rest. These six keys have unlocked the door and welcomed us into the strange, Narnia-esque world of God's economy we find in Scripture. We've encountered a God who calls us to aim our economic lives at love of God and love of neighbor (Worship and Community). We've discovered an economy designed to welcome every person to the potluck party of Jesus, where everyone gets to bring a plate (Work and Equity). And we've stood awestruck before the incomprehensible generosity of Jesus, who welcomes us into an incredible world (Creation Care) shaped by generous cycles of work and Sabbath (Rest).

In addition to exploring Scripture through these keys, we've also explored stories of fellow believers whose lives represent embodiments of these keys in our own world. Through cross-shaped giving, feasting, gleaning job creation, impact investing, creation care, and practicing Sabbath, these Christ followers have given us glimpses of what it might look like to become, as God's people, a colony of *his* economy in the midst of our own.

Finally, we've discussed a wide variety of ways to embrace formative economic practices, spiritual disciplines for our economic health, that will help us get in shape for God's economy. These practices, applicable for life in our homes, churches, and marketplaces, are almost like a list of potential "exercises" that we hope allow you to customize a King Jesus economic exercise regimen that works for you and your community. Nearly all of them are optional in the sense that you may have found any particular one more or less helpful. But we hope you found plenty that you can use to practice God's economy with God's people today.

We've come a long way. Here are three things we hope you'll remember as you finish this book.

First, practicing the King's economy is all about receiving God's rich, immeasurable, unfathomable, deliriously intoxicating grace. The hope of this book is that by embracing these practices by faith we experience God's transforming, renewing, and restoring power. If we try to come at these practices in a workaholic, legalistic mode, we're missing the point. We believe these practices fit God's generous offer of his kingdom. Exercised by faith in God's generosity (see Eph. 2:4–10; 1 Tim. 6:17–19), they will help train us for godliness (see 1 Tim. 4:7) *and* protect us from "ruin and destruction" (1 Tim. 6:8–11).

Because such disciplines help us "tune in" to God's great gifts, we believe the emotion that most often accompanies these practices is *joy*. In our lives, seeking to embrace God's economic kingdom through such practices has been a glorious adventure—and we recognize we're just getting started. We pray Jesus will give you similar joy on your journey.

Second, if the Scripture, stories, and practices of this book help God's people become more and more the people he is calling us to be, we cannot wait to see what God has in store for his church. As we've heard the stories told in this book and sought to embrace the practices of each key, we've often felt like toddlers taking our very first steps. The transition from crawling to those lurching lunges is breathtaking! But the glory comes in full when the child learns to run.

Remember the illustration of the NFL linemen in the introduction? That's us. This book represents the first stages of our training regimen in trying to become triathletes. Because we're so new to this, we have no idea what it will look like for God's people to run his economic triathlon in the twenty-first century (see 1 Cor. 9:24–27; Heb. 12:1–2). But we believe Scripture and the sorts of stories and disciplines we've shared in this book have the ability to get us moving down the road. As we embrace that journey, we believe we may well see a church whose embodiment of God's economy spills out into the world in all sorts of unique ways, providing us with new, as yet unimagined, ways of loving and serving in neighborhoods, businesses, banks, workplaces, church spaces, and politics. We look forward to hearing your story on that journey and continuing to share ours in the years to come. In particular, we hope this book may help, in some small way, ignite conversations between young, energetic kingdom-minded folks who lack money and experience, and older, wiser kingdom-minded folks looking to bend their assets, influence, and acumen toward God's economy.

Finally, we want to remind you that you can study triathlons all day long, read every book on the subject, and even start calling yourself a triathlete, but if you don't embrace the training regimen, you'll never make it past the first event (see 1 Cor. 9:24–27). Jesus once said, "Now that you know these things, you will be blessed *if you do them*" (John 13:17, emphasis added). So also it is with this book. We hope we've helped you fall more in love with Scripture. We hope we've inspired you with stories from God's church. But if you don't get out there and do *some* practices, ours or someone else's, then you'll never get fit for the kingdom economy of God.

That would be a real shame, because the New Testament teaches that God's kingdom is on the move. Like Rahab, when we look out the window, we see his kingdom coming. Scripture teaches us that we live in the shadow of his return, at which every knee shall bow and every tongue shall confess that Jesus is the King (see Phil. 2:9–11). When he comes, he'll be bringing an economy that the Scriptures bear witness to from Genesis to Revelation.

Here's the craziest part, though: according to 2 Timothy 2:12 and Revelation 20:6, when the kingdom comes, those who are in Jesus will reign with him forever and ever. God will put us in his royal, kingly cabinet.

That means that today, you and I have a choice. We can keep working for an economy that won't last, that rust and moth are already destroying, and that can never satisfy (see Matt. 6:20–21; Heb. 13:5). We can make profit maximizing the sole goal of our market activities. We can aim at the economy of "me and mine" and donate our scraps to the soup kitchen. We can continue to develop economic habits and practices that will leave us clueless when God invites us to join him in establishing his new heavens and new earth economy.

Or we can welcome his kingdom now, we can embrace and embody the good news to the poor declared in our King Jesus, and we can make the economy of God encounterable for the world through the way we live our lives. We can create businesses, churches, families, and homes where the way we worship, work, spend, save, invest, compensate, share, and create all aim at establishing a community where everybody can bring a plate to the potluck.

So dig in! Go back through those chapters where you filled in your commitments to particular practices and start practicing. Invite friends and family members to join you. Be faithful and watch what Jesus does. And:

> May the God of peace, who through the blood of the eternal covenant brought back from the dead our Lord Jesus, that great Shepherd of the sheep, equip you with everything good for doing his will, and may he work in us what is pleasing to him, through Jesus Christ, to whom be glory for ever and ever. Amen. (Heb. 13:20–21)

RESOURCES FOR FURTHER STUDY

For further resources for using this book and practicing all the keys in your context, visit the *Practicing the King's Economy* resources webpage at www.practicingthejesuseconomy.org.

Chapters 1 and 2: Worship Key

Books on Worship (Recalibration)

Beale, G. K. and Mitchell Kim. *God Dwells Among Us: Expanding Eden to the Ends of the Earth*. Downers Grove, IL: InterVarsity Press, 2014.

Keller, Timothy. *Counterfeit Gods*. New York: Penguin, 2011.

Smith, James K. A. *You Are What You Love: The Spiritual Power of Habit*. Grand Rapids: Brazos, 2016.

Warren, Tish Harrison. *Liturgy of the Ordinary: Sacred Practices in Everyday Life*. Downers Grove, IL: InterVarsity, 2016.

Books on Generosity

Blomberg, Craig L. *Christians in an Age of Wealth: A Biblical Theology of Stewardship*. Grand Rapids: Zondervan, 2013.

Corbett, Steve, and Brian Fikkert. *Helping Without Hurting in Church Benevolence: A Practical Guide to Walking with Low-Income People.* Chicago: Moody, 2015.

—————. *When Helping Hurts: How to Alleviate Poverty Without Hurting the Poor . . . and Yourself.* Rev. and expanded ed. Chicago: Moody, 2012.

Kapic, Kelly M., with Justin Borger. *God So Loved He Gave.* Grand Rapids: Zondervan, 2010.

Sider, Ron J. *Rich Christians in an Age of Hunger: Moving from Affluence to Generosity.* 6th ed. Nashville: Thomas Nelson, 2015.

Organizations Devoted to Generosity

Generous Giving (https://generousgiving.org/)

Advent Conspiracy (www.adventconspiracy.org)

Chapters 3 and 4: Community Key

Books on Community

Bonhoeffer, Dietrich. *Life Together.* San Francisco: HarperOne, 2009.

Vanier, Jean. *Community and* Growth. Mahwah, NJ: Paulist Press, 1992.

—————. *From Brokenness to Community.* Mahwah, NJ: Paulist Press, 1992.

Anything by John M. Perkins, the founder of the CCDA. His most recent is *Dream with Me.* Grand Rapids: Baker Books, 2017.

Books on Lament and Reconciliation

Katongole, Emmanuel, and Chris Rice. *Reconciling All Things: A Christian Vision for Justice, Peace, and Healing.* Downers Grove, IL: InterVarsity, 2008.

Rah, Soong-Chan. *Prophetic Lament: A Call for Justice in Troubled Times.* Downers Grove, IL: InterVarsity, 2015.

Chapters 5 and 6: Work Key

Sherman, Amy L. *Kingdom Calling: Vocational Stewardship for the Common Good*. Downers Grove, IL: IVP Academic, 2011.

Van Duzer, Jeff. *Why Business Matters to God: (And What Still Needs to Be Fixed)*. Downers Grove, IL: IVP Academic, 2010.

Organizations Focusing on Job Training

The Chalmers Center and their Work Life program (www.chalmers .org)

Jobs for Life (www.jobsforlife.org)

Resources for Making Your Business More Kingdom-Minded

Benefit Corporations. B-Corps is a new incorporation that seeks to encourage businesses "to become a force for good in the world" (good for workers, good for the community, good for the environment, good for the long term, and good to the core). Their business assessment, which can be previewed through https://b-lab.secure .force.com/bcorp/impactassessmentdemo, includes a variety of metrics that would allow any business to consider some ways to become more kingdom-focused. See for further research: www .bcorporation.net.

Resources for Starting a Social Enterprise

Academies for Social Enterprise. Founded by serial entrepreneur Betsy Densmore (who provided helpful feedback and encouragement for both the Work Key and Equity Key), this organization mentors and trains emerging social entrepreneurs by convening, mentoring, consulting, etc. (www.academies-se.org/).

Alternative Staffing Alliance. This group is devoted to social enterprise staffing services like the one run by Advance Memphis (http://altstaff ing.org/).

Co.Starters for Causes. The Co.Starters curriculum (used by LAUNCH Chattanooga and Advance Memphis) offers a version aimed at social entrepreneurs called Co.Starters for Causes. To learn more or to bring Co.Starters to your community, you can begin by checking out their website at https://costarters.co/.

How to Build a Startup: Lean LaunchPad Free Online Course. Entrepreneurship expert and teacher Steve Blanks has a free Udacity course on how to build a startup using the "lean start" method. This course is helpful and easy to use (https://www.udacity.com/course /how-to-build-a-startup--ep245).

REDF. REDF is a historic leader in the field of social enterprise. Their work focuses on social enterprises related to job creation. Visit their website (www.redf.org) for more information. By creating a free account on their "workshop" page (https://redfworkshop.org/), you can access cutting-edge tools for coming up with, testing, and launching new social enterprise ideas.

Social Enterprise Alliance. There are sixteen local Social Enterprise Alliance chapters across the country and many resources on launching and leading a social enterprise (https://socialenterprise.us/).

Chapters 7 and 8: Equity Key

Books on Cooperatives

Nembhard, Jessica Gordon. *Collective Courage: A History of African American Cooperative Thought and Practice.* University Park, PA: Penn State University Press, 2014.

Whyte, William Foote, and Kathleen K. Whyte. *Making Mondragon: The Growth and Dynamics of the Worker Cooperative Complex.* Ithaca, NY: Cornell University Press, 1991.

Additional Resources

The Chalmers Center. The Chalmers Center's *Faith & Finances* program is a financial literacy curriculum with a kingdom focus designed for

low-income learners (https://www.chalmers.org/our-work/us-church
-training/why-faith-and-finances/). Also check out the Chalmers Center's IDA resource page. This page has numerous video and written
resources for churches or nonprofits starting an IDA program (https://
www.chalmers.org/matched-savings-ida-toolkit).

The Christian Community Development Association. Check out their
website at www.ccda.org and in particular any of the many excellent
books by John M. Perkins.

The Criterion Institute. Started by Joy Anderson, a social entrepreneur
with long-term experience in impact investing, Criterion is a think
tank that seeks to use finance as a tool for social change (https://
criterioninstitute.org/).

Democracy Collaborative. This group provides countless articles, research, and how-to guides for all sorts of community wealth strategies,
including IDAs, ESOPs, and worker-owner cooperatives (they were
involved with the Evergreen Cooperatives. Check out their website
(http://democracycollaborative.org/) and their Community Wealth
Project website (http://community-wealth.org/).

Kiva. The easiest way to get started with impact investing is to contribute to a loan on Kiva for as little as $25 (https://www.kiva.org
/lend/kiva-u-s).

LAUNCH Chattanooga. In addition to equipping underserved entrepreneurs in Chattanooga, LAUNCH helps other cities across the country
create similar programs. They're working to establish LAUNCH in
twenty cities by 2020 (http://www.launchchattanooga.org/).

Memphis Teacher Residency. For information on one program working
to recruit and equip Christians to serve as public school teachers in
struggling schools, visit www.memphistr.org.

Neighborhood Economics. Founded by Tim Soerens, Neighborhood
Economics seeks to build resilient community wealth through local
economies. This group helped establish the friends and family CD
and have partnered with SOCAP, the world's largest impact investing
gathering (http://socialcapitalmarkets.net/).

Partners Worldwide. Among other things, Partners Worldwide connects successful business people to emerging entrepreneurs in the United States and around the world (www.partnersworldwide.org/).

Praxis Labs. Praxis runs an accelerator and mobilizes impact investing dollars to create cultural and social impact through entrepreneurship (http://praxislabs.org/).

Stanford Social Innovation Review. The Review inspires "social change leaders from around the world and from all sectors of society . . . with webinars, conferences, magazines, online articles, podcasts, and more." Their free weekly electronic newsletter is absolutely essential for anyone interested in social innovation, social enterprise, impact investing, etc. (www.ssir.org).

Writings of Bob Goudzwaard. One scholar whose work has inspired all three of us regarding a number of economic issues is the economist Dr. Bob Goudzwaard. He has relentlessly raised questions about the relationship between Scripture and our economic lives. Even when we disagree with a particular conclusion, we find him challenging in the best ways. You can access numerous free articles and even books of Goudzwaard's writings (from 1967 to the present) at http://www .allofliferedeemed.co.uk/goudzwaard.htm.

Chapters 9 and 10: Creation Care Key[1]

Books on Creation Care

Bauckham, Richard. *The Bible and Ecology: Rediscovering the Community of Creation.* Waco: Baylor University Press, 2010.

———. *Living with Other Creatures: Green Exegesis and Theology.* Waco: Baylor University Press, 2011.

Berry, Wendell. *What Matters? Economics for a Renewed Commonwealth.* Berkeley, CA: Counterpoint, 2010.

Moo, Jonathan A., and Robert S. White. *Let Creation Rejoice: Biblical Hope and Ecological Crisis.* Downers Grove, IL: InterVarsity, 2014.

General Creation Care Resources

Look into this website for help finding programs to recruit others or educate yourself: http://www.sustainabilitydegrees.com/degrees/sustainable-business/.

Au Sable. The Au Sable Institute "offers environmental science programs for students and adults of all ages" (www.ausable.org).

Blessed Earth. A Christian ministry run by Matthew and Nancy Sleeth (blessedearth.org).

Care of Creation. The mission of Care of Creation "is to pursue a God-centered response to environmental challenges that brings glory to the Creator, advances the cause of Christ, and leads to a transformation of the people and the land that sustains them" (http://www.careofcreation.net/).

Energy for the Mission. A new organization that includes collaboration between Rusty Pritchard, Tearfund, and Micah Challenge to help churches, colleges, and Christian businesses with energy stewardship, with the expressed goal of dedicating financial savings from energy efficiency to common-good projects (www.energyformission.org).

The Faraday Institute of Science and Religion. The Faraday Institute is an interdisciplinary research enterprise based at St. Edmund's College, Cambridge. In addition to academic research, the Institute engages in the public understanding of science and religion. Here you can see, watch, or listen to all sorts of free lectures and papers from Christian scholars, such as John Polkinghorn, Richard Bauckham, Alistair McGrath, R. J. Bell, and more (www.faraday-institute.org).

Micah Challenge USA. This evangelical, justice-oriented organization has recently begun working on environmental issues in the context of justice. Their small group study *Live Justly* includes environmental issues in its second edition (www.micahchallengeusa.org).

Plant with Purpose. A US-based development organization doing excellent development work around the world. They offer curricula for church use (plantwithpurpose.org).

Renewal. Renewal "is a Christ-centered and student-driven creation care network that strives to inspire, connect and equip college students in their sustainability efforts" (www.renewingcreation.org).

Restoring Eden. (http://restoringeden.org/)

Tearfund. Tearfund is ramping up their work, including their creation care efforts, in the United States. They root their environmental concerns in both Scripture and care for people and creation (www.tearfund.org).

Tilth Alliance. Memphis Tilth, launched by the Memphis Center for Food and Faith, was modeled after this Seattle-based organization (http://www.seattletilth.org/).

USA A Rocha. (https://arocha.us/)

Resources for Comparing Labels

Food labels are controversial, and Christians can disagree about how to approach this issue. However, it's our belief that Christians can practice creation care by purchasing products that support producers who treat animals and land with dignity.

- For a comparison on a number of technical differences between various certifications for meat products, see https://awionline.org /sites/default/files/uploads/documents/FA-AWI-standardscomparis ontable-070816.pdf.

- For an article on differences between various egg labels, see http:// health.usnews.com/health-news/blogs/eat-run/articles/2016-07-25 /whats-the-difference-between-pasture-raised-and-free-range-eggs.

- For an overview of labels pertaining to animal welfare that is fairly comprehensive, see https://awionline.org/sites/default/files/products /FA-AWI-FoodLabelGuide-Web.pdf.

Chapters 11 and 12: Rest Key

Recommended Books

Berry, Wendell. *A Timbered Choir: The Sabbath Poems 1979–1997.* Washington, DC: Counterpoint, 1998.

Brueggemann, Walter. *Sabbath as Resistance: Saying No to the Culture of Now*. Louisville: Westminster John Knox, 2014.

Wirzba, Norman. *Living the Sabbath: Discovering the Rhythms of Rest and Delight*. Grand Rapids: Brazos, 2006.

Recommended Website

Rolling Jubilee. Check out their website at http://rollingjubilee.org/.

NOTES

Preface

1. See in particular: Chris Wright, *Old Testament Ethics for the People of God* (Downers Grove, IL: InterVarsity, 2004).

2. We got most of the principles and practices for this sort of work from Dr. John Perkins and the Christian Community Development Association.

3. Steve Corbett and Brian Fikkert, *When Helping Hurts: How to Alleviate Poverty without Hurting the Poor . . . and Yourself*, 2nd ed. (Chicago: Moody, 2012).

Introduction

1. English Bibles usually translate God's name Yahweh (or YHWH) as LORD, in all capital letters.

2. My thanks to Andrew Vincent, who I first heard describing the temptation in this way.

3. Corbett and Fikkert, *When Helping Hurts*, 54–62.

4. Thus we are not surprised that after mentioning how God made us alive in King Jesus by "having canceled the charge of our legal indebtedness, which stood against us . . . he has taken it away, nailing it to the cross," Paul then writes he "disarmed the powers and authorities, he made a public spectacle of them, triumphing over them by the cross" (Col. 2:14–15). We'll discuss it later in this book. But here's a summary of what Jesus is doing in Colossians 1: the same Son in whom we receive forgiveness is (1) the agent of the creation of all things; (2) the one sustaining all things; (3) the goal of all things; (4) the head of God's new humanity—the church; and (5) the agent who has accomplished the work.

5. On the implications for the resurrection in general, we highly recommend N. T. Wright, *Surprised by Hope* (New York: HarperCollins, 2008).

6. Thus, throughout this book, when we refer to the coming of the kingdom, seeking the kingdom, bearing witness to the kingdom, giving to the kingdom, or anything similar, we are referring to the full restoration of God's good creation, including the reconciliation of saved sinners. A restoration that Jesus has inaugurated by his death and resurrection and will consummate at his glorious return. There is a legitimate priority within this account on God rescuing sinners because this key relationship is the central key to all the rest. If there is one God and we are not reconciled to him, what does it profit us if we gain or improve the whole world but forfeit our very lives (see Luke 9:24–26)?

7. We recognize that the use of words like *colony* or *empire* to describe God's kingdom could prove controversial or even painful, particularly for those people who've suffered under oppressive colonization. Our intent is not in any way to support such historic injustices but, rather, to denounce them by recognizing that the only ultimate empire is the one with God on the throne, and he rules by way of the Suffering Lamb, Jesus. Because we are called to be a colony of that kingdom, we cannot participate in injustice and oppression but, rather, must embrace the mission of God's suffering love expanding peacefully throughout the world.

8. Campbell R. McConnell and Stanley L. Brue, *Economics: Principles, Problems, and Policies*, 13th ed. (New York: McGraw Hill, 1996), 1.

9. "Suicide Statistics," American Foundation for Suicide Prevention, accessed June 8, 2017, http://afsp.org/about-suicide/suicide-statistics/.

10. Commission on Children at Risk, *Hardwired to Connect: The New Scientific Case for Authoritative Communities* (New York: Institute for American Values, 2003), 6.

11. "Mental Health Facts in America," National Association for Mental Illness, accessed June 8, 2017, https://www.nami.org/NAMI/media/NAMI-Media/Infographics/GeneralMHFacts.pdf.

12. "Nationwide Trends," National Institute on Drug Abuse, accessed June 8, 2017, http://www.drugabuse.gov/publications/drugfacts/nationwide-trends.

13. Ibid.

14. Ibid.

15. Gina Kolata, "Death Rates Rising for Middle-Aged White Americans, Study Finds," *New York Times*, November 2, 2015, http://www.nytimes.com/2015/11/03/health/death-rates-rising-for-middle-aged-white-americans-study-finds.html?.

16. Jean M. Twenge, as quoted in Courtney Hutchison, "Today's Teens More Anxious, Depressed, and Paranoid Than Ever," ABC News, December 10, 2009, http://abcnews.go.com/Health/MindMoodNews/todays-teens-anxious-depressed-paranoid/story?id=9281013. See also Jean M. Twenge, et al., "Birth Cohort Increases in Psychopathology Among Young Americans, 1938–2007: A Cross-Temporal Meta-Analysis of the MMPI," *Clinical Psychology Review* 30 (2010): 145–54.

17. Chris Wright argues that any hermeneutic or organizing scheme we apply to Scripture inevitably emphasizes some things and overlooks other things. He suggests, though, that the same thing is true of maps: reality is portrayed partially and incompletely to help you get to your destination. This, for Wright, is the test of a good hermeneutic: "How faithfully does it interpret the journey for the traveler?" Chris Wright, *The Mission of God* (Downers Grove, IL: InterVarsity, 2006), 26.

18. John Yoder emphasizes the first two of these in his chapter on "Breaking Bread" in John Howard Yoder, *Body Politics: Five Practices of the Christian Community before the Watching World* (Nashville: Discipleship Resources, 1992).

19. David Mathis, "How Your Habits Show and Shape Your Heart," The Gospel Coalition, March 15, 2016, https://www.thegospelcoalition.org/article/how-your-habits-show-and-shape-your-heart.

20. The phrase is Craig Dykstra's, quoted in James K. A. Smith, *Imagining the Kingdom: How Worship Works*, Cultural Liturgies, vol. 2 (Grand Rapids: Baker Academic, 2013), 65.

21. John Howard Yoder, quoted in Paul C. Heidebrecht, *Beyond the Cutting Edge? Yoder, Technology, and the Practices of the Church* (Eugene, OR: Wipf & Stock, 2014), 205.

Chapter 1 "God, Not Mammon"

1. See Kelly Kapic's wonderful book titled *God So Loved He Gave* (Grand Rapids: Zondervan, 2010).

2. Eugene Peterson, *Run with the Horses: The Quest for Life at Its Best*, 2nd ed. (Downers Grove, IL: InterVarsity, 2010), 44.

3. Robert B. Chisholm Jr., "The Polemic against Baalism in Israel's Early History and Literature," *Bibliotheca Sacra* (1994): 270; Leah Bronner, *The Stories of Elijah and Elisha As Polemics against Baal Worship* (Leiden: E. J. Brill, 1968), 43.

4. Bronner, *Stories*, 54.

5. On this, see Brian Rosner, *Greed as Idolatry: The Origin and Meaning of a Pauline Metaphor* (Grand Rapids: Eerdmans, 2007).

6. Jacques Ellul, *Money and Power*, trans. LaVonne Neff (Eugene, OR: Wipf & Stock, 2009), 85.

7. David Boyle, "The Birth of the New Economics," Schumacher Center for a New Economics, accessed June 12, 2017, http://us5.campaign-archive1.com/?u=69d509d11303 2e3126c4543ce&id=e52f23d02b&e=9ad45965c7.

8. William T. Cavanaugh, *Being Consumed: Economics and Christian Desire* (Grand Rapids: Eerdmans, 2008), 46.

9. James K. A. Smith, *Desiring the Kingdom: Worship, Worldview, and Cultural Formation*, Cultural Liturgies, vol. 1 (Grand Rapids: Baker Academic, 2009), 99.

10. See Brian Fikkert and Michael Rhodes, "Homo Economicus versus Homo Imago Dei," *Journal of Markets & Morality* 20, no. 1 (Spring 2017): 101–26.

11. See Daniel M. Bell, *The Economy of Desire: Christianity and Capitalism in a Postmodern World* (Grand Rapids: Baker Academic, 2012), 93–122; D. Stephen Long, *Divine Economy: Theology and the Market* (New York: Routledge, 2000), 68; Scott W. Gustafson, *At the Altar of Wall Street: The Rituals, Myths, Theologies, Sacraments, and Mission of the Religion Known as the Modern Global Economy* (Grand Rapids: Eerdmans, 2015), 83.

12. Ronald J. Sider, *Rich Christians in an Age of Hunger: Moving from Affluence to Generosity*, 5th ed. (Nashville: Thomas Nelson, 2005), 199–200.

13. Commission on Children at Risk, *Hardwired to Connect*, 6.

14. Jean M. Twenge as quoted in Hutchison, "Today's Teens More Anxious, Depressed, and Paranoid Than Ever." See also Twenge et al., "Birth Cohort Increases in Psychopathology among Young Americans."

15. Sider, *Rich Christians*, 32. Adjusted for inflation.

16. Rick Reilly, "Getting By on $14.6 Mil," *Sports Illustrated*, November 15, 2004.

17. Gustafson, *At the Altar*, 15–20.

18. "US Household Debt Is High while Savings Are Low," National Center for Policy Analysis, April 16, 2015, http://www.ncpa.org/sub/dpd/index.php?Article_ID=25565.

19. Ruth Moon, ed., "Are American Evangelicals Stingy?," *Christianity Today*, January 31, 2011.

20. I was first exposed to the idea that where our treasures go shapes our hearts in Randy Alcorn's wonderful book *The Treasure Principle: Discovering the Secret of Joyful Giving* (Colorado Springs: Multnomah, 2001). For a similar interpretation on this whole segment, see Glen Harold Stassen and David P. Gushee, *Kingdom Ethics: Following Jesus in Contemporary Context* (Downers Grove, IL: InterVarsity, 2003), 64.

21. Ellis Smith, "How a Chattanooga Payday Lender Avoided Prosecution Here," *Chattanooga Times Free Press*, August 31, 2014, http://www.timesfreepress.com/news/local /story/2014/aug/31/how-payday-lender-avoided-prosecution-herebut-new/265975/.

22. Gene Edward Veith, "Who Gives Two Cents for Missions?," *World Magazine*, October 22, 2005, https://world.wng.org/2005/10/who_gives_two_cents_for_missions; Nation alChristianPoll.com, *Church Budget Priorities Survey Executive Report: 2009* (Christianity

Today, 2009), http://www.christianitytoday.com/special/ycresources/pdf/exec-report_church
budgetpriorities.pdf.

23. Jason Hood, "Theology in Action: Paul, the Poor, and Christian Mission," *Southeastern Theological Review* 2, no. 2 (Winter 2011): 132.

24. Halvor Moxnes, *The Economy of the Kingdom: Social Conflict and Economic Relations in Luke's Gospel* (Eugene, OR: Wipf & Stock, 1988), 119–25.

25. This phrase is taken from John M. Barclay's outstanding "Manna and the Circulation of Grace: A Study of 2 Corinthians 8:1–15," in J. Ross Wagner, C. Kavin Rowe, and A. Katherine Grieb, eds., *The Word Leaps the Gap: Essays on Scripture and Theology in Honor of Richard B. Hays* (Grand Rapids: Eerdmans, 2008).

Chapter 2 The Worship Key Today

1. My thanks to Daryl Heald for pointing me to this story, as well as bearing witness to the generous life through his teaching and personal example.

2. The video from which these quotes were taken can be viewed at https://vimeo.com/163251947. For more information, see www.generositypath.org.

3. Brian Bakke, Mustard Seed Foundation, personal correspondence.

4. Stats compiled by Scot McKnight on his blog, which you can find here: Scot McKnight, "Who Tithes These Days?," Beliefnet, accessed June 12, 2017, http://www.beliefnet.com/columnists/jesuscreed/2010/06/who-tithes-these-days.html.

5. Quoted in Craig L. Blomberg, *Christians in an Age of Wealth: A Biblical Theology of Stewardship* (Grand Rapids: Zondervan, 2013), 134.

6. Alan Barnhart, "God Owns Our Business," Generous Giving video, accessed August 8, 2017, https://generousgiving.org/media/videos/alan-barnhart-god-owns-our-business.

7. Greg Garrison, "Deep in Debt? Church Pays Off Payday Loans," AlabamaLiving.com, March 7, 2016, http://www.al.com/living/index.ssf/2016/03/deep_in_debt_church_pays_off_4.html.

8. For more information, see www.adventconspiracy.org.

9. Eberhard Arnold, *The Early Christians in Their Own Words*, rev. ed. (Walden, NY: Plough Publishing, 1998), 87.

10. Sider, *Rich Christians*, 183–205.

11. We need to be careful of phrases found in extremely popular financial material often used by Christians in the church, such as "Live like nobody else now so you can live like nobody else later" (Dave Ramsey, *The Total Money Makeover Workbook* [Nashville: Thomas Nelson, 2003], 218). While we are troubled by the many bad ways to interpret the quote above, we do wholeheartedly acknowledge and rejoice over the fact that Ramsey has helped countless Americans get out of debt. Since debt is an obstacle to the kind of King Jesus practices we recommend here and throughout this book, we celebrate this fact. But we suggest that avoiding or escaping debt needs to be understood within a larger narrative like the one we're trying to communicate throughout this book.

Chapter 3 "One Table, One Baptism, No Distinction"

1. This story is derived directly from Susan Rans and Hilary Altman, *Asset-Based Strategies for Faith Communities* (ABCD Institute, 2002), 18–25.

2. Ibid.

3. Ibid.

4. Many thanks to Amanda Coop and Justin Lonas for assisting us in creating these images.

5. Corbett and Fikkert, *When Helping Hurts*, 154. Originally adapted from Craig Storti, *Figuring Foreigners Out: A Practical Guide* (Yarmouth, ME: Intercultural Press, 1999), 52.

6. Wright, *Old Testament Ethics*, 363–65.

7. Ibid., 204–5.

8. Ibid., 208.

9. Duane Christensen, *Deuteronomy 21:10–34:12*, Word Biblical Commentary 6B (Grand Rapids: Zondervan, 2015), 632.

10. Mark Glanville, "Communities of Gratitude, Celebration, and Justice: A Missional Reading of Deuteronomy," in Mike Goheen, ed., *Reading the Bible Missionally* (Grand Rapids: Eerdmans, 2016).

11. Ibid.

12. Georg Braulik, *The Theology of Deuteronomy: Collected Essays of Georg Braulik*, trans. Ulrika Lindblad (North Richland Hills, TX: D & F Scott Publishing, 1998), 41.

13. Ibid., 51.

14. Ibid.

15. J. Gordon McConville, *Deuteronomy* (Downers Grove, IL: InterVarsity, 2002), 384. McConville rightly calls this one of the "great themes of the book."

16. On this point, see Braulik, *Theology*, 43.

17. It may not be accidental that Deuteronomy 15, one of the high points in all of Scripture in terms of God's command to care for the poor, falls between Deuteronomy 14 and 16, which command God's people to feast together.

18. Joel Green, *The Gospel of Luke* (Grand Rapids: Eerdmans, 1997), 179.

19. Ibid., 658–59.

20. Reta Halteman Finger, *Of Widows and Meals: Communal Meals in the Book of Acts* (Grand Rapids: Eerdmans, 2007), 128.

21. Ibid., 129.

22. Ibid., 131.

23. Ibid., 132.

24. For those who, in my view rightly, see the meal in Acts as the Lord's Supper, see among others, I. Howard Marshall, "Lord's Supper," *Dictionary of Paul and His Letters* (Downers Grove, IL: InterVarsity, 1993), 569–75 (574); Wright, *Old Testament Ethics*, 360.

25. On this, see Yoder, *Body Politics*, 20–21.

26. Robert Jewett, *Paul the Apostle to America: Cultural Trends and Pauline Scholarship* (Louisville: Westminster John Knox, 1994), 82.

27. Ibid., 73.

28. Translation for verses 17, 20, and 22 is my own.

29. See Anthony C. Thiselton, *The First Epistle to the Corinthians: A Commentary on the Greek Text* (Grand Rapids: Eerdmans, 2000), 850; Jerome Murphy-O'Connor, *Keys to First Corinthians* (Oxford: Oxford University Press, 2009), 153–61; Gordon D. Fee, *The First Epistle to the Corinthians*, rev. ed. (Grand Rapids: Eerdmans, 2014), 599–600; Suzanne Watts Henderson, "'If Anyone Hungers . . .': An Integrated Reading of 1 Cor. 11:17–34," *New Testament Series* 48, no. 2 (2002): 197; Mark P. Surburg, "The Situation at the Corinthian Lord's Supper in Light of 1 Corinthians 11:21: A Reconsideration," *Concordia Journal* 32, no. 1 (2006): 36–37.

30. Some scholars question whether there would have been the very wealthy Christians in Corinth that this reconstruction assumes. This is a complicated historical question, but even if the community did not have very wealthy patrons, it's clear that similar mechanisms of social exclusion and ostracizing were occurring. In other words, whether the very rich were shaming the very poor or the "just a bit richer than you" were shaming the "slightly poorer

than them," the overall point remains the same. My thanks to John Barclay for originally pointing this out to me (personal correspondence).

31. Fee, *First Epistle*, 623.

32. On this specifically and this entire section in general, see Michael Rhodes, "Forward unto Virtue: Formative Practices and 1 Corinthians 11:17–34," *Journal for Theological Interpretation* 11, no. 1 (2017): 119–38.

33. Fee, *First Epistle*, 603.

34. Richard S. Ascough, "Social and Political Characteristics of Greco-Roman Association Meals," in *Meals in the Early Christian World: Social Formation, Experimentation, and Conflict at the Table*, ed. Dennis E. Smith and Hal Taussig (New York: Palgrave MacMillan, 2012), 61.

35. Tim Chester, *A Meal with Jesus: Discovering Grace, Community, and Mission around the Table* (Wheaton: Crossway, 2011), 49.

36. Stanley Hauerwas, *With the Grain of the Universe: The Church's Witness and Natural Theology*, rev. ed. (Grand Rapids: Baker Academic, 2013), 214.

37. This title is a play on John Barclay's excellent "Manna and the Circulation of Grace: A Study of 2 Corinthians 8:1–15," in *The Word Leaps the Gap: Essays on Scripture and Theology in Honor of Richard B. Hays*, ed. J. R. Wagner, C. Kavin Rowe, and A. K. Grieb (Grand Rapids: Eerdmans, 2008), 422–23, on which see below.

38. Some scholars see the Greek financial givers as receiving spiritual gifts from Jerusalem, drawing on Paul's discussion of just this issue in Romans. However, the language of equality leads me to believe that Paul envisioned both physical and spiritual reciprocity, with giving and receiving flowing back and forth between the two communities. See Barclay, "Manna and the Circulation of Grace," 422–23.

39. Ibid.

40. St. Basil the Great, "Sermon to the Rich," accessed September 13, 2017, https://bekkos.wordpress.com/st-basils-sermon-to-the-rich/.

41. Rodney Stark, *The Rise of Christianity: A Sociologist Reconsiders History* (Princeton, NJ: Princeton University Press, 1996), 188.

42. Emmanuel Katongole and Chris Rice, *Reconciling All Things: A Christian Vision for Justice, Peace, and Healing* (Downers Grove, IL: InterVarsity, 2008), 78.

43. Walter Brueggemann, *The Prophetic Imagination*, 2nd ed. (Minneapolis: Fortress, 2001), 56.

44. Soong-Chan Rah, *Prophetic Lament: A Call for Justice in Troubled Times* (Downers Grove, IL: InterVarsity, 2015), 103.

45. Brueggemann, *Prophetic Imagination*, 67.

46. Both Soong-Chan Rah's *Prophetic Lament* and Katongole and Rice's *Reconciling All Things* provide excellent guidance and resources in learning this language.

47. Fee, *First Epistle*, 608. Some commentators argue that the reference is to God handing over Jesus for the sake of his people (see Thiselton, *Corinthians*, 870). However, I would argue that while God's divine handing over may be in view, the betrayal of Jesus is also alluded to. Indeed, these may not be mutually exclusive.

Chapter 4 The Community Key Today

1. Quoted in Chester, *Meal with Jesus*, 51.

2. Robert D. Putnam, *Bowling Alone: The Collapse and Revival of American Community* (New York: Simon & Schuster, 2000), 98.

3. Mark R. Gornik, *To Live in Peace: Biblical Faith and the Changing Inner City* (Grand Rapids: Eerdmans, 2002), 2. I personally find Gornik's book one of the most helpful books on ministry in marginalized communities in the United States.

4. Morgan Shoaff, "A Soup Kitchen Disguised as a Restaurant Is Making a Big Difference in Kansas City," Upworthy, March 2, 2016, http://www.upworthy.com/a-soup-kitchen-dis guised-as-a-restaurant-is-making-a-big-difference-in-kansas-city?g=2&c=ufb4.

5. Ibid.

6. Ibid.

7. Derived from a Christian Community Development Association talk. Recording available here: http://www.urbanministry.org/f/audio/including-excluded-mental-illness-and-re covery-jimmy-dorrell-shannon-ford-mary-girard-matthe.

8. Kara Bettis, "How Refugees Revived One White Iowa Church: Meet the Congregation That Traded in a Homogenous Heritage for a Diverse Future," *Christianity Today*, July 2016, accessed June 15, 2017, http://www.christianitytoday.com/local-church/2016/july /how-refugees-revived-one-white-iowa-church.html.

9. Glen Kehrein, "The Local Church and Christian Community Development," in *Restoring At-Risk Communities*, ed. John Perkins (Grand Rapids: Baker, 1995), 168.

10. Ibid., 175–76.

11. Quoted in Chester, *Meal with Jesus*, 50.

12. Ibid., 102.

13. Quoted in Stanley Sanders and Charles Campbell, *The Word on the Street: Performing the Scriptures in the Urban Context* (Eugene, OR: Wipf & Stock, 2006), 175.

14. Philip Hallie, *Lest Innocent Blood Be Shed: The Story of the Village of Le Chambon and How Goodness Happened There* (New York: HarperCollins, 1994), 284. See also Christine D. Pohl, *Making Room: Recovering Hospitality as a Christian Tradition* (Grand Rapids: Eerdmans, 1999), 83, 175.

15. Jean Vanier, *Community and Growth* (Mahwah, NJ: Paulist Press, 1992), 59.

Chapter 5 "Work and Wages, Gleaning and Giving"

1. For videos of Prime, and Lauren's story in particular, see https://vimeo.com/115020023 and https://vimeo.com/157796091.

2. Wes Gardner, personal conversation.

3. Compare also 1 Thessalonians 4:11–12.

4. Paul here used the same Greek word for hard labor that he used in Ephesians 4:28.

5. Andrew Lincoln, *Ephesians* (Grand Rapids: Zondervan, 1990), 304.

6. "Ex-Cons Face Tough Path Back into Work Force: Advocates Hope Federal Program Will Encourage Employers to Take a Chance," NBC News, July 30, 2009, http://www.nbc news.com/id/32208419/ns/business-careers/t/ex-cons-face-tough-path-back-work-force/# .VmdYCr9sGug.

7. Steven Raphael, "The Employment Prospects of Ex-Offenders," *Focus* 25, no. 2 (Fall–Winter 2007–08): 21–26, http://www.irp.wisc.edu/publications/focus/pdfs/foc252d.pdf.

8. Bruce Western, "The Impact of Incarceration on Wage Mobility and Inequality," *American Sociological Review* 67 (August 2002): 526–27, http://scholar.harvard.edu/files /brucewestern/files/western_asr.pdf.

9. Charles Wilbanks, "Temp Work Raises Long-Term Questions for Economy," CBS News, March 7, 2013, http://www.cbsnews.com/news/temp-work-raises-long-term-quest ions-for-economy/.

10. "About Advance Memphis," Advance Memphis, accessed June 19, 2017, http://advancememphis.org/about/.

11. "The Low-Wage Recovery: Industry Employment and Wages Four Years into the Recovery," National Employment Law Project, April 2014, http://www.nelp.org/content/uploads/2015/03/Low-Wage-Recovery-Industry-Employment-Wages-2014-Report.pdf.

12. "Poverty and Hunger in America," Feeding America, accessed June 19, 2017, http://www.feedingamerica.org/hunger-in-america//hunger-and-poverty-facts.html.

13. "Low Wage America and the Working Poor," My Budget 360, accessed June 17, 2017, http://www.mybudget360.com/low-wage-america-middle-class-incomes-and-employment-fields-income-growth-average-incomes/.

14. For these and other stats on implicit bias in recent research, see Sendhil Mullainathan, "Racial Bias, Even When We Have Good Intentions," *New York Times*, January 3, 2015, http://www.nytimes.com/2015/01/04/upshot/the-measuring-sticks-of-racial-bias-.html?_r=0.

15. Given the patriarchal character of the ancient world, at least the vast majority of landowners would have been men. For powerful, countercultural examples in Scripture, see Job 42:15 and Numbers 36.

16. For this stat, check out Jobs for Life's "Flip the List" page on their website at http://www.jobsforlife.org/FliptheList.

17. Although both markets and government policy were important to Israel. In fact, God gave laws that ensured markets would function relatively well (property laws) and created an extensive system of redistribution for the poor (the triennial tithe). It is equally important, though, to say that as a paradigm, the primary, though certainly not only, application of Israel's example is to the church, not the nation-state.

18. E. F. Davis, *Scripture, Culture, and Agriculture: An Agrarian Reading of the Bible* (New York: Cambridge University Press, 2009), 69, 71–72. The Lord's intention to liberate his people was grounded in this economic oppression of his people under their "taskmasters" (see Exod. 3:7–8).

19. Albert M. Wolters, *Creation Regained: Biblical Basics for a Reformational Worldview*, 2nd ed. (Grand Rapids: Eerdmans, 2005), 73.

20. Finger, *Of Widows and Meals*, 75.

21. Wright, *Old Testament Ethics*, 62–74.

Chapter 6 The Work Key Today

1. Lynne Golodner, "Welfare to Career: Plastics Company Helps People Break Barriers to Success," Everything Business Corp!, December 23, 2015, http://www.corpmagazine.com/human-resources/welfare-career-plastics-company-helps-people-break-barriers-success/2/.

2. On Broetje Orchards and all that follows, see their website (http://firstfruits.com/); Kenman Wong and Scott B. Rae, *Business for the Common Good: A Christian Vision for the Marketplace* (Downers Grove, IL: IVP Academic, 2011), 252; and Stan Friedman, "First Fruits: Broetje Orchards Puts People before Profits," *The Christian Century*, November 18, 2008, https://www.christiancentury.org/article/2008-11/first-fruits.

3. Wong and Rae, *Business for the Common Good*, 251–54.

4. Friedman, "First Fruits."

5. Ibid.

6. You can see videos of three other NGP employees who went through Advance's program on Advance's success stories page here: http://advancememphis.org/success-stories/. Andre, Lonnie, and Ray talk about going from Advance to NGP (none of these folks are the person whose story I share in the text). The "More About Advance Memphis"

video includes images from NGP as well as segments from an interview with their hiring manager.

7. "What Is Social Enterprise?," Social Enterprise Alliance, accessed June 20, 2017, https://socialenterprise.us/about/social-enterprise/.

8. For more on ThriftSmart, see http://www.thriftsmart.com/ and https://releaseyourraise.wordpress.com/2014/12/04/resources-in-action-thrift-smart/.

9. For more on Justin Beene and his work, see http://www.povertycure.org/tag/justin-beene/; http://hosted.verticalresponse.com/255160/e1fab87f5d/1304000891/6e3ebbfc3f/; and https://vimeo.com/192781531.

10. "The Problem," AutonomyWorks, accessed June 20, 2017, http://www.autonomy-works.com/About/The-Problem#.VrWStVKVuug.

11. B-Corps is a new incorporation that seeks to encourage businesses "to become a force for good in the world" (good for workers, good for the community, good for the environment, good for the long term, and good to the core). Their business assessment, which can be previewed through https://b-lab.secure.force.com/bcorp/impactassessmentdemo, includes a variety of metrics that would allow any business to consider some ways to become more kingdom focused. See for further research: www.bcorporation.net. For more on GiveGood, see www.givegoodco.com/.

12. Colby Itkowitz, "This Republican Mayor Has an Incredibly Simple Idea to Help the Homeless. And It Seems to Be Working," *Washington Post*, August 11, 2016, https://www.washingtonpost.com/news/inspired-life/wp/2016/08/11/this-republican-mayor-has-an-incredibly-simple-idea-to-help-the-homeless-and-it-seems-to-be-working/?utm_term=.2747bf35e58b. See also a video on this program at https://www.facebook.com/Upworthy/videos/1268563466517842/.

13. "Home," Hospitality Hub, accessed June 21, 2017, http://www.hospitalityhub.org/.

14. Bob Lupton, "Christmas Again!," November 11, 2015, http://www.fcsministries.org/blog/2015/11/5/christmas-again.

15. Jann Ingmire, "Chicago Summer Jobs Program for High School Students Dramatically Reduces Youth Violence," UChicago News, December 4, 2014, http://news.uchicago.edu/article/2014/12/04/chicago-summer-jobs-program-students-dramatically-reduces-youth-violence.

16. "Does It Matter How We Help People?," Covenant Presbyterian Church, accessed June 21, 2017, http://www.covhsv.org/does-it-matter-how-we-help-people/.

Chapter 7 "No Poor among You"

1. Walter Brueggemann, *God, Neighbor, Empire: The Excess of Divine Fidelity and the Command of Common Good* (Waco: Baylor University Press, 2016), 70.

2. Walter Brueggemann, *The Land: Place As Gift, Promise, and Challenge in Biblical Faith* (Minneapolis: Fortress, 2002), 32.

3. Davis, *Scripture, Culture, and Agriculture*, 66.

4. Wright, *Old Testament Ethics*, 64.

5. Ibid., 56.

6. Leslie Hoppe, *There Shall Be No Poor among You: Poverty in the Bible* (Nashville: Abingdon, 2004), 9.

7. Ibid.

8. Jason Hood, *Imitating God in Christ: Recapturing a Biblical Pattern* (Downers Grove, IL: IVP Academic, 2013), 21.

9. Some people have raised questions as to whether the Jubilee Year was ever observed. But that is irrelevant . . . God commanded it, and it was to be obeyed. Period. Of course, we

know that Israel was sent into captivity—in part—for failing to care for the poor in the way God commanded in the Old Testament (see Isa. 1 and 58; Ezek. 16:49). Maybe Israel's failure to observe the year of Jubilee was part of what had God so upset. If so, it merely proves the point that God really cares about this . . . so much so that he sent his only Son to bring the Year of Jubilee as part of his kingdom (see Luke 4).

10. I would also add that trying to make the economic message of these texts that the church's economic communalism didn't work reflects horrendous hermeneutics. It's like suggesting that racial reconciliation doesn't "work" based on Peter's troubles with the Jerusalem church after the business with Cornelius. Nothing shows the contemporary American ideological rejection of God's economy clearer than the tortured interpretations and qualifications we come up with while trying to "deal with" the Jubilee and the early church's practice. Walter Houston's suggestion that our incredulity over the Jubilee legislation is primarily the result of our (often unacknowledged) economic ideology is equally appropriate here (Walter Houston, *Contending for Justice: Ideologies and Theologies of Social Justice in the Old Testament*, 2nd ed. (New York: T & T Clark, 2008), 195–96.

11. Finger, *Of Widows and Meals*, 75–128.

Chapter 8 The Equity Key Today

1. Mark Charles, "The Doctrine of Discovery—A Buried Apology and an Empty Chair," December 22, 2014, http://wirelesshogan.blogspot.com/2014/12/doctrine-of-discovery.html.

2. "The Christian Doctrine of Discovery: A North American History," Christian Reformed Centre for Public Dialogue, November 2013, https://www.crcna.org/sites/default /files/lit_review.pdf.

3. Charles, "The Doctrine of Discovery."

4. Quoted in Gene L. Green, "Immigration and Migration: The Gospel and the Indigenous-European Encounter on Turtle Island," presented at the 2016 Evangelical Theological Society proceedings.

5. Jennifer Clark, "Native Americans Voice Their Support of Social Security," National Academy of Social Insurance, June 20, 2012, https://www.nasi.org/discuss/2012/06/native -americans-voice-their-support-social-security.

6. Algernon Austin, "Native Americans and Jobs: The Challenge and the Promise," Economic Policy Institute, December 17, 2013, http://www.epi.org/publication/bp370-native -americans-jobs/.

7. "How to Redeem Thanksgiving," *Christianity Today*, November 22, 2016, http:// www.christianitytoday.com/ct/2016/november-web-only/how-to-redeem-thanksgiving.html.

8. Elizabeth Jemison, "Black Churches in the Memphis Massacre," *Memphis Massacre 1866* (blog), March 29, 2016, https://blogs.memphis.edu/memphismassacre1866/2016/03/29 /black-churches-in-the-memphis-massacre/.

9. Check out the Chalmers Center's Individual Development Account handbook at https:// www.chalmers.org/matched-savings-ida-toolkit.

10. Ta-Nehisi Coates, "The Case for Reparations," *Atlantic*, June 2014, http://www .theatlantic.com/magazine/archive/2014/06/the-case-for-reparations/361631/.

11. Ibid.

12. Ibid. Note the firsthand accounts Coates collects from people still living who experienced such predation in Chicago.

13. Preston Lauterbach, "Memphis Burning," *Places Journal*, March 2016, https://places journal.org/article/memphis-burning/.

14. James O'Toole, "Wells Fargo Pledges $432.5 Million in Lending, Payments to Settle Lawsuit," CNN Money, May 31, 2012, http://money.cnn.com/2012/05/30/news/companies /wells-fargo-memphis/index.htm.

15. Ken Sweet, "Regulators Fine BancorpSouth $10.6 Million for Redlining," Associated Press, June 2016, http://bigstory.ap.org/article/c018fd2a637244e58a0a44a44f0847b4/regula tors-fine-bancorpsouth-106-million-redlining.

16. See, for instance, Rakesh Kochhar and Richard Fry, "Wealth Inequality Has Widened Along Racial, Ethnic Lines Since End of Great Recession," Pew Research Center, December 2014, http://www.pewresearch.org/fact-tank/2014/12/12/racial-wealth-gaps-great-recession/.

17. For what followed, see Mondragon's history as recorded on their webpage, http:// www.mondragon-corporation.com/wp-content/themes/mondragon/docs/History-MON DRAGON.pdf.

18. Frank Islam and Ed Crego, "A Formula for Reawakening Labor: Capitalism, Communities, and Cooperatives," Huffington Post, November 13, 2013, http://www.huffingtonpost .com/frank-islam/a-formula-for-reawakening_b_3914914.html.

19. Jessica Gordon Nembhard, "African American Cooperatives," prepared for the Babson-Equal Exchange Cooperative Curriculum, June 18, 2012, http://institute.coop/sites /default/files/resources/Black-Coops-GordonNembhard.pdf.

20. Ibid., 15.

21. Ibid., 7.

22. David Brodwin, "A Cleveland Success Story," *US News and World Report*, July 21, 2016, http://www.usnews.com/opinion/articles/2016-07-21/evergreen-cooperative-is-a-cleve land-jobs-success-story.

23. Douglas Trattner, "Worker-Owned Green City Growers Is on the Path to Profits While Giving Refugees and Ex-Cons Gainful Employment," Scene, March 15, 2017, https://www .clevescene.com/cleveland/worker-owned-green-city-growers-is-on-the-path-to-profits-while -giving-refugees-and-ex-cons-gainful-employment/Content?oid=5740258.

24. Prospera, *2015 Annual Report*, accessed June 22, 2017, http://prosperacoops.org /sites/default/files/prospera_2015_annual_report_1.pdf.

25. "Lupita," Prospera, accessed June 22, 2017, http://prosperacoops.org/lupita.

26. On this, see Community-Wealth.org's outstanding resources on ESOPs. Quotes taken from http://community-wealth.org/strategies/panel/esops/index.html.

27. Co.Starters is "a nine-week cohort based program that equips aspiring entrepreneurs with the insights, relationships, and tools needed to turn ideas into action and turn a passion into a sustainable and thriving endeavor." The curriculum helpfully draws on the business model canvas concept. LAUNCH uses the Co.Starters Urban curriculum, but Co.Starters also offers adaptations aimed at causes or social enterprises, rural communities, and teens. See https://costarters.co/.

28. See http://www.pep.org/. For more on Kevin's story specifically, check out https:// www.youtube.com/watch?v=umlFcy5qZxs&feature=youtu.be; https://www.kiva.org/lend /1081289; and http://www.pep.org/kevin-r-testimony/.

29. To watch the video from which most of this content was derived, check out https:// vimeo.com/146304308.

30. For more information on Circles USA, see http://www.circlesusa.org/kettering/.

31. Technically, what we're describing as impact investments are sometimes specified as concessionary impact investments. Non-concessionary impact investments seek to achieve normal market returns. See, for instance, Paul Brest and Kelly Born, "Unpacking the Impact in Impact Investing," *Stanford Social Innovation Review*, August 14, 2013, https://ssir.org /articles/entry/unpacking_the_impact_in_impact_investing.

32. "About Us," Kiva, accessed June 22, 2017, https://www.kiva.org.

33. "The Victor Story," Kiva, accessed August 9, 2017, http://us.kiva.org/stories/lender/jonny/.

34. Oscar Perry Abello, "Closing the 'Friends and Family' Capital Gap for Entrepreneurs of Color," Next City, October 25, 2016, https://nextcity.org/daily/entry/runway-project-friends-family-capital-gap-entrepreneurs.

35. Ibid.

36. Check out the Chalmers Center's resource page on IDAs here: https://www.chalmers.org/matched-savings-ida-toolkit.

37. The Memphis Leadership Foundation, founded by Dr. Larry Lloyd, has been a tremendous force for catalyzing Christian Community Development in our city. Check out their website at www.memphisleadershipfoundation.org. The Alcy Ball Development Corporation, led by my good friend, former coworker, and current next door neighbor Chris Oliver, is a nonprofit that makes partnering with churches a core aspect of their work. They're helping churches in one neighborhood offer *Faith & Finances* and Work Life courses, as well as offering a LAUNCH-style entrepreneurship course later this year. Whereas many nonprofits end up accidentally sidelining or ignoring local churches, Chris and ABDC are trying to equip and empower neighborhood churches. This approach has made them a perfect partner for our IDA pilot. Learn more at http://www.alcyball.org/

38. Broadly speaking, we're pursuing what Bob Lupton calls "gentrification with justice." The idea is that in communities of concentrated poverty, there is a need for greater economic investment, rising home values, etc., but that, left to the market, this gentrifying process will unjustly push out the poor and marginalize neighbors who are the historic residents of the community. Gentrification with justice seeks to prevent this by slowing the process and allowing historic neighbors to become homeowners and business owners so that they benefit economically and remain in place when a community's economic prospects begin to improve. For New City Housing, though, a challenge is that our efforts depend on loans and investments primarily from folks who are not the historic residents of the community (even if we currently live there). A second phase of our work will be to see if we can help historic neighbors become economic stakeholders in the business as well. On gentrification with justice, see Bob Lupton, "Gentrification with Justice," *byFaith Online*, accessed August 9, 2017, http://sites.silaspartners.com/partner/Article_Display_Page/0,,PTID323422_CHID664014_CIID2235910,00.html.

39. The College Board, *Trends in College Pricing 2014* (College Board, 2014), https://secure-media.collegeboard.org/digitalServices/misc/trends/2014-trends-college-pricing-report-final.pdf.

40. My thanks to Pete Selden, associate vice chancellor for workforce programs for Arkansas State University, Mid-South, for helping me find these statistics and opening my eyes to the power of vocational training for economic empowerment. ASU's excellent technical programs helped me see my own biases toward "traditional" college experiences.

41. Jonathan Rothwell, "The Hidden STEM Economy," Brookings Institute, June 10, 2013, https://www.brookings.edu/research/the-hidden-stem-economy/.

42. Benjamin Keylor, "6 Skills Gap Statistics that Continue to Impact Hiring," Davis Companies, July 14, 2016, http://www.davisco.com/6-skills-gap-statistics-that-continue-to-impact-hiring-infographic/.

43. Mark Schneider, *Higher Education Pays: But a Lot More for Some Graduates Than for Others* (College Measure, 2013), http://www.air.org/sites/default/files/Higher_Education_Pays_Sep_13.pdf.

44. See "CTE Today" from the Association for Career and Technical Education (2017) available at https://www.acteonline.org/uploadedFiles/What_is_CTE/Fact_Sheets/CTE_Today_Fact_Sheet_2017.pdf.

45. "Investment Pathways," Criterion Institute, accessed June 23, 2017, https://criterion institute.org/our-church-work/1kchurches/investment-pathways/.

Chapter 9 "The Heavens Declare the Glory"

1. Ann Coulter, "Oil Good; Democrats Bad," Townhall, October 12, 2000, http://town hall.com/columnists/anncoulter/2000/10/12/oil_good;_democrats_bad.

2. Wendell Berry, "The Pleasures of Eating," in *Sex, Economy, Freedom, and Community: Eight Essays* (New York: Pantheon, 1993).

3. Wright, *Mission of God*, 398–99.

4. Scripture is clear about ownership: the whole creation is God's possession. "All the earth is mine" (Exod. 19:5 ESV; see also Deut. 10:14; Pss. 24:1; and 89:11). Receiving the *management* of creation as God's gift-task is foundational for our economic lives. God's gifts are his to give. He shares his bounty with us at his discretion.

5. Coulter, "Oil Good; Democrats Bad."

6. From her outstanding article "Environmental Law in Deuteronomy: One Lens on a Biblical Theology of Creation Care," *Bulletin for Biblical Research* 20, no. 3 (2010): 356, 376, respectively. Richard Bauckham translates this phrase "to till it and keep it" and asserts that "to work" or "to cultivate" is "the obvious meaning in Genesis 2," in *The Bible in the Contemporary World: Hermeneutical Ventures* (Grand Rapids: Eerdmans, 2015), 92. Bauckham, whose extensive and helpful writings on Scripture and ecology we deeply appreciate, may be underplaying the "cosmic temple"/"sacred garden" background that orients one to accept "serve" as a reasonable translation, since *adam avads* the *adamah* in Yahweh's temple. For collections of much of his excellent work in this regard, see ibid., plus *The Bible and Ecology: Rediscovering the Community of Creation* (Waco: Baylor University Press, 2010) and *Living With Other Creatures: Green Exegesis and Theology* (Waco: Baylor University Press, 2011). For recent research and updated bibliography on cosmic temple background to Genesis 2, see Catherine L. McDowell, *The Image of God in the Garden of Eden* (Warsaw, IN: Eisenbrauns, 2015).

However, Bauckham's work is vital for recovering the teaching of Scripture for our relationship with the rest of the creation. His reading of Genesis 1–2 helpfully "distinguishes between human use of the earth, with its vegetation, for human life and flourishing, a right to be exercised responsibly, and human dominion over the rest of the animate creation, for which humans have a responsibility of care" (*The Bible and Ecology*, 90). We are hardly doing his work justice with such swift references. *Tolle lege!*

7. Psalm 19:1–6 famously celebrates the role of creation as teacher. Isaiah 28:23–29 is a wonderful parallel to Psalm 19, which also overlaps with Genesis 2. The farmer, by careful attention to his work of plowing in God's ordered creation "is rightly instructed; his God teaches him" (Isa. 28:26 ESV). And as one learns how to create food with harvested seeds, "this also comes from Yahweh . . . the source of great counsel and wisdom" (28:29, author's own translation).

8. Corbett and Fikkert, *When Helping Hurts*, 54–59.

9. Maltbie Davenport Babcock, "This Is My Father's World" (1915).

10. Here lies the answer to our introductory question: *How far shall our Redeemer's blessing flow?* From "Joy to the World," third stanza, Isaac Watts's wonderful Advent interpretation of Psalm 98!

11. Notice the genealogical contrast represented in Genesis 4:17–5:32. The primary speakers in both lines are named Lamech. The Lamech in the line of Cain represents the "seed of the serpent" and the Lamech in the line of Seth represents the "seed of the woman." The Lamech in Cain's line also alludes to words from the Lord. He multiplies Yahweh's protective speech over Cain, who murdered his brother Abel (see Gen. 4:15), with radical, violent boasting. The number 7 figures prominently in his violent speech (see v. 24). Lamech in the line of Seth, who replaced Abel at the time when his family began to worship in humility (see vv. 25–26), named his son Noah, alluding to Genesis 3:15, and lived 777 years.

12. The order of the descriptions of human sin, God's favor for Noah, and Noah's character seem intentional: all are wicked and God will blot them out (see Gen. 6:5), but Noah received God's favor (see v. 8). And Noah was righteous, blameless, and walked with God (see v. 9). This last line is meant to foreground the flood narrative in a fashion parallel to how 6:1–8 functions.

13. The first two are in verse 11; the third is in verse 15.

14. Davis, *Scripture, Culture, and Agriculture*, 19.

15. The covenant with Noah shows us something about the scope of God's redemption—the whole creation and all creatures are included. The covenant with Abraham points to sequence. God rescued the peoples of the nations, the stewards, first. Romans 8 provides a parallel reflection on the relationship between these covenants.

16. For this phrase, see Hauerwas, *With the Grain of the Universe*.

17. On this point, see Wright, *Mission of God*, 397.

18. Something similar may be at work in Yahweh's command that mother birds not be taken with their eggs. If one came across a bird's nest, the means of life (the mother) had to be preserved even when taking the production (the eggs). See Deuteronomy 22:6–7.

19. These statistics apply to an average family in ancient Israel. See Richter, "Environmental Law," 371–72, and the scholarship she summarizes there.

20. As we will see, these themes continue in the New Testament and reach their climax in Romans 8 and Revelation 21–22.

21. This becomes even clearer once we realize that the Behemoth and Leviathan Yahweh celebrates are probably simultaneously representative of the hippopotamus and crocodile, fearsome creatures in their own right, as well as cosmic destructive characters in the mythologies of the nations around Israel. For many in the ancient Near East, such sea creatures were part of the dark stories of the world's beginning in the violence and war of the gods, and their existence reflected the ongoing chaos and evil at work in the world. Against such stories, Yahweh's poetry proclaims that he alone is Lord of heaven and earth, Creator of a world made good from the heavens above to the ocean floor below.

22. Davis, *Scripture, Culture, and Agriculture*, 46.

23. See Psalms 65:6–13; 69:34; 89:11–17 (esp. vv. 11–12); 96:1–13 (esp. vv. 1, 11–13); 97:1–7; 98:7–9; 103:22; 104:1–35; 145:10; 148:1–14; 150:6.

24. Walter Harrelson, "On God's Care for the Earth: Psalm 104," *Currents in Theology and Mission* 2 (1975): 20–21.

25. See especially Bauckham, *The Bible and Ecology*, 64–91, and *Living with Other Creatures*, 1–13, 163–84. Further, Bauckham's historical account on the reception of, modern and reductionist misunderstandings of, and potential recovery of the "dominion" concept is superlatively helpful for twenty-first-century Bible readers (*Living with Other Creatures*, 14–62).

26. See William P. Brown, *Wisdom's Wonder: Character, Creation, and Crisis in the Bible's Wisdom Literature* (Grand Rapids: Eerdmans, 2014), 39.

27. See Matthew 1:18–23; Luke 1:26–38; John 1:1–18; 8:48–59; 13:1–4; 17:1–5; Galatians 4:4; Philippians 2:5–11; Colossians 2:9–10; Titus 2:11–14; Hebrews 1–2; Revelation 4–5.

28. See John 1:1–4; Colossians 1:16; Hebrews 1:2. He also *sustains* all things (see Col. 1:17 and Heb. 1:3).

29. See Galatians 4:4; Philippians 2:6–8; 1 Timothy 2:1–5. Note the four uses of *anthropos*: in 1 Timothy 2:1, 4 and then two in verse 5. In the ESV, for example, in verses 1 and 4 this Greek word is translated "people," as in "regular old humans—normal people." Then the same term, *anthropos*, is translated "men" (same meaning as "people" and "man"—referring to Jesus—in 1 Timothy 2:5). So 1 Timothy 2:1–5 teaches that Jesus became a man, a real human being. The glorious Son described in Hebrews 1:1–3 was temporarily "made lower than the angels" and even suffered death (Heb. 2:9), was perfected as our redeemer through suffering (see v. 10), and was even made like us "in every way" (see vv. 14–18).

30. See Colossians 1:16–20; Ephesians 1:10. Jesus (see Matt. 19:28) and Peter (see Acts 3:21) allude to parallels of what Paul writes in Ephesians 1 and Colossians 1.

31. See Philippians 2:5–11; Colossians 1:15–20; Hebrews 1:4–13; Revelation 5:3–14; in all of life (see Rom. 14:6–12).

32. Matthew, Mark, and Luke all narrate Jesus's baptism and subsequent temptation. Luke's narrative helps the reader see correspondences with Adam in the garden (largely by placing a genealogy between the baptism scene and the temptation scene, which moves from Jesus all the way back to Adam; see Luke 3:38). Jesus obeyed in the barren wilderness where Adam failed in the lush garden. Matthew helps the reader see particularly correspondences with the story of Israel, where Israel rebelled on the borders of the promised land and wandered for forty years. Jesus was tempted in the wilderness for forty days, facing temptations that paralleled those faced by the Israelites.

33. Wright, *Mission of God*, 403.

34. The "already" and "not yet" pattern parallels the pattern of salvation for those who believe—with good reason.

The kingdom is inaugurated, growing, and will be consummated.

Our salvation is accomplished, growing, and will be completed.

(Justification has happened.) (Sanctification is happening.) (Glorification will happen.)

35. Wright, *Mission of God*, 409.

36. Wendell Berry, *Hannah Coulter* (Berkeley: Shoemaker & Hoard, 2005), 43. Of course, this is a mystery. There are enormous questions about the relationship between this age and the age to come, and the discontinuity and continuity between them. But what we stand firm on is a commitment to real redemption of God's good creation, including culture, of which Jesus's own resurrection is the firstfruits (see 1 Cor. 15; Rev. 21:24).

Chapter 10 The Creation Care Key Today

1. See the discussion of terrestrial ecologists from Stanford in Davis, *Scripture, Culture, and Agriculture*, 54–55.

2. Please note: the authors of this book believe in the cultural mandate and absolutely affirm that, because everyone is made in God's image, work is good. We also are pro-development (one of us is a development economist) and celebrate cultural developments that lead to things such as the computers we're using to write this book. However, in this chapter, we're focusing specifically on the creation care aspect of God's economy, which we believe is an essential, and often missing, piece of a Christian understanding of work and development. We believe there must be great development, including technological advancement, that respects the rest of the creation as God's good gift.

3. See Al Wolters, "The Story: Creation," *Comment* (Spring 2010), https://www.cardus.ca/comment/article/2022/creation; we believe the best descriptions of creation as a biblical

doctrine include "everything which God has ordained to exist, what he has put into place as part of his creative workmanship." Similar to Bauckham (*Living with Other Creatures*, 14–62), Wolters notes the danger of post-Enlightenment worldviews that divorce "the natural world from human worlds, so that the standards of human life and culture are no longer sought in a given and external order that has divine authority, but rather in the human subject itself which produces its own order out of its own authority." Wolters's earlier book, *Creation Regained*, is a standard bearer for this broader perspective on the meaning of creation.

4. Athanasius, *On the Incarnation of the World*, New Advent, accessed August 9, 2017, http://www.newadvent.org/fathers/2802.htm.

5. Twenty-one of the original twenty-two men who gathered were committed Christians. This group included the famous and tireless abolitionist, William Wilberforce. The remaining member was a Jewish activist. See Philip Johnson, "Revered Author Broome Founder of RSPCA (Part One)," *Animals Matter to God*, June 16, 2012, https://animalsmattertogod .com/2012/06/16/reverend-arthur-broome-founder-of-rspca-part-one/.

6. Ibid.

7. Ibid.

8. Ibid. Queen Victoria's reign began on June 20, 1837. She was crowned on June 28, 1838. "In 1840, sixteen years after it was founded (and which was sadly three years after Broome's death in 1837), Queen Victoria granted [them] official royal patronage. . . . That patronage, which continues to the present-day, has elevated the RSPCA's status and helped to ensure that it is the oldest and longest-running animal protection organisation in the world (with its bicentenary approaching on Sunday, 16 June 2024).

9. See https://edenthistle.myshopify.com/.

10. Marshall Teague, personal conversation.

11. Richter, "Environmental Law," 373–74.

12. "9 Facts about Factory Farming That Will Break Your Heart," Huffington Post, March 17, 2014, http://www.huffingtonpost.com/2014/03/17/factory-farming-facts_n_4063892.html.

13. On dead zones in the Gulf, see http://oceanservice.noaa.gov/facts/deadzone.html; http://oceanservice.noaa.gov/education/classroom/lessons/13_ecoforecasting_deadzone .pdf; http://www.noaa.gov/media-release/average-dead-zone-for-gulf-of-mexico-predicted.

14. Centers for Disease Control and Prevention, "CDC Links Improved Air Quality with Decreased Emergency Visits for Asthma," news release, February 21, 2001, https://www .cdc.gov/media/pressrel/r010221.htm.

15. Daron Babcock uses this phrase to describe how the urban farm he founded "to create jobs and provide fresh food" (where previously none was available) is "a catalyst" for cultivating much more than new jobs and better food. See the excellent video capturing their inspiring vision at http://bontonfarms.org.

16. "Our Story," Bonton Farms, accessed June 26, 2017, http://bontonfarms.org/our-story/.

17. Courtney Gilmore, "Texas Connects Us: Bonton Farms Plants Hope in the Middle of Dallas Food Desert," NBCDFW.com, December 20, 2016, www.nbcdfw.com/news/local /City-Farm-Grows-Hope--407668165.html.

18. H.I.S. BridgeBuilders is a community development nonprofit in Dallas, Texas, focusing on a holistic, relational approach to poverty. They serve there, "working to mobilize the Body of Christ to cure poverty in our city," because Dallas is leading the nation in childhood poverty, second in the nation in growing rate of poverty, and third nationally in overall poverty rate for cities with a population over one million. See their website for their holistic approach to community transformation: https://www.hisbridgebuilders.org/.

19. "More Than a Farm," Bonton Farms, accessed June 27, 2017, http://bontonfarms .org/our-farm/, italics added.

20. Ibid.

21. See the discussion of "four foundational relationships" in Corbett and Fikkert, *When Helping Hurts*, 54–63, building off Bryant Myers, *Walking with the Poor: Principles and Practices of Transformational Development* (Maryknoll, NY: Orbis, 1999). More and more urban farms exist to address such needs. Hope for the Inner City in Chattanooga, Tennessee, is another example. In their own words, "Urban agriculture is a way for people to reclaim their connections to nature, to the act of eating, and to each other through the act of growing food, all without leaving the city. It's also a movement through which people are gaining more independence from the current industrial food system, which is expensive and inefficient and relies on petrochemicals." See "What We Do: Urban Agriculture," Hope for the Inner City, accessed June 27, 2017, https://www.hopefortheinnercity.org/growhope/#.

22. Wendell Berry, "The Pleasures of Eating," Center for Ecoliteracy, accessed August 9, 2017, https://www.ecoliteracy.org/article/wendell-berry-pleasures-eating.

23. For more on the Center and their partner organizations Memphis Tilth and Bring It Food Hub, see http://memphisfoodandfaith.com/our-work/; http://bringitfoodhub.com/about-us/; and http://www.memphistilth.org/.

24. Memphis Tilth, *Memphis Tilth 2016 Annual Report*, accessed June 27, 2017, https://static1.squarespace.com/static/58b448a0414fb5caa4f2502d/t/58b4dff417bffc8838231cb8/1488248889464/2016+Public+Annual+Report.pdf.

25. "Land of Waste: American Landfills and Waste Production," SaveonEnergy.com, accessed June 27, 2017, https://www.saveonenergy.com/land-of-waste/.

26. Ibid.

27. Ibid.

28. The Au Sable Institute (www.ausable.org) "offers environmental science programs for students and adults of all ages." The group Renewal (www.renewingcreation.org) is a "Christ-centered and student-driven creation care network that strives to inspire, connect and equip college students in their sustainability efforts."

29. Like Bonton Farms and Grow Hope Urban Farm, more and more urban farms exist to address such needs: "Agriculture in the city is different from traditional farming. It often involves growing food within a limited space and sometimes, with limited resources. Ideally, urban agriculture represents the place where environmentally sustainable methods, the local economy, and relationships between people intersect, creating a thriving local food system and ensuring greater access to healthy food—community food security" ("Urban Agriculture," Hope for the Inner City, accessed August 9, 2017, https://www.hopefortheinnercity.org/growhope/).

Chapter 11 "The Lord Has Given the Sabbath"

1. These metaphors are so familiar we employ them to mean different things depending on context. Thus, "I'm chasing my tail" typically connotes "futility" but captures the busyness behind our sense of futility. Remarkably, for as tired and busy as we are, we also have a rich supply of metaphors for futility that assume we're busy and accomplishing little: "I'm spinning my wheels," "I'm going nowhere fast," and "I'm losing traction."

2. Sandra Richter, *The Epic of Eden: A Christian Entry into the Old Testament* (Downers Grove, IL: IVP Academic, 2008), 105. But as Richter notes, the Hebrew word that an ancient person would expect to express a king's rest sounds a lot like Noah's name to us. But here in Genesis 2:1–3, God takes a "Sabbath." The play on words depends on expecting a common verb for rest and getting another verb, *shabat*, which the Israelites would have readily associated with the Sabbath.

3. This inelegant translation is our own and tries to follow the Hebrew text as closely as possible.

4. Walter Brueggemann, *Sabbath as Resistance: Saying No to the Culture of Now* (Louisville: Westminster John Knox, 2014), 29.

5. Chris Wright, "Biblical Paradigms of Redemption," in *Transforming the World? The Gospel and Social Responsibility*, eds. Jamie A. Grant and Dewi A. Hughes (Downers Grove, IL: InterVarsity, 2009), 79.

6. Davis, *Scripture, Culture, and Agriculture*, 71–72.

7. We realize that Sabbath was central and basic to Yahweh's law for Israel. Our "300 level" metaphor relates to Yahweh's economics training. On the way to Sinai he proved he was the Provider, giving water and comfort (15:22–27) and then manna (16:1–26). The gift of manna undergirds the Sabbath in its six-day program. On the heels of these gifts and in the context of unbelieving, grumbling, and disobedience, Moses declares, "See! Yahweh has GIVEN you the Sabbath; therefore on the sixth day he GIVES bread for two days" (author's translation).

8. Brueggemann, *Sabbath as Resistance*, 45.

9. The phrase is Walter Brueggemann's, whose provocative work has inspired much of this book in myriad ways.

10. Davis, *Scripture, Culture, and Agriculture*, 70.

11. Ibid., 71.

12. The redemption dynamic is also present in Exodus, as can be seen in the prologue to the Ten Commandments, which recounts the story of Yahweh's liberation of Israel from Egypt. Like the call of Abraham to bless all the families of the earth, Exodus 19 prepares the reader for this connection between redemption and creation. Yahweh rescued Israel to be royal priests because the whole earth is his (see vv. 5–6).

13. G. K. Chesterton, *Orthodoxy* (Snowball Publishing, 2015), 41.

14. Brueggemann, *Sabbath as Resistance*, 40.

15. Ibid., 40–41.

16. Mark Glanville, "Family for the Displaced: A New Paradigm for the Ger in Deuteronomy" (unpublished PhD dissertation, University of Bristol, 2016), 128.

17. The first reference to this ethical orientation of empathy led straight into care for widows and orphans (see Exod. 22:21–22). See also Leviticus 19:33–34 and Deuteronomy 10:12–22.

18. Walter Brueggemann, *Money and Possessions* (Louisville: Westminster John Knox, 2016), 51.

19. Ibid., 23.

20. This is actually a bit difficult to see in the English translations of the Bible because Leviticus 25:5 makes it sound a bit like they won't eat the gleanings, while verse 6 makes it clear that they will. We take verse 5 essentially to be prohibiting any organized farming, while verse 6 explains that all will eat the natural harvest of the land together.

21. Note that some scholars believe the Year of Jubilee occurred in the forty-ninth year.

22. Wright, *Mission of God*, 299.

23. "The jubilee had two major thrusts: release/liberty and return/restoration (Lev. 25:10). Both of these were easily transferred from the strictly economic provision of the jubilee itself to a wider metaphorical application. That is, these economic terms became terms of hope and longing for the future, and thus entered into prophetic eschatology" (Wright, *Mission of God*, 300). Wright's work here and elsewhere is excellent. He demonstrates that all the Sabbath legislation, including the weekly Sabbath, the sabbatical year, and the Jubilee required a Godwardness, complete with trust in God's sovereignty, providence, redemptive acts, and forgiveness (ibid., 299).

24. Wright, *Mission of God*, 299.
25. Willard M. Swartley, "Sabbath," in *Dictionary of Scripture and Ethics*, ed. Joel Green (Grand Rapids: Baker Academic, 2011), 695.
26. Brueggemann, *Sabbath as Resistance*, 66.
27. One thinks of Augustine's wonderful adage regarding true spirituality: "Do you wish your prayer to fly towards God? Give it two wings: fasting and almsgiving."
28. See also Luke 8:1–3 and 16:16.
29. On the preceding interpretation, see N. T. Wright, *The Resurrection of the Son of God* (Minneapolis: Fortress, 2003), 667.
30. Brueggemann, *Sabbath as Resistance*, 31.
31. Ibid., 29–30.
32. Obviously our salvation includes an ongoing process. But this is a recovery of what we are—God's image-bearing stewards—by his finished creative power (see Gen. 2:1). Grace restores God's good work (see Eph. 4:20–24; Col. 3:10–11). Even in the ongoing renewal happening in us, the Creator/Redeemer/Renewing God will bring what he has begun (our recovery by grace) to completion (full recovery—called glorification in the New Testament; see Phil. 1:6).

Chapter 12 The Rest Key Today

1. Dean Schabner, "Americans Work More Than Anyone," ABC News, accessed August 9, 2017, http://abcnews.go.com/US/story?id=93364&page=1.
2. Allison Linn, "Workaholic Americans Don't Take All Their Vacation," CNBC, April 13, 2014, http://www.cnbc.com/2014/04/02/workaholic-americans-dont-take-all-their-vacation.html.
3. "Workaholics May Face Poor Physical and Mental Well-Being, Study Suggests," Huffington Post, April 1, 2015, http://www.huffingtonpost.com/2013/09/06/workaholics-well-being-physical-mental-health_n_3795626.html.
4. Ian Sample, "Are Smartphones Making Our Work More Stressful?" *The Guardian*, September 18, 2014, https://www.theguardian.com/technology/2014/sep/18/smartphones-making-working-lives-more-stressful.
5. Amy Morin, "Is Technology Ruining Our Ability to Read Emotions? Study Says Yes," *Forbes*, August 2014, http://www.forbes.com/sites/amymorin/2014/08/26/is-technology-ruining-our-ability-to-read-emotions-study-says-yes/#f2c2f8d12ca3.
6. Timothy Keller, *Every Good Endeavor: Connecting Your Work to God's Work* (New York: Penguin, 2012), 226.
7. At this point, Rhodes cries, "Guilty!"
8. Brueggemann, *Sabbath as Resistance*, xiv.
9. Paul Heintzman, "What We Do for Rest and Enjoyment," in *Living the Good Life on God's Good Earth*, ed. David S. Koetje (Grand Rapids: Faith Alive Christian Resources, 2006), 73.
10. As an emergency room doctor, Collins in particular does occasionally have to work on Sundays. But unless absolutely impossible, both he and Jonathan continue to pursue a weekly day of rest.
11. Tim Keller, "Wisdom and Sabbath Rest," Q, accessed August 9, 2017, http://qideas.org/articles/wisdom-and-sabbath-rest/.
12. Judith Shulevitz, "Bring Back the Sabbath," *New York Times Magazine*, March 2, 2003, http://www.nytimes.com/2003/03/02/magazine/bring-back-the-sabbath.html.
13. In the church, any concept of "family" must include widows, orphans, and the single members of the body who need connection and are God's gift to us (see 1 Cor. 7:8–9, 32–35).

14. Nick Wing and Carly Schwartz, "Here's the Painful Truth about What It Means to Be 'Working Poor' in America," Huffington Post, May 19, 2014, http://www.huffingtonpost.com/2014/05/19/working-poor-stories_n_5297694.html.

15. "What Is Refuge Coffee Co.?," Refuge Coffee Company, accessed June 29, 2017, http://www.refugecoffeeco.com/about/.

16. "Refugee Community in Georgia Town Thrives," CNN, accessed June 28, 2017, http://www.cnn.com/videos/us/2015/11/21/clarkston-georgia-refugee-community-valencia-dnt-nr.cnn/video/playlists/refugee-stories/.

17. "What Is Refuge Coffee Co.?"

18. Wong and Rae, *Business for the Common Good*, 252.

19. "A Bailout of the People by the People," RollingJubilee.org, accessed June 28, 2017, http://rollingjubilee.org/.

Resources for Further Study

1. Our deep gratitude to Rusty Pritchard for his help in thinking through the creation care chapters as a whole, and the resources section in particular. Of course, final decisions about such things, as well as any mistakes, belong to us alone.

INDEX

Michael Rhodes is the director of community transformation and an instructor at the Memphis Center for Urban and Theological Studies, where he heads up efforts to equip urban pastors and community development practitioners with theologically informed tools for community transformation.

Robby Holt is the senior pastor at North Shore Fellowship in Chattanooga, Tennessee. He teaches theology of work and New Testament courses for the Chattanooga Fellows Initiative, and is a teacher and theological dean for the Chattanooga Institute for Faith and Work.

Brian Fikkert is the founder and president of the Chalmers Center for Economic Development at Covenant College in Lookout Mountain, Georgia, where he also serves as a professor of economics and community development. He is the coauthor of several books, including *When Helping Hurts* and *From Dependence to Dignity*.

expect more

At Covenant, we expect more of our college community.

More than four years of entertainment. More than four years of cruising by. More than just a place to get a degree. Covenant students, faculty, and staff are eager to tackle the difficult questions of our time and are passionate about living out their faith in every area of life—in business, ministry, school, and home.

For more than sixty years, Covenant College has shaped curricula and experiences to equip generations of men and women to embrace their vocations as they serve the church, their communities, and a changing world.

Ask hard questions. Pursue your calling.
*Join us at **covenant.edu**.*

Pictured: Covenant alumni teaching music to children in their community.

COVENANT
COLLEGE

IN ALL THINGS CHRIST PREEMINENT

Ready to live out the King's economy in your community?

Put your learning into action with additional resources to help you take your next step—and start applying what you've learned where you live!

Discover more resources at:
PracticingTheKingsEconomy.org